Child Development in Educational Settings

Child Development in Educational Settings provides a comprehensive introduction to traditional and contemporary theories of development and learning in the contexts of early childhood and primary education.

Drawing upon the experiences and perspectives of children, families, educators and Aboriginal and Torres Strait Islander scholars, Marilyn Fleer provides insights into significant theories and approaches, including cultural-historical, constructivist, social constructivist, maturational and ecological systems. The book features four major case studies, which are revisited throughout, to examine how learning and development can be reimagined within socially, culturally and linguistically diverse communities. This approach enables readers to use theories to analyse and measure learning and development in planning and curriculum, and to feel empowered to enact change in their educational settings.

Written in an engaging and accessible style, *Child Development in Educational Settings* is an essential resource for pre-service teachers and professionals alike.

Marilyn Fleer is Professor of Early Childhood Education and Development at Monash University, Australia, and is an Honorary Research Fellow at the University of Oxford, UK.

Child Development in Educational Settings

Marilyn Fleer

CAMBRIDGE
UNIVERSITY PRESS

CAMBRIDGE
UNIVERSITY PRESS

University Printing House, Cambridge CB2 8BS, United Kingdom

One Liberty Plaza, 20th Floor, New York, NY 10006, USA

477 Williamstown Road, Port Melbourne, VIC 3207, Australia

314–321, 3rd Floor, Plot 3, Splendor Forum, Jasola District Centre, New Delhi – 110025, India

79 Anson Road, #06–04/06, Singapore 079906

Cambridge University Press is part of the University of Cambridge.

It furthers the University's mission by disseminating knowledge in the pursuit of education, learning and research at the highest international levels of excellence

www.cambridge.org
Information on this title: www.cambridge.org/9781316631881

First published 2018

Cover designed by Leigh Ashforth, watershed art + design
Typeset by SPi Global
Printed in Singapore by Markono Print Media Pte Ltd, November 2017

A catalogue record for this publication is available from the British Library

A Cataloguing-in-Publication entry is available from the catalogue of the National Library of Australia at www.nla.gov.au

ISBN 978-1-316-63188-1 Paperback

Additional resources for this publication at www.cambridge.edu.au/academic/childdevelopment

Contents

Part II: Using child development theory: What does theory
allow us to see?

Part III: Critiquing theory: Thinking critically about child development

Case studies

Preface: My journey

This textbook is an important book to me because it represents a reclaiming of the field of child development by and for early childhood educationalists. For far too long we have been told from outside our profession what we should think and do. Many of those who have advised the field of early childhood education have not even stepped into a early childhood centre, let alone worked together with such young children and their families. But of course many have, and their research has been informative. However, I feel we need to support our profession with research conducted from within our own field. We should be building capacity within our own profession, but also valuing what it is we know about our practice that can meaningfully inform new ways of thinking about children's development.

Observing children through the eyes of a researcher is very different from being an educator working with a group of 25 to 30 children, so this book is written through the eyes of someone who has been a preschool teacher, in both child-care settings and in government- and community-funded kindergartens in Australia. As a teacher, I ask different questions about the conditions we create to support children's development. I don't just focus on the child, but also look closely at the contexts we create for children's development. My own experience has shaped the way this book has emerged.

I began my career as an early childhood educator, having worked in child care and preschool education, as well as acting as an educational adviser in Aboriginal education, as an adviser on information and communication technology (ICT) and as a researcher undertaking many studies in child development with my colleague Professor Mariane Hedegaard, from the University of Copenhagen in Denmark. Together, these experiences laid the foundations for me in terms of thinking through the key theories of child development that contemporary early childhood education students would find most helpful to support the important work they do with young children and their families.

Consequently, this book does not follow the traditional norms of psychology; rather, it takes the essence of what matters for education and discusses only those child development theories used in education. Many of the child development theories that can be found in traditional educational psychology textbooks cover traditional theories. Some of these theories are still relevant, but many do not say much about contemporary children, who live in different contexts, have different digital and virtual experiences, travel the world in real time and through new media, and simply do not fit the patterns of 'growing up' described by traditional theorists such as Piaget or as speculated on by Freud. The studies that sit under many of the child development theories were done on children who have grown up and are now in their old age, or have passed away. I wondered why we still draw on these theories. My response has been to go back to the original writing of each theorist and to study closely at what they said, rather than just drawing on secondary sources. Some interesting differences have emerged through this research method.

In drawing upon primary sources to support the content of this book, many anomalies have emerged between what is traditionally presented in child development textbooks and what I present here. This means that some sections will feel familiar to the experienced reader, but other sections will challenge and disrupt what some have come to know as the 'truth' about child development. Further, many traditional theories that are viewed as old-fashioned in the field have not been covered. Other theories that are being used in education, but are not always covered in traditional child development textbooks, are included. Further, the concepts that are discussed in this textbook focus on the essence of the particular child development theories. Rather than covering many different concepts, this book seeks to cover fewer, but to do so more comprehensively. Student teachers have busy lives, often supporting their study through part-time work. I wanted to make sure that the content was concise and immediately relevant to today's context. I wanted this book to be about theories that are talked about by students' peers, theories with which they grapple through the introduction of the Early Years Learning Framework and the National Curriculum, and theories that are relevant to children living in today's world.

When I was a student, I had the good fortune to be taught by a child development lecturer who had grown up in a family of theorists. She set a foundation of questioning many of the taken-for-granted theories of children's development. Now, when I look at the available textbooks, and seek to set a textbook to support my own university students' learning, I continue to be amazed that the same content I learned so long ago is still presented – albeit with much more relevant examples and photographs of children today. So why has theory not developed further? I was a student of the late 1970s!

I continued to wonder. When my first child was born, I watched him closely, drawing upon the theories I had learned as a student to see and understand his development. But the theories I had learned about were all formed in different countries. Key ideas were framed in relation to milestones, but these milestones didn't really fit what with what I was seeing. This was also the case when I was teaching in the field. I recall a conversation with a colleague who was teaching babies and toddlers. I asked her whether she thought the stages of play so carefully illustrated by Parten actually explained the development of the infants and toddlers in her room. I explicitly asked whether she ever saw babies playing imaginatively. She said, 'Yes, of course – many times!' Parten's theory suggests that infants shouldn't be doing that. Later, when my daughter was born, I watched her in relation to this curiosity. I have a lovely set of photographs of her role-playing at 8 months – just sitting and using a spoon to feed her brother, who was being the baby. I also remember a moment when my partner changed her nappy. She pointed to him and said 'woof'. She was engaging her father in role-play – child-initiated play. She wanted him to be a dog – we are a dog-loving family, and this was an important part of her life. She was less than 12 months old and just starting to say the odd word. So these experiences have informed how I wanted this book on child development to be.

The intent of this textbook is to inform, challenge and provoke, so that the student will emerge from the pages of this book with a solid understanding of a few key child development theories, and have a toolkit of concepts for critiquing theory. It is hoped that students will adopt an open mind towards new thinking in the future, when a comprehensive Australian theory of child development is finally researched and written. The beginning of an Australian theory of child development is presented in Chapter 8. Our early childhood profession should continue to do this important work from within, so that we have theories of child development based on Australian children.

Acknowledgements

In the many chapters of this book are the stories of exemplary leaders, such as Dr Esme Capp, teachers from her school and preschool teachers of distinction. The book also features analyses of data from a range of research projects, funded through different sources, such as the Australian Research Council (ARC) Discovery Grant Scheme, Early Childhood Australia and the deLissa Institute in South Australia. Common to many of the ARC discovery projects has been my amazing research assistant and PhD student, Sue March.

New insights from Associate Professor Karen Martin (Griffith University) and Associate Professor Peter Anderson (Queensland University of Technology), examined through their scholarly writing, dialogue and interviews, are presented in the latter part of this book. Their scholarly contribution is important for paving the way for the new work that is still to be done. Collectively, these experiences and my own journey with co-collaborator Professor Mariane Hedegaard (University of Copenhagen), along with the scholarly women who have, at different times, supported my thinking, such as Professors Anne Edwards (University of Oxford), Elena Kravtsova (formerly Vygotsky Institute, Russian State University for the Humanities), Barbara Rogoff (University of California – Santa Cruz), Iram Siraj (University of London) and Joy Cullen (formerly Massey University), and Dr Valda Kirkwood, Dr Anne Hone and Dr Margaret Bearlin (formerly University of Canberra), have contributed to the way this book has ultimately been shaped – even though they have not seen a single page of the manuscript.

There have also been teams of research assistants over the years who have helped me with my data collection at different times, colleagues at Monash who have positively challenged my thinking and a former Vice Chancellor of the University of Canberra, Professor Don Aitkin, who believed enough in my scholarship to give me a personal chair at the age of 40. Last but not least, Cambridge University Press, with their amazing team, including Vilija Stephens, who joined the journey through her continual encouragement and patience, and her colleagues, Tanya Bastrakova and Georgina Lowe, for their editorial support. I thank them all!

PART I

The need for theory: Understanding the different contexts of child development

CHAPTER 1

Introduction: Starting your journey

In this book, you will meet the children, families and teachers from four educational communities. Through entering into these communities through the pages of this textbook, you will:

- learn how theory guides what you see
- be introduced to a range of ways in which teachers understand children's development
- draw on theories to frame educational practice
- reflect on the power of theories to support inclusion and enable diversity, but also to detect marginalisation.

In Part I, you will be introduced to the four case studies and be shown how to gather and analyse your own observational data and undertake analyses of children's development. As you continue to read, you will learn more about each case study and find out how theory helps with understanding children's development. Additional content about the lives of the children, families and teachers will be presented in each chapter, alongside different theories of child development. You will meet interesting problems that you will need to solve using the different theories of child development.

Part II presents explanations of the main theories of child development that guide early childhood and primary teachers today. This book is focused on the core theories that guide contemporary practice in playgroups, childcare centres, preschools and schools – maturational and developmental theories, constructivist and socio-constructivist theories, bioecological theory, socio-behavourist theories and sociocultural – or, as it is increasingly becoming known, cultural-historical – theory. Because of this focus, some long-standing theories of development and learning have not been included – for example, Freud's psycho-sexual theory and others have not been detailed – for example, behaviourism. The focus is on theories that guide practice, so the case examples and the core theories introduced have been chosen with this goal in mind. Australian contexts and examples of development are theorised in Chapters 7 and 8, with Chapter 8 examining the perspectives of Karen Martin and Peter Anderson, two of Australia's leading scholars in educational and child development theory.

Part III turns to the critiquing of child development theories in the context of what guides our practices and the curriculum – the Early Years Learning Framework (EYLF) and the National Curriculum. We look closely at the different theories that are reported in the EYLF and discuss which could be considered theories of child development. We do this alongside a critique of existing theories because the theories were researched and theorised outside Australia.

The *Child Development in Educational Settings* companion website provides links to additional resources, videos and activities to expand upon the content of the book. Throughout the book, the ideal point at which to view these resources is identified with this margin icon.

Your professional journey

Struggles with understanding child development and learning theories continue throughout our professional career, as Figures 1.1 and 1.2 show. Figure 1.2 is a poster that was prepared by the experienced teachers shown in Figure 1.1, who were analysing their pedagogy in relation to their assessment and asking questions about their alignment through examining the different theories of child development.

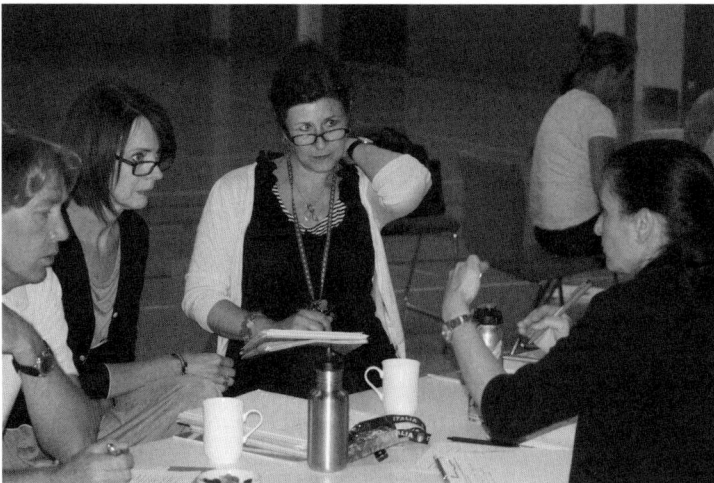

Figure 1.1 What theory of child development informs our pedagogy? What theory is guiding our school and early childhood setting?

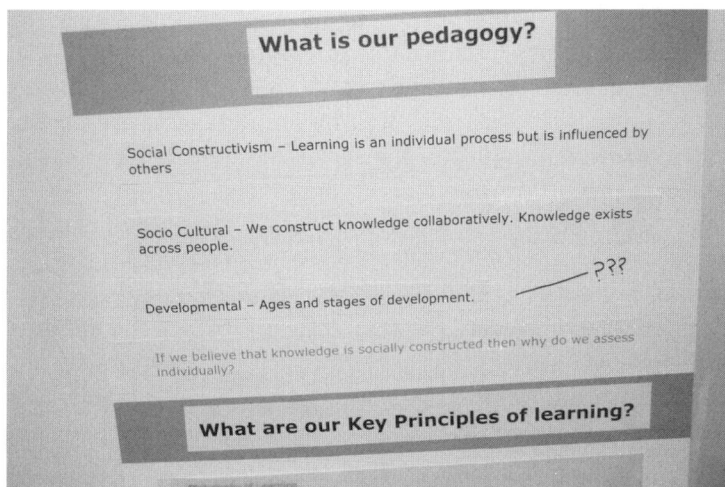

Figure 1.2 Critiquing the child development theories that guide our pedagogy and principles of learning in our school

They wanted to know which theory of child development they should support in their school. As seen in the poster, they initially examined social constructivism by asking questions about this theory. Was it a theory of learning? Was it a theory of child development? What approaches to teaching are related to this particular theory? They asked similar questions about sociocultural theory, later deciding that the term 'cultural-historical theory' was much more closely aligned with their beliefs about how children develop and learn. Finally, they asked questions about the theories of development that underpinned their state (Victorian Curriculum and Assessment Authority, 2017) and national curricula (Australian Curriculum and Reporting Assessment Authority, 2017). They wondered whether the developmental perspective that appeared to sit under these documents reflected contemporary thinking about child development.

Understanding what theory of child development underpins a curriculum is also a core issue raised in the EYLF, the national curriculum that guides educators working with children in the birth to 5 years period (DEEWR, 2009). It is also foundational to using the National Curriculum – even though the theory of child development on which it is based is not made explicit. It is much clearer in the EYLF because the document has made a special feature of child development. Educators are encouraged to think about and discuss different theoretical positions of child development and learning. For instance, the EYLF (DEEWR, 2009: 11) states:

> Different theories about early childhood inform approaches to children's learning and development. Early childhood educators draw upon a range of perspectives in their work.

The theoretical perspectives named and explained in the EYLF are listed below. As you read through the different chapters of this book, you will be introduced to each of these theories:

- developmental theories that focus on describing and understanding the processes of change in children's learning and development over time
- sociocultural theories that emphasise the central role played by families and cultural groups in children's learning and the importance of respectful relationships, which provide insight into the social and cultural contexts of learning and development
- socio-behaviourist theories that focus on the role of experiences in shaping children's behaviour
- critical theories that invite early childhood educators to challenge assumptions about curriculum, and consider how their decisions may affect children differently
- post-structuralist theories that offer insights into issues of power, equity and social justice in early childhood settings (DEEWR, 2009: 11).

This is not unique to Australia. Different theoretical perspectives are also reflected in the recently released curriculum for early childhood teachers in New Zealand, Te Whāriki (Ministry of Education New Zealand, 2017). Te Whāriki draws upon Vygotsky's sociocultural theories, Bronfenbrenner's bioecological model and Kaupapa Māori theory.

It is interesting to note that the Australian curriculum provides no sense of what theory of child development should be supported. This is a question to ponder as you read through the book. You should consider what theories of child development might underpin the Australian curriculum and, further, what theories could inform your thinking in relation to the development of school-aged children. This book seeks to foreground child development for both school and preschool (e.g. early childhood and kindergarten) contexts.

Your personal journey

The theories discussed in the EYLF and those shown in the poster in Figure 1.2, which was made by primary teachers in a school, demonstrate that learning about child development continues throughout your professional career. Using theory to guide your practice in an informed way underpins your personal journey. Thinking critically about these theories (Part III) is key to taking scholarship forward and being open to new ideas about children's development.

Your journey into comprehensive learning about the different theories of child development begins at university and sometimes before, when studying courses at TAFEs and secondary colleges/schools. However, you will continue to return to your beliefs and practices as you encounter new challenges in different educational settings. The case studies in this book show real-life contexts in which real-world problems arose that needed to be solved by the professionals working with the children and their families, in conjunction with the children and family members.

In using the theories of child development and learning presented in the chapters of this book, you will come to better understand the families, teachers and curricula discussed throughout each case study. As the children's lives unfold through the pages of the book, and as you use theory to analyse the children's development, you will begin to make informed decisions about the learning possibilities for the particular children about whom you are reading. You will bring to these problem situations your own personal or professional experiences of being in communities, preschools and schools, where you will meet similar children, families and teachers to those introduced in this book.

Please think about the case examples and the problem scenarios introduced in this book as part of your personal journey. You will revisit content, reanalyse case studies, compare and contrast theories, and eventually come to an informed judgement about your own philosophy of teaching and learning, in the context of your emerging understanding of how child development informs practice.

The intention of this book is to support you to build foundational knowledge of child development in ways that encourage you to reach out to the communities in which you will be teaching so that you can learn about what matters for a particular community. It is through this knowledge that you will be more informed, and thus better able to better read the children's development in that community and then use this to inform your practice. It is through researching communities in the context of a deep knowledge of child development that you will be more likely to be able to make informed decisions about the best approaches and optimal conditions for children's development. As noted in the EYLF:

> Drawing on a range of perspectives and theories can challenge traditional ways of seeing children, teaching and learning, and encourage educators, as individuals and with colleagues, to:
>
> - investigate why they act in the ways that they do
> - discuss and debate theories to identify strengths and limitations
> - recognise how the theories and beliefs that they use to make sense of their work enable, but also limit, their actions and thoughts
> - consider the consequences of their actions for children's experiences
> - find new ways of working fairly and justly (DEEWR, 2009: 11).

Challenging traditional ways of seeing children

You will return to this analytical frame at different points throughout this book.

ONGOING REFLECTION: KEEPING A JOURNAL TO DOCUMENT YOUR JOURNEY

You are encouraged to keep a journal and to enter into it your thinking, analysis and research. The Child Development Reflections in each chapter are designed to support your learning journey to discover the different theories of child

(continued)

development. You will be invited to reflect on the case studies and to consider how you would respond if you were the educator. As you gain more insights into child development theories, you will then be challenged to reconsider your initial views. In some chapters, you will be invited to explicitly reflect on a case study scenario, drawing upon a particular theory of child development. This will help you to engage with the particular concepts and principles underpinning each theory, enabling you to better understand what each theory allows you to see and how each theory informs your judgements about children and families.

References

Australian Curriculum and Reporting Assessment Authority 2017, *Australian Curriculum*. Available at: https://www.acara.edu.au/curriculum [Accessed 20 April 2017].

Department of Education, Employment and Workplace Relations (DEEWR) 2009, *Belonging, Being and Becoming: The Early Years Learning Framework for Australia*, Canberra: Commonwealth Government.

Ministry of Education New Zealand 2017, *Te Whāriki: He whāriki mātauranga mōngā mokopuna o Aotearoa: Early childhood curriculum*, Wellington: New Zealand Government.

Victorian Curriculum and Assessment Authority (VCAA) 2017, *Victorian Curriculum: Foundation–10*. Available at: http://www.vcaa.vic.edu.au/Pages/foundation10/f10index.aspx [Accessed 20 June 2017].

CHAPTER 2

Understanding and using theory in educational settings

Introduction

In this chapter and those that follow, you will meet the children, families and teachers who are part of four different communities that form the case studies for this book. The case studies are:

- *The Resourceful Community case study*. The first case study is of two families with a similar profile who live in a resourceful, but poor community. They are the Peninsula family and the Westernport family. The community has been labelled the Resourceful Community because the families are able to reuse, recycle and invent in resourceful ways.
- *The Collective Inquiry School case study*. The second case study is of a primary school in a community that has creative families, professional families, poor families and newly arrived immigrant families.
- *The Building Bridges case study*. The third case study is of a group of Aboriginal and Torres Strait Islander families from different parts of Australia who came together to talk about what mattered for their children's learning and development and what non-Aboriginal and Torres Strait Islander teachers needed to know about growing up in Australia as an Aboriginal child (Fleer & Williams-Kennedy, 2002). Some core ideas, rather than definitive views, are presented in Chapter 3.

- *The Culturally Diverse Preschool case study.* The final case study is of a group of preschool children who come from culturally diverse families. You will be introduced to this case study in Chapter 3.

To protect the anonymity of the families, pseudonyms and non-identifying material have been used. Only images and work samples of children from families who have given permission have been included in this book.

You are now introduced to the first two of the four case studies. Each case study finishes with a problem situation that you will work towards solving as you read the child development and learning theories presented throughout this book. Enter your reflections on each case scenario and problem situation into your journal. Your responses over time will contribute to building a collective and holistic picture of the development of the children discussed throughout this book.

Through engaging with the content of this chapter, it is anticipated that you will:

- think about child development in the context of families and communities and the conditions that you, as an educator, create in child-care centres, preschools and primary schools
- be oriented to some of the major theories of child development that inform education
- begin to appreciate that theories of child development determine what you see and shape how you might act
- consider the importance of using child development theory to inform your thinking and practice.

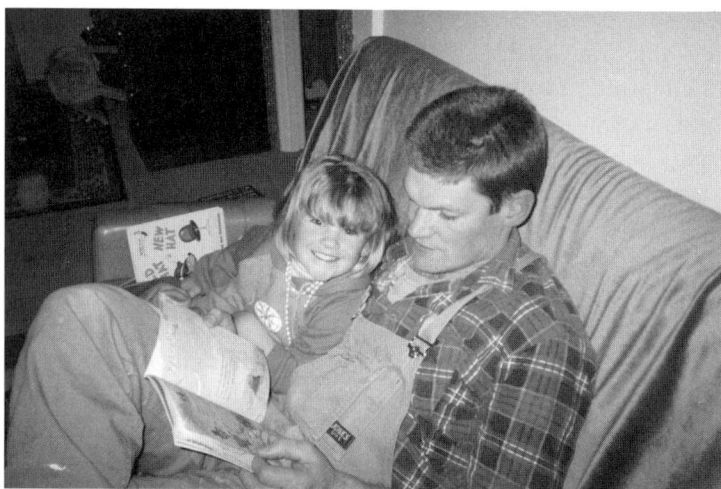

Figure 2.1 A father reads to his daughter

RESOURCEFUL COMMUNITY CASE STUDY

PART 1: MEETING THE FAMILIES, CHILDREN AND TEACHERS

The members of the Peninsula family live in a resourceful community. Many of the families in this community are poor, but they appear to be able to cleverly turn their hand to recycling materials in ways that solve everyday problems in cost-neutral or minimal ways. For instance, the community has an abundance of metal, wood and clothing recycling centres, along with staff who appear to give advice on doing things in a cost-effective manner. This is not only an assumed everyday practice, but is something that families expect and grow up with in their community. William, the principal of one of the local schools, drew upon this strength and, with the support of the local Rotary Club, set up an after-school tinkering club.

> The children in this community live in homes where families are poor. The families are very resourceful in making things, figuring out cost-effective ways to fix things, and have really highly developed problem-solving skills. So I thought, let's capitalise on this strength, and set up a tinkering club after school. So I asked the local Rotary Club to help. We had people from the community come in and work with the children. We also had a lot of broken things donated, such as lawn mowers – which we know are always breaking down. Well, would you believe it, the children not only 'tinkered' but they actually fixed up the lawnmowers. (Field notes, interview with Principal William)

It is important to know that William grew up in this community and went to school with many of the parents whose children now attend his school. He was therefore very keen to support the strengths of the community through the after-school activity of a Tinkering Club.

Further, many families in the community either run home businesses or do their own repairs, such as servicing cars in the back yard. Children in this community have the opportunity to observe or be part of resourceful home practices from an early age. For example, the photograph shown in Figure 2.2 was taken by Katrina, who photographed her everyday family practices at home, and who was interviewed about her

Figure 2.2 Helping to service the family car

photographs. She said she helped her father to service the family car in the home garage (Fleer & Robbins, 2005a, 2005b).

In this community, some people drive through the township and notice poverty. But the community has a depth and richness that are often invisible to someone driving through, and even to some teachers who have a different view of what matters for children's development, as the following comment shows:

> Well, all the children in this community do not have much happening at home. I don't expect much. They don't even have paper and pencils for drawing. (Field notes, interview with classroom teacher)

This teacher, along with others from this community, was invited to comment on what literacy and numeracy practices they thought were occurring in the children's homes. In contrast to what the teachers said, the study of the children's home practices (Fleer & Robbins, 2005a, 2005b; Fleer & Quiñones, 2009) showed something very different. For instance, the images taken by the families of their everyday practices show fathers at home reading quality books to their children (Figure 2.1), as well as children using toys to sort and classify, and children engaging in measurement strategies, such as establishing a baseline for fair comparisons of toys (Figure 2.3). (For further details of the studies from this community, see Fleer & Robbins, 2005a, 2005b; Fleer & Quiñones, 2009; Kennedy, Ridgway & Surman, 2006.)

Figure 2.3 Children line up their toys – establishing a baseline for a fair comparison

When we showed these and other photographs to the teachers from the schools and preschools in this community, they were surprised, as the following comment illustrates:

> I can't believe they are doing that at home. I am just so surprised. I had not expected that. (Field notes from community workshop and focus group interviews, October)

It is within this community and educational context that the Peninsula and Western-port families are introduced (Hedegaard & Fleer, 2013).

Peninsula family

Figure 2.4 The children from the Peninsula family who live in this resourceful community

The Peninsula family does not own a car. The family lives approximately 5 km from the local school, preschool and child-care centre. The transport system does not appear to be useful for the route the children must take each day to get to and from these educational institutions, so the family must walk. The 10 km walk takes the family approximately one hour (Fleer & Hedegaard, 2010).

The parents are in their early thirties and are of European background. The father discussed his own difficulties at school, reporting that he had a form of dyslexia. He appears to be unable to read or write, while the mother is literate.

The family participated in an 18-month child development study. The children were observed in their everyday family practices, breakfast routines, evening activities, walking to school, preschool and child care, and also while attending class and playing in the playground at school. At the beginning of the study, the children were all under 5 years of age: Louise (16 months), JJ (2 years), Nick (4 years) and Andrew (5 years). The family was observed over three periods, approximately three to four months apart. Digital video cameras were used to film the family's everyday practices, and nearly 100 hours of digital observations were made in the overall study.

The home is sparsely furnished. It is clean, tidy and well organised. The adults and children appear to walk and run around the various rooms in the house and backyard, and rarely sit down in the available chairs. Fewer chairs than people were evident on each visit over the 18-month period.

On each occasion when the evening meal was observed, the children sat at the table briefly, then moved to different parts of the house to finish their meal. The common practice was for the mother or the father to cook and then to serve the food at the kitchen table, before retiring to another room. The children managed their meals independently.

When Louise was 18 months old, she was observed at the evening meal. She was placed in a high chair and given her food by the mother, but it was her siblings who supported her with eating her meal. Prior to this age, her mother fed her and then left the table. At 18 months, Louise stayed in her high chair for an extended period, and called out to her parents when she had finished eating. While she waited, her siblings ran from room to room and engaged with her momentarily as they passed by, so she was never alone. When Louise was in the outdoor area and seated on the ground, the children also continually ran past her and engaged momentarily with her. Except for Louise, the children were continually moving around, both inside and outside. They appeared to manage climbing furniture and unstable outdoor fixtures with great ease and dexterity. The children and the adults rarely sat or stood still.

Louise was observed at home being moved from her high chair to the floor, and from her cot to her pram (when going out) or to the floor/outdoor ground. Later, when play equipment (swing and slide set) was gifted to the children at Christmas, she was picked up and placed in the swing and supported. Louise walked at 2 years of age (Fleer, 2014).

The Peninsula family was visited regularly by government officials. It was reported by the parents that the officers were worried by Louise's development because she could not walk. The mother said:

> We have community services in our lives. They have told us that Louise should be walking by now. (Observation Period 1, Visit 3)

The school was also worried about Andrew, who was in his first year of school. Both the mother and teacher reported that he had difficulties settling into school and sitting still in class. The mother said:

> His teacher has told me to stop him moving around all the time and to make him sit still. They are worried about his behavior, and I don't want him to have to stay down a grade. (Observation Period 1, Visit 1)

On a subsequent visit to the home, the children were observed as the mother spoke to the researcher about her worries (Fleer & Hedegaard, 2010; Hedegaard & Fleer, 2013).

> The mother is in the kitchen making a cup of coffee. Andrew is running from the family room to the kitchen and back. He has new shoes on, which have lights in their sole, and as he runs the light flashes. He appears to be delighted by his new runners, predominantly looking to the observers as he runs in and out of the kitchen. The mother tells the researcher, 'The school has said that I need to work on his behaviours.' She then turns to Andrew as he is running through the kitchen, and says gruffly, 'Andrew, stop showing off.' She points her finger at Andrew to punctuate her point. (Observation Period 2, Visit 1)

In this active family context, the family organised Andrew's homework routine. Each child in their first year of school was given a homework folder that they took back and forth to school. The folders contained flash cards (sight words printed on light card the size of playing cards), a reading book and sometimes notes for families. During the 18 months of observations, one home reading session and one homework period were observed:

One late afternoon the mother takes out of Andrew's bag his home reader and flash cards. She stands next to Andrew and asks him to read. Both mother and child are standing in the lounge room. The other children (except Louise) are running between rooms. Andrew looks at the book and the mother points to the words. Andrew says 'The' and then does not say any more. The mother points to each word and reads the text, while Andrew repeats shortly after her each word. The sequence lasts approximately one minute. The mother puts away the book and cards, and Andrew joins the others, running from room to room around the house. (Observation Period 2, Visit 1)

CHILD DEVELOPMENT REFLECTION 2.1: ANALYSING THE CASE STUDY

What is your view about family life for Louise and Andrew? What do you feel is interesting about this family that could impact upon the children's development? Write one thing about family life from each of the following perspectives:

- What is the mother's perspective?
- What is the teacher's perspective?
- What is the government official's perspective?
- What is your perspective?
- What do you need to know in order to support your perspective?

We will come back to these questions and your initial response as we progress through the chapters of this book, where more information about the family will be presented and where you will encounter different theories of child development. You will be invited to analyse the Peninsula family in light of increased knowledge about the different theories of child development.

Westernport family

Members of the Westernport family are pictured in Figure 2.5 and discussed further in the chapters of this book. The family comprises four children, Jason (5 years), Alex (4 years), Cam (3 years) and Mandy (16 months), who live with both parents. However, the uncle and grandmother (shown in Figure 2.5) are also an integral part of the children's lives, visiting regularly and playing an important role in the children's development and learning (Fleer & Hedegaard, 2010).

The family lives within walking distance of the school and owns a car. The family receives financial support from the government to assist with food and housing. Like

Figure 2.5 The children and extended members of the Westernport family who live in this resourceful community

the Peninsula family, the Westernport family lives in a government house and pays subsidised rent, and receives financial assistance with living expenses. The eldest child attends the same school as the Peninsula family.

The children in the Westernport family are also active, but not as active as the Peninsula family children. There are some family practices that appear to follow those of the school, one of which is homework (Fleer, 2013).

> Since Jason began school, the mother has transformed the kitchen table each afternoon for 15 minutes into a homework space. This is a whole family event, because all the children are assembled, keenly observing this new family routine, except Jason who is in another room watching TV and playing. The mother calls Jason to sit at the table and do his homework. However, he usually groans and insists that his father participate, rejecting his mother. On this particular occasion, the grandmother and uncle are visiting. Jason, in a whining tone, asks for the father to do the flash cards rather than the mother. The father sits down and begins to shuffle the cards. As he does, he turns the context of reading sight words into a card game. The grandmother asks whether she can join the game, and on this being accepted by Jason, she slides closer to Jason and the father. As the father talks, he takes a card from the pack and holds it up. The grandmother says, 'Oh this is tricky, I wonder if I can get the word right.' Jason responds immediately and tries to sound out the word, while the grandmother gives an incorrect response. This makes Jason laugh. The flash card game continues in this manner until Jason has correctly identified all the sight words, at which point the father says, 'Give me a high five!' and the mother and grandmother cheer. Jason smiles widely, appearing to beam with pride. (Field notes, Family Observations, Period 3, Visit 2)

CHILD DEVELOPMENT REFLECTION 2.2: ANALYSING THE CASE STUDY

1   What is your view about family life? What is happening here to support the children's development?
2   Write one thing about family life from each of the following perspectives:
    - What is the father's perspective? What is he doing to support learning and development?
    - What is the grandmother doing to support Jason's development?
    - What is your perspective on the opportunities for development in this everyday practice?
3   Write down your thoughts. Note your feelings, values and beliefs. What do you need to know in order to be more confident about your initial thoughts?
4   When you consider family life for both the Peninsula family and the Westernport family, what things are similar and what things are different? Do the differences matter?

Using theory to understand families

A group of pre-service teachers was asked to analyse the Resourceful Community case study, drawing upon their own intuitive beliefs about children's development. Comments included the following:

Alicia: I noticed that the Peninsula family was very active. The children moved around a lot.

Jason: I was surprised that Andrew had such a short time in which to read his 'school reader'. Actually, I was trying to imagine how he could be paying attention to the book while standing and having all of his siblings running about. I would find it hard to concentrate.

Rowan: I thought that Louise should be walking by now.

These comments are different to those of the teachers from the school, who did not have the opportunity for home visits. Their comments were based solely on what they observed in the school:

Andrew just does not sit down at school. He finds it really hard to concentrate. He needs some behaviour modification. I have organised for him to be tested. (Prep teacher)

We have spoken to the family, and asked the mother to work on his behaviour. Because he does not sit still and concentrate, he has not picked up the basics, and he is now a struggling reader. I try to get him to focus on his work. (Year 1 teacher)

A group of policy-makers were also invited to analyse the practices of the Peninsula family in relation to their policy work. They said:

Yow: In preparing policy, how might we change practice and better support teachers, the children and families? How do we work with teachers in the early years of school so that children who come from active homes can access learning more easily?

Helen: This is about the need for effective transition statements. What did the preschool teachers give to the school teachers?

Carmel: Do we change schools or do we change children?

Stephen: I think we need to do a careful diagnostic test on Andrew. Does he have attention deficit hyperactivity disorder? What are the range of testing tools we can use to better understand his problems?

Chandra: A maturational view of child development would suggest that Louise is not developing as is expected or shown in the standardised profiles of normal child development.

Finally, video clips of the family practices were shared with conference attendees, who said the following:

Jasmine: We need to go beyond thinking about the child as a consumer of a stepped approach to curriculum. This is a maturational view of the typical learner. We have to have a new way of thinking about child development. It cannot be about the age of the child and what they should be learning in Prep or Year 1. We have to think about the learner and child development in a different way – as interrelated.

Elin: What is needed is for us think about family pedagogy and school pedagogy, rather than the individual child. A checklist of what Andrew can do is not going to be so helpful. But an understanding of Andrew as learning through participation, as an active participant, may be a way forward. That view demands a theory of child development that captures more than the individual child, but the child as they are participating in a broad range of social practices.

Jules: How might we bring together the family pedagogy and the home pedagogy? How can the experience of Andrew be seamless as he transitions to school?

Marilyn: Louise is living in a very active family. She has no need to walk. So why would she develop this capacity? Does this mean her development will be different? Should the government officials really be worried about her development? If the government officials believe Louise develops in relation to milestones associated with age, then yes. But is this the whole picture? They visited the home. They have a profile of the family and the children's development.

CHILD DEVELOPMENT REFLECTION 2.3: THEORETICALLY ORIENTING TO THE LANGUAGE OF CHILD DEVELOPMENT

1   Do any of the comments made by the student teachers, teachers, policy-makers and conference attendees reflect the views you documented in Child Development Reflection 2.1 and 2.2?
2   What child development terms are being used? Document each of the terms by listing:
    •   the child development term
    •   what it might mean
    •   what you would like to know more about.

We will come back to these terms and your questions in subsequent chapters where more detail about the family practices and school context will be presented.

COLLECTIVE INQUIRY SCHOOL CASE STUDY

PART 1: MEETING THE CHILDREN AND TEACHERS

In the Resourceful Community case study, we looked at the everyday lives of children and families from their perspective and reflected on child development as it was discussed by a range of professionals. In this section, we enter the Collective Inquiry School, to look at child development from the perspectives of a group of student teachers. We will follow the group of student teachers as they observe classrooms, speak to children, and experience how school teachers discuss and conceptualise their philosophy of learning and development, both individually and collectively as a school community.

This school is found in a community that has many newly arrived families from Africa (Sudan, Ethiopia, Somalia) and Asia (Korea, China, Vietnam), as well as European heritage families (Greece, Italy, France). It also has professional families from artistic and corporate employment contexts. The school does not have classrooms with children of the same age, but rather neighbourhood communities in which multi-age groupings are the norm (except for the first year of school) and where two teachers co-teach one neighbourhood community. This means that the spaces in the school do not look like classrooms; instead, there are 'home groups with two teachers' and 'home spaces', and collective spaces that all the children use with the support of other teachers.

Rather than lessons, the multi-age groups or neighbourhood communities have a big conceptual idea, such as 'Time', or 'Why write?' to which children and families are introduced as inquiry projects that they jointly seek to solve with their teachers over an extended period of time. The children ask their own research questions in relation to the big ideas, such as 'How do you measure time?' or 'Where did writing begin?' Groups of children research their own questions as part of the overall inquiry (see Figure 2.6). These inquiries collectively constitute a project that is fully documented and jointly assessed (see Fleer, 2015 for an overview of the assessment in the school).

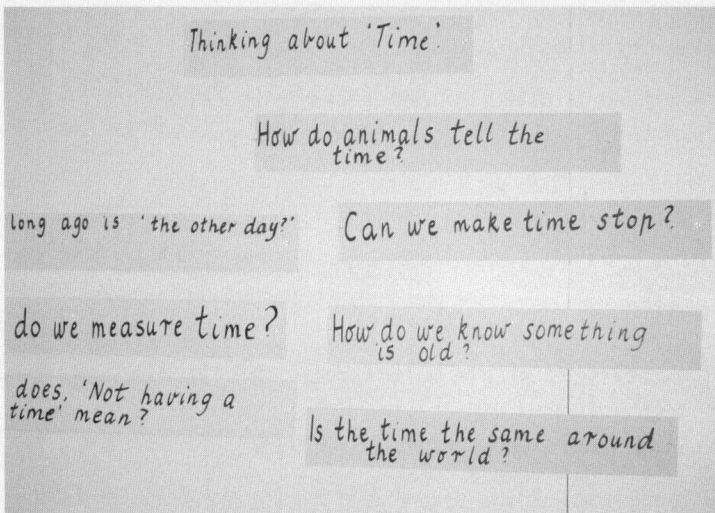

Thinking about 'Time'

How do animals tell the time?

long ago is 'the other day?'   Can we make time stop?

do we measure time?   How do we know something is old?

does. 'Not having a time' mean?

Is the time the same around the world?

Figure 2.6 Inquiry questions that the children investigated about the big idea of 'Time'

CHILD DEVELOPMENT REFLECTION 2.4: WHAT IS THE PHILOSOPHY OF THIS SCHOOL?

As you read the details of this case study, document your growing ideas about the child development terms being used to inform the teachers in this school. What child development terms are the teachers using to inform their pedagogy? Add the terms to your responses to Child Development Reflection 2.3.

We will return to these terms in subsequent chapters, where you will be provided with more case study content and child development theories.

The Collective Inquiry School has many visitors. Student teachers from a university were invited to visit the school and spend a full day observing and experiencing the school with the support of Lilly, a Student Council member, Esme, the leader of the senior leadership team, and Marilyn, a university lecturer who was a critical friend to the school. The student teachers sought to determine the theory of child development that was informing the teachers' pedagogical practices and observations of children's learning and development in the school (see Child Development Reflections 2.3, 2.4 and 2.5).

The university students were greeted by Lilly, aged 11. She oriented the group to the school by talking about how it was organised.

Lilly: Our school is different from other schools. We have learning inquiries and learning agreement times (Figure 2.7). We have a lot of freedom to follow what we are interested in, and can make decisions about how we want to find out the answers to the research questions.

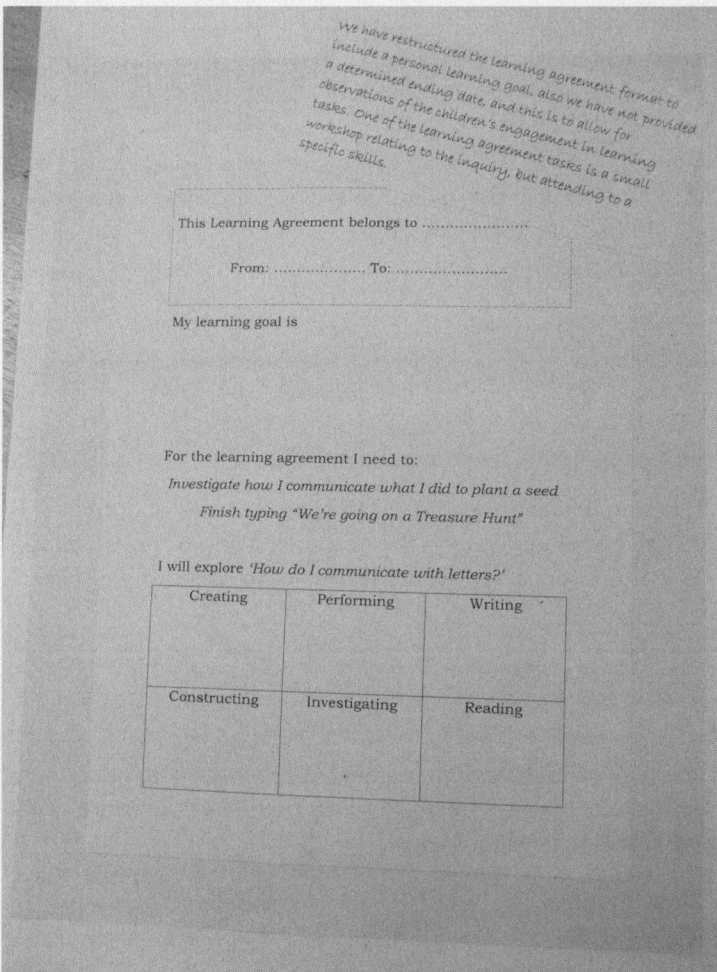

We have restructured the learning agreement format to include a personal learning goal, also we have not provided a determined ending date, and this is to allow for observations of the children's engagement in learning tasks. One of the learning agreement tasks is a small workshop relating to the inquiry, but attending to a specific skills.

This Learning Agreement belongs to ....

From: .... To: ....

My learning goal is

For the learning agreement I need to:

Investigate how I communicate what I did to plant a seed

Finish typing "We're going on a Treasure Hunt"

I will explore *'How do I communicate with letters?'*

Creating	Performing	Writing
Constructing	Investigating	Reading

Figure 2.7 Learning agreements: A child's perspective from the Collective Inquiry School

Student teacher: Really? What do you mean you 'do research'?

Lilly: We have to think about the big idea we are working on that term (Figure 2.6). We have an inquiry and we do our own research. I am a Student Councillor, and I meet with the teachers in my neighbourhood community to talk about what we need for the research we are doing.

Student teacher: What other things do you talk about at those Student Council meetings?

Lilly: Well, we talk about the big ideas that the teachers want us to learn, and me and the other Student Councillors plan with the teachers. They listen to our views. But they also challenge us. We often make surveys and interview other children in the school. We have different roles on the Student Council. Matt, who is also on the Student Council, is on the Finance and Fundraising Committee. I am on the Pedagogy and Curriculum Committee . . . [continues]

Lilly escorted the student teachers around her school. They were encouraged by Lilly and the teachers they met to not just observe the practices, but also to talk to the children about their projects.

On this particular visit to the school, Learning Inquiry Time was taking place. There were small groups of children actively discussing, role-playing, writing, undertaking experiments and more. No two groups were doing the same activity, yet all the children were working towards the big idea that was the focus for the term.

CHILD DEVELOPMENT REFLECTION 2.5: ANALYSING OBSERVATIONS

As you read the following, write down the questions you have about child development so you can better understand the practices being observed and discussed. Record some questions you would like to have asked if you had been there.

To determine the theory of child development that the teachers were using in the school to inform teaching practices, the student teachers asked key questions of the children, as the following three observations show.

Observation 1: Lilly takes the children into the Year 1/2 Neighbourhood Community, where the children are exploring time. There are small groups of children scattered all around the expansive spaces. They hone in on a small group of children who are creating a timeline around the walls of one of the rooms.

The children are placing photographs of events from their school, from their families and from their community on to the timeline while discussing the sequence and debating the chronology.

Observation 2: Another group of children is looking at a range of clocks, timers and other devices for measuring time. The children are drawing pictures of the tools in a thinking book, where they also record information they have found on the school intranet. The children discuss the nature of the measurements and then the usefulness of the tools with each other.

Figure 2.8 Learning Inquiry Time

Observation 3: Sitting with one of the teachers are three children who are looking at the photographs of the teacher. The children are laughing and squealing as they try to put the teacher's photographs from when the teacher was a baby on to a timeline. One child picks up a digital device and photographs the teacher, then places the image on the timeline. The children discuss their own photographs, then add these to the timeline.

After visiting the neighbourhood, one of the student teachers reported the following to Marilyn and the other students:

Student teacher: We were talking with Lilly about how, when we were at primary school, we had to sit at desks, and Lilly said, 'At this school, everyone listens and it works well, when everyone is engaged and hands-on.' Can you believe that?

Marilyn: Was it the content of what Lilly said or her ability to reflect that impressed you?

Student teacher: Both what she said, using pedagogical language, and that she consciously knows and analyses student engagement.

As a result of visiting the neighbourhood communities and talking to Lilly, the student teachers had a lot of questions that they wanted answered. They asked the following questions of the senior leadership team about what they had observed:

Student teacher: Can you talk about the idea of neighbourhood communities? What is the theory underpinning this?

Esme: A community of learners and the idea of a community of practice underpin this idea. In most other schools, traditionally each classroom is autonomous. But for us, we were looking at what is our community of practice across the whole school: how do we bring in resources, what are the practices throughout the day, such as, agreement time, targeted teaching, etc.? This is now leading us to the concept of a community of researchers. Everyone is a researcher: teachers are researchers, children are researchers, everyone is involved in the learning inquiries. What is particularly exciting is to see the School Council as researchers, and to observe them trying to interpret the resource needs of the neighbourhood communities, playgrounds, etc.

Student teacher: What are the structures you had set up in the school so that inquiries could be developed by the children? What theory of child development informs these structures?

Esme: The inquiries that were developed came about because children sat in planning sessions with teachers, discussing it with us as we were developing the programs. It's about negotiated learning – children have a voice in what is included in the curriculum, where is it moving to next – and it is about transformation through participation. Our theory of child development informed this practice, but so did the structures we put in place:

- *memoranda of intent* – this is about a team coming together to discuss how they are going to work together as a team throughout the year
- an *inquiry-based learning approach* – we have guidelines for that

- *big ideas* – which we discussed at staff meetings. These big ideas underpin the conceptual framing of the inquiries, which are continually re-visited. Big ideas such as sustainability, interdependence, time and 'Why write?'
- *embedding curriculum* – for instance, how are mathematical concepts embedded in these big ideas? This is a challenge for the maths leaders in the school. How are we engaging children in meaningful, real-world experiences to learn mathematics?

We were using a cultural-historical approach to frame our thinking about children's development and the aligned pedagogy. Sometimes this is called sociocultural theory. So it is not so much about the ages and stages of children's development (see Figure 1.2). We were questioning that view of development. Instead, we were focused on learning through participation, and creating a learning community. These terms come directly from a cultural-historical view of child development.

CHILD DEVELOPMENT REFLECTION 2.6: EXPERIENCED TEACHERS TALK THEORY AND PRACTICE

1   What kind of school practice did you notice?
2   What were the key terms used by Esme to describe the practices in the school?
3   How is the school practice different or the same as the practice you experienced when you were at school?
4   What child development terms did Esme introduce to the student teachers? What might these terms mean?

We will return to these terms in subsequent chapters, where we will discuss the child development theory that is informing the teaching practices in this school.

Conclusion

In this chapter, you have looked closely at a group of student teachers trying to figure out what theory of child development underpins the teaching practices found in the Collective Inquiry School. You have also looked at the family practices of the Peninsula family and Westernport family and thought about the children's development.

You were invited to respond to the problem situation found in each of the case studies following your own intuition. You were asked to think about how you felt about the situation, what you noticed and what mattered to you. Your responses were based on intuitive reactions to each case study. Intuitive reflection is a normal practice, and we frequently see this in reports presented on TV or radio, or read about views in the social media and in newspapers. However, as professionals we need to go beyond intuition and to draw upon theories to inform our analysis and build evidence. Chapter 1 showed the importance of educators in engaging with child development theory for understanding and working with the EYLF.

In the chapters that follow, we invite you to go beyond your initial – but important – everyday analysis, and to consider the particular theories of child development presented as a way of guiding your judgements. These theories act as conceptual tools for professionally analysing and thinking about children's development.

A theory is usually developed on the basis of empirical evidence that has been gained through systematic research. A theory has its own system of concepts, which have been proven to be useful for analysing children's development. By using theory rather than intuition, we are acting as professionals, using powerful concepts and being informed by evidence. The important aspect here is that the theory of child development:

- has been validated in the education community and is based on empirical evidence
- is made up of a system of concepts that are coherent and logical
- is known, and can be talked about to others and immediately understood, as the logic being applied to the particular situation – we have a common knowledge of and approach to analysis and confidence in the results
- is a powerful tool for analysis, reporting and planning for the conditions that best support the learning and development of all children.

However, how we feel and respond intuitively must also be acknowledged because it reveals something about our own belief system. If we follow our intuition, it is more difficult for us to logically analyse, talk with others and feel confident that our analysis is rigorous and based on evidence.

Each of the chapters that follow will offer different insights into the problem situations that emerged and that you were invited to consider in this chapter (Child Development Reflections 2.1 to 2.6). In the final part of the book, you will need to decide upon which theory of child development appears to have the most analytical power for informing the kinds of conditions you want to create for the teaching and learning of young children in the communities in which you will work.

References

Fleer, M 2013, 'Examining the relations between a play motive and a learning motive for enhancing school achievement', in K Ku & S Phillipson (eds), *Constructing achievement: A sociocultural perspective*, London: Routledge, pp. 105–17.

——2014, 'Cultural-historical theories of child development', in T Maynard, S Powell & N Thomas (eds), *An introduction to early childhood studies*, 3rd ed., London: Sage, pp. 127–44.

—— 2015, 'Developing an assessment pedagogy: The tensions and struggles in re-theorising assessment from a cultural–historical perspective', *Assessment in Education: Principles, Policy & Practice*, 22(2), 224–46.

Fleer, M & Hedegaard, M 2010, 'Children's development as participation in everyday practices across different institutions: A child's changing relations to reality', *Mind, Culture and Activity*, 17(2), 149–68.

Fleer, M & Quiñones, G 2009, 'Assessment of children's technological funds of knowledge as embedded community practices', in A Jones & M de Vries (eds), *Handbook for research and development in technology education*, Rotterdam: Sense, pp. 477–92.

Fleer, M & Robbins, J 2005a, 'Broadening the circumference: A socio-historical analysis of family enactments of literacy and numeracy within the official script of middle class early childhood discourse', *Outline*, 6(20), 17–24.

—— 2005b, '"There is much more to this literacy and numeracy than you realise ...": Family enactments of literacy and numeracy versus educators' constructions of learning in home contexts', *Journal of Australian Research in Early Childhood Education*, 12(1), 23–42.

Fleer, M & Williams-Kennedy, D 2002, *Building bridges: Researching literacy development for young Indigenous children*, Canberra: Australian Early Childhood Association.

Hedegaard, M & Fleer, M 2013, *Play, learning and children's development: Everyday life in families and transition to school*, New York: Cambridge University Press.

Kennedy, A, Ridgway, A & Surman, L 2006, '"Boundary crossing": Negotiating understandings of early literacy and numeracy pathways', *Australian Journal of Early Childhood*, 31(4), 15–22.

CHAPTER 3

Observing children and using theory to analyse learning and development

Introduction

In this chapter, the focus will be on observing children and using theory to analyse learning and development. Two related sets of theories of child development are introduced as the framework for making observations of children: sociocultural/ cultural-historical theory; and maturational developmental theories. The intention of this chapter is to support you to actively engage in creating knowledge about child development through learning how to observe and analyse children in school/ centre and home communities. To achieve this, a range of examples of observing and analysing will be provided, and examples of how to make quality observations of children will be presented through the eyes of university students. The nuts and bolts of observing and analysing will be illustrated through the challenges and successes identified by these student teachers (see also Fleer & Robbins, 2004a, 2004b). Protocols for respectful and ethical practices when observing children will be highlighted in relation to culture, community and country. Country foregrounds Aboriginal and Torres Strait Islander perspectives.

Through engaging with the content of this chapter, it is anticipated that you will:

- be able to make holistic observations of child development in the family, community, preschool and school
- become aware of the importance of listening to the voice of the Aboriginal and Torres Strait Islander community in the context in which you will be teaching
- develop insights into the range of ways in which analysis can be framed, such as a sociocultural approach, as shown through Barbara Rogoff's three planes/ lenses of analysis; and maturational developmental views, through milestones and checklists

- learn that theories determine what you see and how you act
- be sensitive to cultural validity and ethical practices, where cultural ways of engaging with communities are central.

Figure 3.1 Observing children

In this chapter, we link back to Chapter 2 and examine and build on the content of the Resourceful Community case study. The final two case studies, the Culturally Diverse Preschool and the Building Bridges Community, will be introduced briefly in this chapter. Together, this chapter and those that follow will provide you with the source material you need to successfully observe children and use theory to ana-lyse learning and development.

Approaches to gathering information about children

Researching children's development: Capturing the child's perspective

There are many different ways to observe children's development (Fleer, 2005a, 2005b; Hedegaard, 2012; Stetsenko & Arievitch, 2004). Each approach to studying children is informed by a particular theoretical perspective (e.g. Ochs & Izguierdo, 2009). While it is not possible to cover all the methodologies and their correspond-ing methods, we can examine two common ways of observing and analysing children's development:

- a developmental approach to observing and studying children development
- a cultural-historical, or sociocultural, approach to observing and studying children's development.

A key analytical question that will inform the presentation of these two approaches is: How do we follow, capture and gain an understanding of the child's perspective when observing and studying their development?

As you read this chapter, reflect upon how well the two approaches to observing and studying children's development capture (or not) the child's perspective.

Over the years, many critiques have been undertaken of how to study children's development (e.g. Correa-Chavez, Mejia-Arauz & Rogoff, 2015; Farquhar & Fleer, 2007; Saracho, 2015). A range of theoretical orientations informing the critiques can be observed (Burman, 2008; Nsamenang, 2009). However, what appears to be common to these critiques is the view that many traditional approaches have not taken into consideration:

- the societal conditions
- the values and expectations within particular communities
- the diversity of what informs, and therefore constitutes evidence of children's development
- the tools used for gathering evidence – do they capture what matters for a particular cultural community, education system, family, or even the society at large?(Hedegaard & Fleer, 2008)

But how might we capture these important dimensions of the context in which children develop? In the next section, we begin answering this question by examining the dominant theory that has guided how we make observations and how we analyse those observations: developmental or maturational theory.

Developmental or maturational theories guiding observations and analysis

Developmental or maturational traditions for researching children's development can be captured through three key approaches:

- laboratory experiments
- observations
- child study approach (Hedegaard & Fleer, 2008).

Observations and the child study approach are of relevance to this book.

Observations

An observational approach seeks to carefully document and describe what is observed and spoken about. Key here is ensuring that the observer does not contaminate the research context and that the observations are objectively written – that is, they do not make judgements in their descriptions, such as 'The child was happy', but rather give a clear behavioural account of the observation, such as 'The child smiled widely' (see also Whitebread, 2012). It is important to ensure that the observation is written as descriptively as possible. This is foundational advice given when following a developmental or maturational theory of child development.

Two key aspects are important: observer bias and the effect of the observer.

- *Observer's bias.* It is suggested by Szarkowicz (2006) that when writing observations, the observer needs to be aware of distractions, cultural perspectives, feelings about the focus child, potential bias, their own comfort and, importantly, their own level of fatigue. These all affect the quality of the observations being made.
- *Observer influencing the observations.* The role of the observer is to be a 'fly on the wall' or to use a 'one-way screen' so that the observer does not influence the situation being documented. Observations are made of children in actual and local situations.

Writing observations: Following a maturational or development view of child development

How to write objective observations of children

Once both bias and influencing factors have been taken into account, the observer will do the following:

Setting up
- locate themselves in a place that does not interrupt the follow of traffic in the classroom or centre room.
- not draw attention to themselves in any way or interrupt the teacher or the children
- write down the name of the focus child (pseudonym is preferred if the observer is not a member of the staff working in the centre/classroom)
- note the date of the observation and the time period when it began (and later when it ends)
- describe the observation context – for example, standing at the back of the classroom or seated on child's chair in the reading corner
- if using paper and pencil to document in a notebook, draw a floor plan of the centre/classroom

- if using digital means, such as a mobile phone, or a mobile digital device or tablet, then set up their equipment to record and store the observation (without running out of memory or power). A folder should be created, in which a photograph of the context of the classroom or centre is included, and any notes needed to contextualise these photographs should be added. Some instructions for producing quality digital documentation follow later in the chapter.

Writing the observation

1 When using your preferred mode of observing (pen and paper, digital audio or digital video) document what the focus child does, such as:

- Focus child is seated on the floor in the book corner in the primary classroom. She is holding the story of *The Hungry Caterpillar*. Next to her is another child who is leaning over on the right side of the focus child. This child is standing. The focus child looks up to this child and says in a loud and forceful voice, 'Get away!' She then uses her right arm to push the other child, connecting directly onto the left leg of the other child. The child falls down (observation continues).

2 This observation can be done in situ when you are in the classroom; if you are using digital means, then simple field notes will be enough (as described above in 'Setting Up'). If you are digitally documenting, then you are likely to write up your observations later in written form. This means you need to follow the following steps after you have digitally documented and are working directly from your digital observations.

3 Make sure that descriptive language is used – such as, 'She then uses her right arm to push the other child, connecting directly onto the left leg of the other child.' Here the focus is on the behaviour – no inferences are made; only descriptions of behaviours are given.

4 Include what the child says and how it is expressed, such as 'says in a loud and forceful voice, "Get away!"'.

5 Make sure you document any key aspects, such as what the child is holding – the storybook – the name of the book may be important, so include that.

6 Include the context in the observation – such as, 'Focus child is seated on the floor in the book corner in the primary classroom.'

7 Record the time sequence – the beginning and end of the episode.

8 If you are using time sampling observations (see detailed examples below), such as when making observations for five-minute intervals where you might break for a period, include exactly when you start and when you finish for each five-minute observation (not the gap when you take a break – it is hard to keep observing non-stop, while writing what is going on). If you are doing this digitally, then you should set up your smartphone or tablet accordingly (if that is possible; otherwise time yourself and make each observation as a five-minute clip).

We now turn to an example of an observation for you to analyse.

CHILD DEVELOPMENT REFLECTION 3.2: ANALYSING BEHAVIOURALLY WRITTEN OBSERVATIONS

Examine the following observation. Circle the descriptive language, and cross out any emotive or subjective language.

Observation context: Block area – inside
Observation period: Morning session – 15 minutes

I observed Finlay playing with some animals in the block area, not very far from the home area.

He sings softly to himself and I can hear him naming and seriating the animals while playing. Finlay seemed oblivious to the other children in the room, especially to Charlie who is standing nearby, holding two dolls and calling Zak.

Zak came, and Charlie handed him a doll.

Charlie: My baby is a boy.

Zak: My baby is a boy.

Few words were spoken, a glance or look seemed to be sufficient to create the necessary link between both children who engaged in some kind of associative/co-operative play, each caring for a doll. Charlie and Zak commented on their babies' sex.

At this moment, Ethan, who had just arrived, joined in the play by stating, 'They can't do wee.'

Zak: . . . or poo.

Trish: Oh, that's interesting.

Ethan: Yeah, they don't have anything, only bum.

Trish: Hum, only bum.

Ethan: They don't have penises, so they can't do wee.

Zak: . . . and they don't have 'doodles' [pointing to sexual organs].

Charlie stayed at the periphery of the play, silently observing the boys as they talked. At this moment, I moved away from the play but stayed close by in order to observe and record their interactions. Finlay, who up to now had been playing with his animals and who remained a silent observer, pushed the magnifying glass towards the group of children, as if wanting to verify Ethan's and Zak's theory.

Finlay: Let's look under there.

Finlay concluded by saying, 'See they don't have anything and they can't move.'

The large group of children who were playing in the home corner started showing signs of uneasiness. This was soon followed by one child in the home

(continued)

corner, Ben, throwing a chair across the floor, thus indicating his needs to the whole group. This action stopped the children's thread of thought and the teacher ended the activity time and called all the children to a large group story time.

1 Who was the focus child?
2 What did you notice about the language used to describe the focus child in this observation?
3 What was the observer doing? Is there any information about the observer?
4 Was any contextual information given?
5 What cultural insights were reported, if any?

Mentioned briefly in the section above on how to write observations was how to record the setting. A key part of writing observations is the context. We now turn to this important aspect of making observations of children in school classrooms and early childhood settings.

Context

Observations in naturalistic settings, such as child-care centres and primary class-rooms, or the family home, are very different from writing observations in laboratory-based settings. Centres and classrooms are naturalistic settings. They include all the day-to-day activities that make up a particular educational setting. For instance, in preschools they include routines such as snack time or learning activities such as table top activities, floor activities such as puzzles, or even free play time inside and outside the centre. In primary classrooms, they include routines such as lunch breaks, learning activities such as specially planned lessons at the desk, whole-group instruction or even specialist classes such as physical education. All of these contexts are naturalistic settings because they are where we normally find children. These settings are complex to observe because many children are interacting and every one of these contexts is different and affords different kinds of opportunities for children's development and learning.

In contrast, laboratory-based settings are created specifically to study children, and they have their own protocols for what is to be observed and how the interactions are to be framed. These protocols are usually centred on how to set up the situation, how to enter these different observational settings, how to elicit the behaviours that the observer is seeking to document, how to record the observations in the laboratory or naturalistic setting (e.g. camera placement) and what the role of the experimenter is in the laboratory – or how to be the 'fly on the wall' in the naturalistic setting.

For example, in studying children's ability to learn by observing others, some researchers will set up a paper-folding activity for a pair of children. For instance, one child is shown how to make a paper plane. The other child is seated nearby but is not with the first child. The second child can observe the other child learning how to fold the paper plane if they pay attention. In this example, the observations are made of both children, but particular focus is on whether and how the second child observes the adult and child making a paper plane. The idea is to see whether the second child learns through observation, as evidenced by their glancing towards the adult and child, and whether they keenly observe (or not) the making of the paper plane. The role of the observer is to record (digitally or through note-taking). The observer acts as though they are not there watching/documenting the pair of children and the adult. Sometimes the laboratory setting is set up so that there is a one-way mirror/window in the room. The observer can record unseen what is going on in the laboratory. The children think they are in a room with a mirror.

Examples of these dimensions of undertaking developmental observations in laboratory and naturalistic settings can be found on the companion website. Also found there are protocols for using digital tools to make quality observations.

Digital tools can support you in undertaking observations. A summary is provided in the box.

Using digital tools for making quality digital observations

CHECK ON ARRIVAL AND DURING FILMING

- Check sound quality on entering site.
- Ensure the camera does not point directly towards a light source, such as a window.
- Stand filming away from machinery or rustling paper, or windy areas, as this will reduce the sound quality.
- Make sure the microphone is actually recording sound.
- Hold the camera at hip height with the viewfinder up, rather than placing the camera near your face. (Facial communication with participants is important for observing more broadly what is going on and it is respectful to the participants.)

CHECK DURING FILMING

- Ensure movement of camera is smooth as it follows the focus child.
- Keep the camera on, even if you are helping a child, such as if they fall over (this is contextually important).
- Turn the camera away if requested not to film something, but keep the camera running if appropriate.

CHECK AFTER FILMING

- Check the quality of the sound.
- Check the quality of the video images.

Types of observational records

There are different types of observational records, including:

- running records
- anecdotal records
- time sample records
- sociograms
- child study approach records.

Time sample records

Time sampling was mentioned briefly earlier in the context of writing an observation. Children in early childhood settings and primary classrooms do different things at different times during the day. Making observations of children at different times is important in order to gain a holistic view of their development. In the Westernport family in the Resourceful Community case study, the eldest child had a particular routine that he followed at school, and a timetable of activities he undertook with his peers. But how Andrew behaved and what he did when seated on the carpet in front of the teacher during story reading time were different from the way he acted at playtime or in the afternoons when he was tired. A time sample observation can be used to capture what children do at different times during the day. How a child interacts and what the child does in group time, when working on their own, and when playing with peers at playtime can provide insights into the child's development.

As an observer, you set up time sample records by making a decision about the time period during which an observation will be made and for how long. Deciding upon the different activities, such as play time or group time, will give certain information. You must also decide how long the observation will last – for example, a five-minute observation every 20 minutes will provide a sense of the child's activity for the duration of the period being observed.

Table 3.1 An example of a time sample format

Focus child:		Date:	
Time: Duration: Interval:			
Time:		Event:	Comments:

Running records

Running records capture a great deal of detail. They are used when a detailed observation of an event or a child is needed. When keeping running records, it is important to document everything that is seen and heard at that moment. Running records require a lot of concentration, as they are intense, and there is a need for fast typing or writing.

Decisions have to be made about how many children will be observed at one time. For instance, a group setting invites complex interactions. But this means documenting all of the children simultaneously, which is difficult. Often a focus child is chosen and that child followed. In this situation, the interactions of the other children are briefer and often missed or summarised, while the actions and words of the focus child are captured in detail.

Anecdotal records

Anecdotal records allow the observer to be flexible about when and how they document. This approach is in contrast to a time sample record, where the observer strictly follows the chosen time period for observing. Anecdotal records involve the observer noting something and later, when the opportunity is available, writing it down as an observation. Sometimes this means an observation of an event is not documented fully, due to not being able to physically record the observation. Anecdotal records are often made of events that are noteworthy.

Anecdotal records may be brief points that are elaborated more fully later, when the observer has time. It is usually a summary of what you have observed. Anecdotal records are a flexible approach to observing children, because they are done at any time. However, it is important to try to document fully as soon as practically possible, due to the risk of forgetting the necessary detail.

Sociograms

Sociograms are maps of observations of children interacting, such as during children's play or movement around a classroom. Often sociograms are done because of a worry about how a particular child or group of children may be interacting with eachother. There are many different ways by which sociograms are created by observers. The essence of the sociogram is to plot the interactions between children as arrows – with the head of the arrow indicating who initiated the interaction. Figure 3.2 shows an example of a sociogram where the triangle represents the focus child and the squares are the other children. It is possible to see at a glance who the child interacts with, and who has initiated the interaction. As with other types of observations, the observer needs to decide upon the time period for the observations – when, the interval, and the length of the observation. For instance, the time period might be at playtime. This is helpful if there is a need to know about who the child is playing with, and the interaction dynamics of the group of players. The time period might be every 20 minutes for five minutes throughout a whole day. This enables a holistic picture of the focus child's interactions over an extended period of time to be created.

Sociograms could be done of all the children in a group for a period of 15 minutes. Using this approach, it becomes possible to capture the general dynamics of a group. This means it will be necessary to document the name of each child being followed, in order to capture who they interact with and who initiates the interaction, and possibly even to record how long the interaction lasts (e.g. by jotting with the arrow a time period, such as five minutes or three seconds).

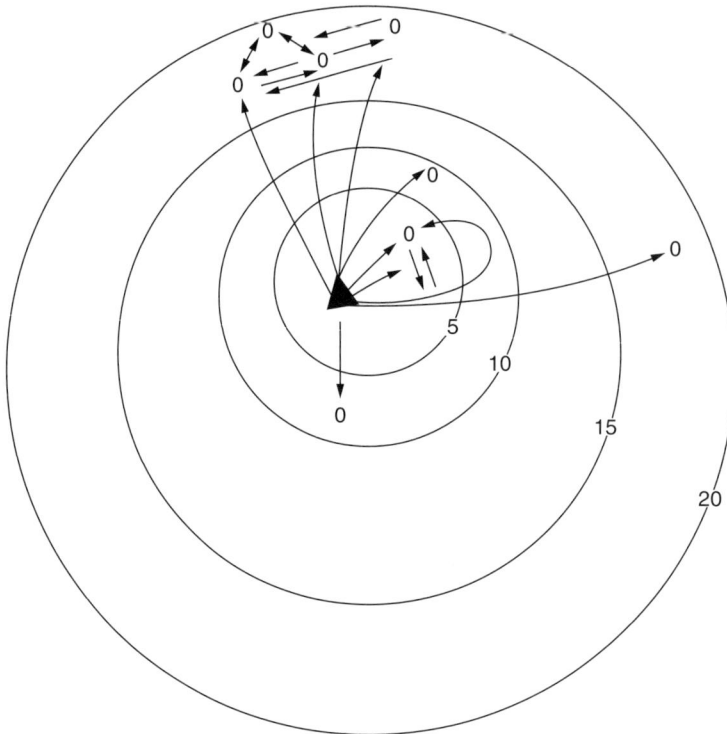

Figure 3.2 An example of a sociogram

Child study approach

The child study approach is an important observational technique for early child-hood education. This approach is thought to have originated through the rigors of developing a scientific approach to the study of pedagogy through the child study movement of G Stanley Hall. The approach that is the legacy of this work, and the directions it took – although diverse – now tends to focus on observations of children over extended periods of time (e.g. 12 months) so as to capture their development. Child development studies have been important for building evidence of the typical development of infants, toddlers and preschool children. This evidence has produced milestones of children's development. These child studies have given educators trajectories of typical development that they can use for assessing whether the child being observed is developing in the expected way. For example, infants will crawl, stand and then walk at particular age periods.

The key aspect is that child development studies are carried out over an extended period, rather than for short periods of time in a laboratory or a naturalistic setting. This affords different insights about a child's development. In the laboratory setting, we can look explicitly at one factor, such as learning by observing another child or adult, but this does not tell us much about how a child might do this in a classroom – or even whether they do this in a classroom. In a naturalistic setting, if we wanted to learn about a child's learning by observing, we would have to spend a longer time observing them – in different contexts, at different times of the day and with different children. This takes time. But we could feel more confident about our analysis because we would determine how and when a child learns by observing them in the context in which they would naturally be learning – their early childhood centre or primary classroom. It is richer but much more time-consuming. In research, it means that you would only be able to study a small sample of children because it would take too long to use this approach with, for example, 100 children. In a laboratory setting, it is possible to study many more children and be able to study them under the same conditions, and therefore to determine the results more confidently because more children were studied.

Developmental milestones

Milestones focus on what a child can do at a particular age. Age determines the child's development and key milestones usually include such things as when a child learns to walk and when they begin talking. They are usually grouped under domains, such as physical or social development. Schools do not usually focus on these groupings as explicitly, but rather focus predominantly on learning outcomes, as can be seen in the Australian National Curriculum. Milestones are often used to look for expected development when conducting child development studies.

A document called *Developmental Milestones* has been prepared as a resource to support educators using the EYLF (DEEWR, 2014). This resource mirrors the developmental or maturational view of child development that is shown in the EYLF (from the selection of child development theories shown). The material provided to educators to support the implementation of the EYLF includes the following developmental areas:

- physical
- social
- emotional
- cognitive
- language.

These are provided for the following age groups:

- birth to 4 months
- 4 to 8 months
- 8 to 12 months
- 1 to 2 years
- 2 to 3 years
- 3 to 5 years.

Examples of physical development for the 1 to 2 years period show the following observations:

- walks, climbs and runs
- takes two or three steps without support, legs wide and hand up for balance

- crawls up steps
- climbs up a chair
- kicks and throws a ball.

....

🌐 Developmental milestones

....

Challenges to maturational or developmental theories

The findings that have come from child development studies are still used by many professionals in the health and medical fields, where stages of development related to a child's age have acted as a guide for the assessment and care of children. Some of the tools developed have been shown to be problematic. For example, the World Health Organization (WHO) prepared a set of growth charts that advised practitioners not only on children's developmental milestones, but also the expected growth of infants after birth. These growth charts were used worldwide from 1977 through to 2006. These basic growth charts were developed on the basis of data on standard infant growth gathered in Ohio in the United States (Coghlan, 2007). Unfortunately, the growth charts were developed by studying formula-fed infants. This means that the expected growth of babies was normed on heavier babies than if the norming had been done on breastfed infants. Consequently, maternal health nurses across many countries who used the WHO growth chart were advising mothers who breastfed their babies that their infants were underweight. Further, the WHO growth charts did not recognise the diverse cultural communities around the world. Rather, the growth charts were norming babies to US infants from Ohio rather than relevant cultural communities, such as China, Vietnam and Bangladesh, where the height and weight of infants are very different. The tools that are created to measure child development must be examined carefully to see what data were gathered and used to develop these tools. Expectations and norms may not work across different cultures.

In returning to the Resourceful Community case study, it is known that Louise from the Peninsula family learned to walk at the age of 2 years (Fleer, 2014). If you used a maturational theory of child development to analyse Louise's development, you would draw upon the milestones of development and would determine that Louise should have been walking well before she turned 2. This was the assessment of the social workers who visited the Peninsula family home, and who told the mother that they were worried about Louise's development. An analysis of Louise's development (Fleer, 2010) showed that the family context, where moving around was valued, and where Louise's siblings continually went to her, meant she did not have a social need to walk. The adults picked her up. The long walk in the morning to school meant she was in a pram for extended periods of time. Everything and everyone came to Louise. However, just prior to her second birthday, the children were given a slide and swing set. Louise had to be put into the swing by an adult. She was too heavy for her siblings to pick her up and the adults were not always available to pick her up. Louise observed her siblings on the swing and slide set. This play equipment changed the practices in the family and created a need for walking. Louise developed a motive to learn to walk (Fleer, 2010). Understanding Louise's development from a developmental or maturational perspective, where the milestone of walking at a particular age were used to judge Louise's development, did not take into account her motive for walking. Developing a motive for walking was based on Louise's need to walk. A maturational or developmental view of child development does not explain Louise's individual trajectory of development. Rather, it puts a deficit reading on her and blames the family for her lack of development because she did not meet the milestone as was expected by the social workers who visited the Peninsula family home.

In Chapter 2, it was noted that the teachers were also worried about Andrew's development. They did not know that the family pedagogy was to continually be in motion when at home. Sitting still at school was therefore extremely difficult for Andrew (Hedegaard & Fleer, 2013). It was found that Andrew had to focus hard on staying still at school, and this left little capacity to focus on the content of the curriculum. In addition, an analysis of what Andrew paid attention to in school (Fleer & Hedegaard, 2010) showed that he tried to collectively engage with all the children, as was the norm in his family. This meant that Andrew had to continually turn his head to each of the children and the teacher, and to move his body so that he could view everyone. But this behaviour made him appear to his teachers to be a child with attention deficit hyperactivity disorder. A careful study of Andrew's development revealed that he was simply transitioning into school, bringing with him his family pedagogy of engaging collectively with family members, where moving around all the time was a valued home practice. The problem was not with Andrew's development, but rather with the discrepancy between the home and school pedagogy.

A developmental or maturational view of child development has also informed early education practices in the United States, with the US curriculum displaying a developmentally appropriate practice perspective (National Association for the Education of Young Children, 2009). Developmental and maturational views of child development have also led to a particular domains-based conceptualisation of children's development by many early years educators in the United Kingdom (BAECE, 2012). Educators divide development into the domains of physical development; communication and language development; and personal, social and emotional development. Children's cognitive development is focused on literacy, mathematics, understanding the world, expressive arts and design. This framing has been used to support the analysis of children's development in educational settings. For example, Alicia, who undertook a child development study, made the following comment in relation to a developmental view of child development:

> Using the classical developmental domains, we can learn what the child knows and can do in each of the developmental areas – social, cognitive, emotional, and physical. (Third-year student teacher)

Despite the critiques of maturational and developmental views of child development that have underpinned child development studies, milestones and a domains-based approach in the early years of education, important observational techniques have been written about in this body of literature. You will see examples of some of the observations in Chapter 4, where you will look closely at Piaget's theory of child development and a constructivist approach to learning that is related to a developmental view of child development.

Attention is now directed to the second approach to studying children's development: a cultural-historical, or sociocultural, perspective. This approach is examined so that you can learn about what this approach will allow, and what the challenges might be.

A cultural-historical, or sociocultural, approach to observing and studying children's development

Observing children's development from a cultural-historical perspective has attracted increasing attention in recent years, because it offers another way of documenting and analysing children's development. In particular, a cultural-historical perspective casts the observation net much more widely than the individual child, including contextual dimensions, social interactions, cultural values and practices, and a distinctively different role of the observer from a developmental or maturational view of child development.

A cultural-historical or sociocultural view of child development is based on the theoretical writings of Vygotsky, whose work – originally written in Russian – has only been available in English since the late 1960s through to the 1980s. In Russia, the term 'cultural-historical theory' has been used to capture Vygotsky's legacy. In the United States and in some other countries, the term 'sociocultural theory' has been coined (Fleer, 2016). There are other related and merging theories that have their roots in Vygotsky's work, but that have been developed differently. They are not discussed in this book.

Vygotsky's collected works (Volumes 1–6) give details of how development is conceptualised, and what system of concepts make up his theoretical conception of child development (Vygotsky, 1987, 1993, 1997a, 1997b, 1998, 1999). Details of this theory of child development can be found in Chapter 6.

A cultural-historical view of studying children has, in recent times, been developed further through the work of Barbara Rogoff, who choses to use the term 'sociocultural theory', and also through the work of Hedegaard and Fleer (2008), who use the term 'cultural-historical theory'. The former is discussed in this chapter, and the latter is covered in Chapter 6.

In this section, you will study Barbara Rogoff's (2003) sociocultural theory of child development. First, you will critique a maturational view of child development using a set of lenses conceptualised by Rogoff (2003). Second, you will be introduced to the third case study, the Culturally Diverse Preschool, in order to learn about Rogoff's three lenses for observing and analysing children's development from a sociocultural perspective. This is followed by examples and reflections by student teachers who have used Rogoff's theory for framing and analysing their observations.

Look for further insights offered by Barbara Rogoff on her theory of cultural nature of human development, discussed in different parts of this chapter and throughout this book, where she introduces the term 'Learning through Observation and Pitching In (LOPI)'. Finally, in the fourth case study, you will meet the families from the Building Bridges Community, enabling you to draw upon Rogoff's theory to analyse the observations presented. However, before examining Rogoff's theory, it is important to meet the person behind the ideas that have contributed to the development of early childhood and primary education in many countries.

Biography of Barbara Rogoff

Figure 3.3 Barbara Rogoff

Barbara Rogoff is a distinguished Professor of Psychology, and has been studying children's development for many years. She is based at the University of California – Santa Cruz. Her work has been instrumental in guiding researchers and students in undertaking observations in a broad range of cultural communities. Barbara's research, and the discussions that follow in this section, can be found in the key publications:

- *Learning Together* (finalist for the Maccoby Award, APA)
- *The Cultural Nature of Human Development* (APA William James Book Award)
- *Developing Destinies: A Mayan Midwife and Town* (Maccoby Award, APA)
- *Learning by Observing and Pitching In.*

The research and the accompanying theorisation discussed below have received a Distinguished Lifetime Contributions Award from the Society for Research in Child Development.

....

Professor Barbara Rogoff: Talks and LOPI

....

Rogoff's sociocultural approach to observing and analysing children's development

Barbara Rogoff's approach includes the elements discussed below.

Critiquing maturational or developmental theories of child development

In line with the interpretations of both maturational and developmental theories of child development, Rogoff (2003) states that most traditional approaches to studying children focus on the solitary individual child. This is represented in Figure 3.4, taken from the Culturally Diverse Preschool case study.

Figure 3.4 An individual focus: What is the child doing?*

This focus specifically ignores the setting of the activity. What do you think the child is doing? Is this child looking at something? Could this child be hiding something from another child? Has this child been asked to leave the group because of disruptive behaviour? It is not possible to answer these questions because we do not have enough information about the child's relations to others or the purpose of the activity.

How children relate to each other is very important, particularly in group settings such as child-care centres, preschools and schools. In these settings,

* Magnifying glass outline used in Figures 3.4–3.11: © Getty Images/mrgao

parents, peers – even siblings – and teachers are all recognised as relevant. However, Rogoff (2003) argues that, traditionally, we study the child apart from other people. In many traditional observations, teachers have been asked to keep individual portfolios for children, where children are often represented in observations and in analysis as separate from others – especially the teacher, who is usually invisible in all objective observations. Figure 3.5 is an example of this representation, where the focus child on the left – Hugh – is shown alongside another child.

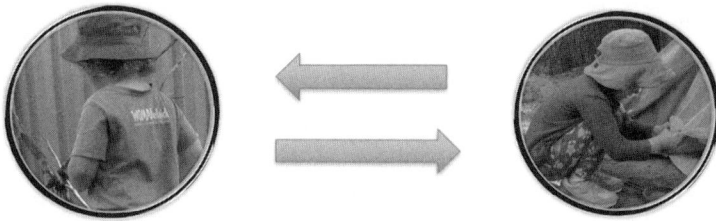

Figure 3.5 Bringing individual observations together: What might each individual be doing?

Rogoff (2003) argues that in this conceptualisation of studying children, the relations between children – even when in the exactly the same situation or activity setting – are usually discussed in terms of social influences. She says that social influences are 'examined through correlating the characteristics or actions of the separate entities' (Rogoff, 2003: 54). Further, Rogoff states that this is often shown through bi-directional arrows, as shown in Figure 3.5.

When you look at this figure, what do you think is happening? Are you able to work out what Hugh is doing and how both children may be relating socially? Once again, it is not possible to answer these questions because not enough information is given about how these two children are – or are not – relating to each other.

In Figure 3.6, it is possible to see the bi-directional arrows, where aspects of the context are now being made visible. The study of children's development is said to be influenced by the cultural factors or contexts surrounding the child. The tent is

Figure 3.6 How is the environment influencing the children?

now visible, and this cultural artefact is influencing the two children in some way. However, Hugh remains separate from the cultural artefacts.

Rogoff (2003: 55) notes that:

> The individual and the rest are taken apart from each other and analyzed without regard for what they are doing together in the sociocultural activities. With this portrayal of 'cultural influences' information, people's guesses about what this child [Hugh] is doing are still not very specific.

What is becoming known is that the child is in a context of camping; however, we do not know much more.

Figures 3.4 to 3.6 represent a typical traditional individualistic approach to observing and studying children's development. Portfolios of individual children frequently line the shelves of school offices and the filing cabinets of preschools and child-care centres. In many countries, it is a requirement that educators keep observations of and assessment records for individual children.

But if we take a cultural-historical conception of studying children's development, then a different relational image is formed. Rogoff (2003) provides insights into how this conceptualisation is different. By introducing the Culturally Diverse Preschool case study, where Rogoff's three lenses are used for reconceptualising Hugh, a different reading of Hugh becomes possible.

A sociocultural approach to observing children's development

Rogoff (2003) argues that when the same child is brought into focus in the observation in the context of the activity and educational setting, we position the child from the perspective of a *transformation-of-participation perspective*. We have information now on the interpersonal relations that are made visible in this observation, as well as the cultural-institutional context in which the child is located. We can see that Hugh is visually engaged with Yijun (Figure 3.7). A general sense of both the

Figure 3.7 First – the individual lens for analysis

cultural-institutional context and interpersonal relations is needed to make a judgement about what Hugh is doing. What do you think is happening here? What sense can you make of what Hugh is doing?

If we were interested in studying the interpersonal relationships, we would pay attention to what the children were collectively doing. This would be an interpersonal analysis. Figure 3.8 visually represents this type of analysis. We would be wondering, for example, if Hugh was just acting as an 'onlooker' or if he was signalling to Yijun that he 'wished to join the play'. We would be studying Yijun's response in relation to Hugh, and also studying Hugh's response in relation to Yijun. Was she inviting Hugh into the play? How was Hugh trying to enter the play? But in this analysis, we would not necessarily be examining the culture of the preschool or the cultural practices that children were bringing into the centre. We would need more information. We would be asking different questions and seeking more information in order to fully understand this interpersonal interaction between Hugh and Yijun.

Figure 3.8 Second – the interpersonal lens for analysis

Figure 3.9 captures the context of culture and community. The lens is over the tent (see also Figure 3.10). In this example, we can focus on what is being brought to this situation. It is clearly a play situation, because the tent is a play tent and not a real tent. This gives different meaning to the observation and to what the children at the back are doing – they have created a campfire. The sticks support a pot, which is dangled over a fire – once again, it is not for a real fire, but rather the setting of a fire. The children are probably in an educational institution because they appear to be of the same age – and this signals a child-care centre or preschool rather than a family setting. The cultural diversity of the children would support this. But we do not know much more than this.

Figure 3.11 constitutes the activity under study, as it captures the child (personal perspective), the interpersonal, and the cultural and institutional

Figure 3.9 Third – the institutional and cultural analysis

Figure 3.10 What do we foreground and what is backgrounded?

dimensions of studying children's development. In this example, we understand Hugh better because we have undertaken an analysis of his development in relation to an analysis of the interpersonal and cultural-institutional dimensions of the activity setting. We understand Hugh because we also understand the other children, their relations, and the cultural and institutional dimensions that shape and are shaped by Hugh's engagement in the activity setting. This is a dynamic context for analysis where we do not consider each of these relations (Figure 3.11) as separate entities. This is different to what is shown in Figures 3.4–3.6.

Rogoff (2003: 58) argues that '*The focus of analysis stems from what we as observers choose to examine*' (emphasis in original). We do not know about the historical or institutional practices, or even the practices that might be changing due to new government legislation about not having a real fire in an educational setting, or philosophical perspectives of the educators, who may wish to promote multi-age

Figure 3.11 Understanding the cultural, interpersonal and personal perspectives holistically

grouping rather than having children of the same age together in one group. This particular observation does not provide answers to these questions. More information is needed. As Rogoff (2003: 58) states, 'It is usually necessary to foreground some aspects of phenomena and background others simply because no one can study everything at once.'

In the next section, you are invited to practise using these three lenses for both observation and analysis.

Practice examples: Making observations and analysing development

We would encourage you to make observations of children and families in your own neighbourhood, preschool and school – potentially while on field placement (if this is an option). These observations, along with the source material provided in this and subsequent chapters, will support you with learning about how and why theory is so important for understanding children's development in educational settings.

CHILD DEVELOPMENT REFLECTION 3.3: REFLECTING UPON THE THREE-LENS APPROACH

Selena is a student teacher in the third year of her degree. You read her observation in Child Development Reflection 3.2. She analysed this observation using Rogoff's three lenses. Before you read her analysis, go back to Child

(continued)

Development Reflection 3.2 and undertake your own analysis using Rogoff's three lenses:

- analysing from a personal lens perspective
- analysing from an interpersonal lens perspective
- analysing from an institutional and cultural perspective.

Now compare your analysis with the one that follows. As you read Selena's analysis, consider whether you agree with her. Think about why you do or do not agree.

PERSONAL FOCUS OF ANALYSIS

Finlay (3 years, 5 months) was actively involved in observing some animals, which he accurately identified while talking and singing softly to himself. He displayed some early mathematical concepts (classifying his animals in order of size). He played in parallel to the other children for some time, then gained access to the play by engaging in conversation with the other children. He displayed the ability to share equipment and knowledge as well as showing interest in science activities, such as the magnifying glass for observing and identifying animals and body parts.

Charlie (3 years), the youngest and only girl of the group, used short sentences to communicate and displayed enjoyment during make-believe play (family activities). She engaged in some associated/cooperative play with Zak while sharing materials. Charlie displayed leadership while instigating play.

Reflections

> Had I limited my interpretation to the personal focus of analysis where I used a more conventional domain approach for recording my observations, I would have obliterated many influencing factors, thus obtaining a more static and narrow image of the child, consequently limited by opportunity to provide a rich learning environment for the children.
>
> Using Rogoff's sociocultural theory, where I used the three lenses of analysis in my observations, allowed for a wide spectrum of data collection, where I could consider the children collectively.

INTERPERSONAL FOCUS OF ANALYSIS

This activity started with two members: Charlie and Zak. Charlie acted as the instigator and first leader (calling Zak, inviting him to the home corner, and handing him a baby). Few words were spoken; a glance or look seemed to be sufficient to create the necessary link between the children, who engaged in some kind of cooperative play, each caring for a doll. Charlie and Zak commented on their babies' gender: 'My baby is a boy.' At this moment, Ethan – who had just arrived – joined in the play by stating, 'They can't do wee.' This moved the focus of the play while changing both Zak's and Charlie's participation.

Zak immediately joined in, moving from his nurturing role of 'family man' to a more scientific role. Charlie's role moved from being the leader to being an observer, standing at the periphery of the group, observing silently. Was she learning by observation, as suggested by Rogoff (2003)?

Finlay, who up until now had been involved in his own play at the periphery of the group, took the leadership of the play by suggesting that they should validate Ethan's and Zak's theory by observing the doll under the magnifying glass, 'Let's look under there.' He then added a new dimension, 'See they don't have anything and they can't move.'

INSTITUTIONAL/CULTURAL FOCUS OF ANALYSIS

Applying the third focus of analysis, I was able to pay attention to the different contextual and community factors that might have a bearing on the children's attitudes and involvement thus influencing the direction of the play.

Space

I considered the space and materials provided for this specific activity, and noted that, as a team, we had divided the space available evenly between the home corner and block corner. However, the block corner did not attract the group's attention except from the four participants named in the observation. They had simply decided to move to this area, as the home corner was overcrowded. This lack of space seemed to be responsible for Ben's frustration, which resulted in the throwing of a chair across the floor, thus communicating his need to the group.

Tools, discourses, attitudes and beliefs

The anatomically correct dolls served as prompts for the discussion on gender and sexuality. Ethan used accurate scientific terms, such as penis, whereas Zak used terms like 'doodle' to describe sexual organs. This choice of words of each participant reflected the influence of family discourse and values.

The nurturing attitude displayed by Charlie and Zak was a reflection of their roles, presumably something that came from their families.

Reflections

I reflected on how my role influenced the children's play. At first, I positioned myself at the peripheral of the activity, observing the children without interfering with them. Then I offered verbal cues to keep the play going. However, when Ethan moved the focus of the play to a scientific one, using terms like 'penis', I immediately felt ill at ease. I analysed this feeling and realised that coming from a developing country, which has a melting pot of cultures – mainly India, Creole and European heritage, plus a range of religions, such as Muslim – it would have been quite inappropriate for a teacher to talk about sexual organs, even while using scientific terms. Consequently, not knowing what the norm was in Australia, and being careful not to offend anyone, I retracted back to my role as observer, and listener to the children's play.

Selena also analysed her own approach to observing and analysing her observations. She reflected on what was important about using Rogoff's three

(continued)

lenses to inform her work as a beginning teacher. Do you agree with her? Why/why not?

> Using Rogoff's three lenses allows the observer to learn more about the children, and the contexts and people surrounding them. By using this perspective, we are no longer exploring children's learning through one lens – the individual focus; instead, we are becoming aware of the other factors in children's lives that are contributing to their learning, understanding and development.
>
> The theory that underpins Rogoff's three lenses was hard to understand at first, and the concepts were hard to grasp, but once an understanding is gained, this theory is powerful. We achieve a greater understanding of the whole dynamic context, not just the individual static child within it.

CHILD DEVELOPMENT REFLECTIONS 3.4: ANALYSING DIFFERENT APPROACHES TO OBSERVING AND ANALYSING CHILDREN'S DEVELOPMENT

How does a sociocultural view of observing and analyzing children's development compare with using maturational or developmental theories of the classical developmental domains (e.g. cognitive, social-emotional, physical)? Record your views. You will add to your reflections again after reading Chapter 4 and 6.

Culturally sensitive approaches to observing and analysing children's development

In this section, you will meet families from different parts of Australia. The families are from the Building Bridges Community case study. The focus of this section is on hearing the stories of the families. You will be invited to use what you have learned in the previous section to analyse the data presented.

BUILDING BRIDGES COMMUNITY CASE STUDY

PART 1: MEETING THE FAMILIES, CHILDREN AND TEACHERS

We begin with snapshots of the families – their stories and what matters to them about their children's development. This is followed by a broad analysis to show how the three lenses are used in another context (Fleer, 2005a).

The families in the Building Bridges Community were from different Aboriginal and Torres Strait Islander communities and had encountered different intergenerational experiences since Australia's colonisation. The cultural knowledge and practices were diverse across the different families, as well as the acknowledgement of the loss of cultural knowledge. However, all agreed that together they had important things to say to teachers about what mattered for children's learning and development in preschool and school. Further details of the families can be found in Fleer and Williams-Kennedy (2002).

The families participated in a study that involved filming their children's everyday practices at home, in the community, and in the preschool. The families specifically wanted to capture cultural practices that were important to them, and that they wanted non-Aboriginal and Torres Strait Islander preschool teachers to know about. The families video-recorded their practices, viewed what they had caught on camera, then shared those aspects of their everyday life that they wished to share when the families came together in Central Australia. The digital video content was initially shown and discussed by the families. This was facilitated by Denise Williams-Kennedy and documented by Marilyn Fleer. Then key aspects of children's development were then shared with the broader early childhood community, through a dialogue about what mattered and why. This was facilitated by Denise over three days.

The facilitation focused around three key questions, which were continually applied to the video snapshots of children's development in everyday family life (see Reflection 3.5).

CHILD DEVELOPMENT REFLECTION 3.5: GENERATING AND ANALYSING DATA

The study reported by Fleer and Williams-Kennedy (2002) used three guiding questions to analyse the practices of the families so that important cultural knowledge could be made visible. The guiding questions for analysing the video material featured three key points of critique:

1   When we look at snapshots of family practices, what is it that everyone can see?
2   There are practices that families have deliberately filmed to make visible what they think is important. But maybe these are not visible to others. What is it that only the families can see?
3   Filming everyday family practices often means filming what is routine, normal and expected. But sometimes these practices are so embedded that even the family can no longer see them. What might be family practices that we can no longer see?

You are invited to examine the family case studies using these three questions. Document one aspect that becomes evident because the families are using these guiding questions.

(continued)

1 What is it that everyone can see?
2 What is it that only the families can see?
3 What might be family practices that we can no longer see?
4 What do you notice? What forms of cultural knowledge are made visible? What aspects of the children's development are discussed?

Seven different family members are seated together watching a video segment of two children who are playing together. The video is playing images of two cousins aged 4 and 5 years. As they go to leave the house, one child helps the other child to tie his shoelaces. As the older child ties the laces of the younger child, he says 'cross over, under', then asks, 'Can you do double knots?' This everyday practice sparks a conversation between the family members. Denise begins the discussion.

Denise: In a school context, sharing knowledge with family members in the classroom is not cheating for Aboriginal children.

Laura: I shared knowledge when I was at school and the teachers used to think that when I used to help my cousins in the classroom that I was cheating. The teacher used to think we were all cheating, just because we were all helping each other, but really that's a cultural thing – if you know the answer then you really need to share it and it works in opposition to competition because the aim is for you to share what you have got and not to keep it to yourself. See, if you look at competition it is an individualistic thing: you are really competing against other individuals; with sharing, you are sharing with everybody. It is a different way of doing things.

Sharon: In school, children didn't want to feel too different and didn't want to not fit in; they are so sensitive to another child's needs; they look like they are sacrificing praise from the teacher for their friend. Our kids are so unselfish in that way.

Laura: The children need a quiet time to let the other child catch up to where they are.

Different forms of cultural knowledge were being discussed by Laura and Sharon. Cultural knowledge in the context of the families from the Building Bridges Community focuses not on ethnicity, but rather on the ways in which families and communities have come to know and act – the particular cultural practices specific to their family but also to the community in which they live.

Rogoff (2003) asks those interested to study children's development to consider what might be the cultural regularities observed in particular communities, and how knowing about these regularities helps with making sense of the cultural aspects of human development. This question is not just about the biology of a person, but rather concerns the ways families know, do and live their lives, passed on intergenerationally. This means both looking at the cultural variations that we see across communities and at the same time foregrounding the commonalities across human beings generally. Documenting the variations and similarities of cultural practices is important for understanding the dynamic cultural nature of human development.

All communities have cultural traditions, as do individual families. Cultural studies help us to better understand our own culture – despite people sometimes being blind to their own taken-for-granted practices. We also notice this in education, where assumptions about how someone develops have been normalised in a particular way. For instance, we saw in the maturational theory of child development discussed above that age is a central criterion for conceptualising development. What is expected is based on a child's age. The institutions of preschool, child care and school all reinforce this conception, because they predominantly place the same-aged children together to learn.

Rogoff (2015) argues that this belief in how children develop has supported particular practices that were based on an industrial model of education. By sorting children into age groups, and placing them into age cohorts in schools and childcare centres, we validate age as the central criterion by which development is measured. We expect a child to do certain things at a particular age. With this has come competition and a view of learning as being about the individual – a private activity that is ultimately their responsibility. Yet as we saw with Laura, she understood this industrial model based on European heritage values. She also knew that this Western cultural practice was different to what mattered for her extended family. Helping and sharing, and waiting for others to catch up, are the antithesis of the education journey that is privileged in many schools today. But what happens if a different view of development is adopted – a view that is focused on the cultural nature of human development? Making this cultural knowledge visible is challenging because the system already privileges one worldview. Documenting important family practices and analysing these so that important regularities and commonalities, but also differences in a dynamic flux of cultural development, emerge is one ethical way forward.

Culturally sensitive approaches to observing and analysing were found in the Building Bridges Community case study. The key was first inviting the families to digitally document everyday practices, and then to decide which material could be shared. Together, this ensured that the families were able to share and talk about everyday family practices that are important for educators to be aware of, so that they can better understand cultural practices, cultural values and know-how to align preschool pedagogy with family pedagogy. The key points for ethical practice in observing and analysing include:

- a mindset that accepts that culture is not what others do – we all have a culture
- a recognition of your own cultural heritage, but also an understanding that knowing about cultural communities requires taking the time and showing a willingness to adopt another's cultural perspective
- an awareness that cultural practices can only be understood as a system of practices that fit together and have cultural coherence for a community or family

- the knowledge that culture is dynamic and communities are always changing – culture is not a static phenomenon
- the knowledge that there are multiple ways of doing the same thing – not one best way
- the understanding that there will be diverse goals for children's development, and that we must find out what they are
- the ability to always position yourself as a learner in others' communities, as it takes time to see, hear and feel the cultural regularities and commonalities across and within communities
- the capacity to go beyond a deficit conception of development to a credit model – finding out what matters for a community is key to understanding how cultural practices are valued and enacted.

Below, you are introduced to a further observation of the families from the Building Bridges Community. Consider your own cultural stance as you analyse and reflect on the observation presented below.

> The seven families are seated around a large screen. Playing on the screen is group time in a preschool. The non-Aboriginal teacher is seated on a chair, and the preschool children are seated in front of her. The teacher is reading a big book. She is smiling, holding the book carefully so all the children can see the images. She uses animated language and facial expressions to give life to the story she is reading. Approximately half of the children are Aboriginal and the other half are of European heritage background. The Aboriginal children are looking away from the book, while the other children are looking at the book.

CHILD DEVELOPMENT REFLECTION 3.6: ANALYSING DATA AND WORKING IN A CULTURALLY SENSITIVE WAY WHEN STUDYING CHILDREN'S DEVELOPMENT

Undertake your own analysis.

1 If you were the teacher, how would you interpret this vignette?
2 What would you do if you were the teacher?
3 How might you change your practice or the children's actions? Record your views.

The following is an analysis by the seven families of the interaction between the children and the teacher during group time. An extract taken from their analysis is shown, with comments from Laura and Karen featured. As you read this analysis, reflect upon what you wrote.

Laura: Teachers are often giving off stiff body messages; those little ones know that. When I want my kids to stop doing something, then I do a freeze movement (shows stiff body). I have noticed that many teachers sit with a stiff body in front of the children. Our kids are getting mixed messages. They read it the way they always read it: the teacher sits still in front of the children; they use language but the teacher forgets about the message their body is giving. The children read the body language and they listen to the words – they then get mixed messages. Some children will turn away; the body is saying a different message to the words, so the child turns and doesn't see the body, so that they can concentrate on what's coming out of the teacher's mouth.

Karen: The kids are looking away – they are listening, but they are turning away so that they can understand; when you listen to music you don't have to look at the stereo!

CHILD DEVELOPMENT REFLECTION 3.7: USING THEORY IN ANALYSIS

1   Did you notice the same things as the families?
2   Was your analysis the same or different?
3   What did you learn from the cultural analysis provided by Laura and Karen?

Figure 3.12 Using theory to analyse observations

Looking to the future: Critiquing the two approaches to observing and analysing children's development

You previously read about Alicia's reflections on the a maturational or developmental view of child development. Her statements are repeated, but now the full reflection is given in relation to the differences between a developmental and a sociocultural view of child development.

> This theory gives us a greater understanding of and insight into children's learning and development. Using the classical developmental domains, we can learn what the child knows and can do it in each of the developmental areas – social, cognitive, emotional, physical. However, by using sociocultural theory, we can learn about children's relationships with others and their environment. We can focus on their participation with peers and the social context of their learning. The three lenses allow us to look beyond the children solely as individuals, and instead to the children as active participants in their social world. The learning and development of the child cannot be understood without paying attention to what else is going on.

Maturational theory and interpretations of developmental theory foreground the individual, with the environment being just one factor influencing the child's development. Attention was drawn to this in the Building Bridges Community case study, where it was shown that it is important to go beyond an individual perspective. In contrast, a sociocultural or cultural-historical perspective highlights the relations between children and families. The families from the Building Bridges Community case study stated that, 'It is not an individual child that goes into the preschool, but it is the whole family and community that is there.' Rogoff's (2003) sociocultural approach makes this visible.

Another key feature of a sociocultural or cultural-historical approach to observing children is the positioning of the observer. A sociocultural or cultural-historical approach seeks to include the observer in the observations. An example of this can be seen in the observations made by Harry, who included himself in his observations:

> Taylah and I are sitting at a small three seated table that has a container of teddy bear counters, when Jennifer joins the table and watches us. Taylah says, 'You have to sit here, Jennifer', pointing to an empty chair. Jennifer sits down and points to the teddy bears, saying 'Teddy bear'. Taylah opens the lid and begins to pull out of the contents of the container. She pulls out a large bear, saying, 'Mummy Bear. Look how cute they are, we can pick out all the same colours.'

This is very different from a maturational or developmental approach, where it is shown that it is important to ensure that the observer is objective and outside the observation frame. What is lost by including the observer in the observation? What is gained? Observations of groups is the norm in a sociocultural approach to observing children. Rather than just observing one child, as discussed previously, it is important that the group interactions are captured in the observation. The perspective of the individual child is noted, but only in the context of what the group is doing.

By using Rogoff's (2003) analytical approach, it is possible to go beyond an individual interpretation of children's development. However, this approach is complex and requires careful consideration of the theory of child development, as noted by Selena, who reflected further on the challenges of using a sociocultural approach:

> When I was first introduced to this theory, I found it very difficult to grasp the concepts and thought that it would be much easier to stick with the developmental, maturational view of child development. However, I am glad I persisted, as I have now come to realise the importance of sociocultural theory and how invaluable a tool it can be. It allows us to view the child through three different lenses, gaining a more in-depth understanding of what the child can do, where the children's interests lie and how we as educators can best adhere to their individual needs. It enables us to look at experiences critically and implement strategies to maximise learning and development.

Another example of reflecting is provided by Alicia:

> I have found, through using the sociocultural approach, that I have been able to record and interpret observations on a much deeper level. It is still a challenge to interpret the observations using the three lenses, but I am determined to grasp it, as I feel it will greatly benefit and strengthen my ability as an educator. It appears that recording observations is much easier using this approach, as I never felt comfortable using the domains-based approach of recording observations, which is due to my inability to remain objective. This approach gives me much more freedom to record observations in a style that suits me. I feel that the sociocultural approach gives me an opportunity to develop my own style of teaching, planning and observing that not only caters for my needs as an educator but also provides me with a richer picture of children, thus allowing me to provide them with meaningful and rich experiences and opportunities.

CHILD DEVELOPMENT REFLECTION 3.8: COMPARING APPROACHES

- Do you agree with Selena and Alicia?
- What was made visible in the analysis of children's development and what was unique to each of the different theoretical lenses?
- What was invisible?

Conclusion

In this chapter, you examined two theoretical framings for observing and analysing children's development. You looked at the essence of maturational or developmental views, and then at a sociocultural or cultural-historical perspective. Although there are many different methods available for observing children, such as checklists and sociograms, this chapter highlighted the essence of two very different theoretical perspectives for framing the methods of observing children's development. This gave you the opportunity to examine the strengths and weakness of both, through critiquing what they afforded and what was silenced by making direct comparisons between the two different orientations. In the next section, you will look closely at the foundations of key theories of child development. You will also critique each of these by using theory to analyse the case study materials that are progressively being built up throughout this book.

References

British Association for Early Childhood Education (BAECE) 2012, *Development matters in the early years foundation stage*. Available at: https://www.foundationyears .org.uk/files/2012/03/Development-Matters-FINAL-PRINT-AMENDED.pdf [Accessed 15 August 2017].

Burman, E 2008, *Deconstructing developmental psychology*, 2nd ed., London: Routledge.

Coghlan, A 2007, 'Babies overfed to meet flawed ideal', *New Scientist*, 28, 6–7.

Correa-Chavez, M, Mejia-Arauz, R & Rogoff, B 2015, *Children learn by observing and contributing to family and community endeavors: A Cultural Paradigm*, Amsterdam: Elsevier.

Department of Education, Employment and Workplace Relations (DEEWR) 2014, *Early Years Learning Framework practice based resources – developmental milestones*. Canberra: Commonwealth Government. Available at: http:// files.acecqa.gov.au/files/QualityInformationSheets/QualityArea1/ DevelopmentalMilestonesEYLFandNQS.pdf [Accessed 17 October 2016].

Farquhar, S & Fleer, M 2007, 'Developmental colonisation of early childhood education in Aotearoa/New Zealand and Australia', in L Keesing-Styles & H Hedges (eds), *Theorising early childhood practice, merging dialogues*, Sydney: Pademelon Press, pp. 27–50.

Fleer, M 2005a, 'Looking in and not seeing yourself mirrored back: Investigations of some Indigenous family views on education', in C Marsh (ed.), *Curriculum controversies: Point and counterpoint 1980–2005*, Canberra: Australian Curriculum Studies Association, pp. 432–7.

—— 2005b, 'Developmental fossils – unearthing the artefacts of early childhood education: The reification of "Child Development"', *Australian Journal of Early Childhood*, 30(2), 2–7.

—— 2010, *Early learning and development: Cultural-historical concepts in play*, Melbourne: Cambridge University Press.

—— 2014, 'Cultural-historical theories of child development', in T Maynard, S Powell & N Thomas (eds), *An introduction to early childhood studies*, 3rd ed., London: Sage, pp. 127–44.

—— 2015, 'A cultural-historical view of child development: Key concepts for contemporary and localised cultural contexts', *Asia-Pacific Journal of Research in Early Childhood Education*, 9(1), 45–64.

—— 2016, 'The Vygotsky project in education – The theoretical foundations for analyzing the relations between the personal, institutional and societal conditions for studying development', in D Gedera & J Williams (eds), *Activity theory in education: Research and practice*, Rotterdam: Sense, pp. 1–15.

Fleer, M & Hedegaard, M 2010, 'Children's development as participation in everyday practices across different institutions: A child's changing relations to reality', *Mind, Culture and Activity*, 17(2), 149–68.

Fleer, M & Robbins, J 2004a, 'Beyond ticking the boxes: From individual developmental domains to a sociocultural framework for observing young children', *New Zealand Research in Early Childhood Education*, 7(1), 23–39.

—— 2004b, '"Yeah that's what they teach you at uni, it's just rubbish": The participatory appropriation of new cultural tools as early childhood student teachers move from a developmental to a sociocultural framework for observing and planning', *Journal of Australian Research in Early Childhood Education*, 11(1), 47–62.

Fleer, M & Williams-Kennedy, D 2002, *Building Bridges: Researching literacy development for young Indigenous children*, Canberra: Australian Early Childhood Association.

Hedegaard, M 2012, 'Analyzing children's learning and development in everyday settings from a cultural-historical wholeness approach', *Mind Culture and Activity*, 19, 1–12.

Hedegaard, M & Fleer, M 2008, *Studying children: A cultural-historical approach*, Maidenhead: Open University Press.

—— 2013, *Play, learning and children's development: Everyday life in families and transition to school*, New York: Cambridge University Press.

National Association for the Education of Young Children 2009, *Developmentally appropriate practice in early childhood programs serving children from birth through Age 8. A position statement of the National Association for the Education of Young Children*. Available at: https://www.naeyc.org/files/naeyc/file/positions/position%20statement%20Web.pdf [Accessed 21 October 2016].

Nsamenang, B 2009, 'Cultures in early childhood', in M Fleer, M Hedegaard & J Tudge (eds), *Childhood studies and the impact of globalisation: Policies and practices at global and local levels. World yearbook of education*, London: Routledge.

Ochs, E & Izguierdo, C 2009, Responsibility in childhood: Three developmental trajectories, *Ethos, Journal of the Society for Psychological Anthropology*, 37, 391–413.

Rogoff, B 2003, *The cultural nature of human development*, New York: Oxford University Press.

Saracho, ON 2015, *Handbook on research methods in early childhood education. Review of research methodologies Volume 1 and 2*, Charlotte, NC: Information Age.

Stetsenko, A & Arievitch, IM 2004, 'The self in cultural-historical activity theory: Reclaiming the unity of social and individual dimensions of human development', *Theory and Psychology*, 14, 475–503.

Szarkowicz, D 2006, *Observations and reflections in childhood*, Melbourne: Thomson/Social Science Press.

Vygotsky, LS 1987, *Problems of general psychology: The collected works of L.S. Vygotsky, vol. 1*, N Minick (trans.), RW Rieber & AS Carton (eds), New York: Plenum Press.

—— 1993, *Fundamentals of defectology: The collected work of L.S. Vygotsky, vol. 2.* JE Knox and CB Stevens (trans.), RW Rieber & AS Carton (eds), New York: Plenum Press.

—— 1997a, *Problems of the theory and history of psychology: The collected works of L.S. Vygotsky, vol. 3*, R Van der Veer (trans.), RW Rieber and J Wollock (eds), New York: Kluwer Academic and Plenum Press.

—— 1997b, *The history of the development of higher mental functions: The collected works of L.S. Vygotsky, vol. 4*, MH Hall (trans.), RW Rieber (ed.), New York: Plenum Press.

—— 1998, *Child psychology: The collected works of L.S. Vygotsky, vol. 5*, MH Hall (trans.), RW Rieber (ed.), New York: Kluwer Academic and Plenum Press.

—— 1999, *Scientific legacy: The collected works of L.S. Vygotsky, vol. 6*, MH Hall (trans.), RW Rieber (ed.), New York: Plenum Press.

Whitebread, D 2012, *Developmental psychology and early childhood education: A guide for students and practitioners*, Thousand Oaks, CA: Sage.

PART II

Using child development theory: What does theory allow us to see?

CHAPTER 4

Using constructivist theory to analyse learning and development

Introduction

One of the key child development theorists who laid the foundations of constructivism was Jean Piaget. In this chapter, you will be introduced to his theory. Through engaging with this content, it is anticipated that you will:

- develop insights into Piaget's theory of child development
- understand what underpins a constructivist view of learning
- become aware of the strengths and limitations of Piaget's theory of child development.

The chapter begins with an overview of Piaget's theory set alongside examples of how this theory can be used to analyse the Culturally Diverse Preschool case study and what it might mean for children and their families from the Building Bridges Community case study. Links will also be made to the Collective Inquiry School case study. However, before you look at Piaget's theory, it is important to meet the person behind the ideas that have shaped curriculum and pedagogy in early childhood and primary education in many countries.

Biography of Piaget

Born in Switzerland in 1896, Jean Piaget showed a deep interest in nature, studying birds, fish and other animals in the environment in which he lived. His focus at school was on the biological sciences. At the age of 11 years, he published his first paper in a magazine on natural history, and thereafter he assisted the director

of the Natural History Museum to classify and catalogue zoological specimens. Between the ages of
15 and 18, he studied molluscs and published a
series of articles on these shellfish.

During his adolescence, Piaget spent time with
his godfather, who introduced him to philosophy,
broadening his interests from the natural sciences
to religion and logic, leading to an interest in epistemology: What is knowledge? How is it acquired? Is it
possible to gain an objective understanding of external reality? His interests led him to consider the need
to bring epistemology and biological sciences together.

Piaget studied biology, completing his under-
graduate studies in 1916, and two years later sub-
mitting his PhD thesis on the study of molluscs of
the Valais region of Switzerland. Interestingly, Piaget
decided to explore psychology after completing his
formal studies. He worked in two psychological
laboratories where he learned about psychoanalysis.

Figure 4.1 Piaget

Source: Wikimedia Commons/1968
Michiganensian, p. 91

Psychoanalysis

What followed was another published article as a result of undertaking further
study in Paris on abnormal psychology (as it was named then).

In 1920, Piaget took up a position in the Binet Laboratory (the foundational
research laboratory for the construction of IQ tests).

Binet Laboratory

In the laboratory, he used strict procedures to determine responses to questions.
This experience led Piaget not only to focus on correct responses to questions,
but also to explore the incorrect responses given by children. What he noticed
was that particular 'wrong answers' appeared at particular ages. Piaget became
curious about why children gave the responses they did, concluding that older
children were not just brighter, but gave qualitatively different answers. He
rejected claims about quantitative responses forming an IQ score and decided
that researching the different methods of thinking at different ages was a productive line of inquiry.

In 1921, Piaget took up the post of Director of the Jean-Jacques Rousseau
Institute in Geneva. From 1923 to 1932, he researched (using naturalistic and
experimental observations) and published a series of books on children's
development.

Piaget's own children were born in 1925, 1927 and 1931, and he and his wife closely observed their children. These observations informed the publication of two books:

- *The Origins of Intelligence in Children* (Piaget, 1952)
- *The Construction of Reality in the Child* (Piaget, 1954)

More research, further publications and further appointments, including to the Geneva University and the University of Paris (Sorbonne) resulted. Most of Piaget's studies and subsequent books were focused on particular problems, such as children's thinking or logic in relation to time, velocity and movement (at the suggestion of Albert Einstein). This resulted in a need for a general understanding of Piaget's theory in one publication. A book by Inhelder and Piaget, titled *The Psychology of the Child*, was published in 1966. Throughout his long career, Piaget continued to research the relations between adaptation to the environment and children's development of logic, bringing together his two passions of epistemology and methods of researching in the natural sciences (Piaget, 1972b).

A constructivist view of learning and development

As you might expect, Piaget's work informed the scope and sequence of mathematics curriculum in many countries around the world. His research also gave new directions for science education – both in his method of studying children's thinking and the kinds of conceptions that children had about their world. For example, Piaget studied children's logic about the natural world. He examined children's explanations of:

- movement – for example, the nature of air, the origins of the wind and of breath
- prediction and explanation – for example, the floating of boats, the problem of shadows
- machines – for example, the mechanism of bicycles, trains, cars and planes.

His approach can be seen in the following example of the problem of shadows:

> GALL (5): Why is there a shadow here? [We make a shadow with the hand] – *Because there is a hand.* – Why is this shadow black? – *Because … because you have bones.* – You see this paper, why is it black here? [the shadow of the paper] – *Because there is a hand* [Gall clings to the idea that the shadow comes from the hand, although there is now only a piece of paper in question] (Piaget, 1972a: 181–2)

In studying children's explanations of their natural world, Piaget developed insights into the kinds of responses children gave at particular ages. In the example of shadows, he determined that there were four stages of development in children's logic:

- *Stage 1:* A shadow is a substance emanating from the object and participating with night.
- *Stage 2:* A shadow is a substance emanating from the object alone.
- *Stage 3:* A shadow is a substance which flees from light.
- *Stage 4:* A scientific explanation is given.

In the first stage, a child believes that a shadow comes from the object itself and is participating with the night. In his early work, Piaget's stages were determined through asking children questions about natural phenomena, as the following explanation of shadows by Roc demonstrates.

> Roc (6;6) also believes in the participation of two origins: Look [the shadow of our hand on the table.] What makes this shadow? – *The trees.* – How is that? – *When they are quite close* [some trees] *to the others.* – But why does that make it dark here? – *Because there is something on to* [because the hand is on the table.] – Then why does that make it black? – *Because there are things on the group.* – What? *Trees sometimes.* (Piaget, 1972a: 182)

Piaget argued that Roc was hesitating between two ideas. One explanation drew upon an analogy between the shadow produced by the hand and that produced by the tree. He also noted that night caused some challenges for children in explaining shadows to the interviewer. For example, in the continuation of the interview with Roc, this conclusion is shown:

> We then make a shadow with a pocket-book. Where does this shadow come from? – *It comes from the sky.* – And there? [in our open hand]? – *No.* – And there? [under the hand and putting the hand on the table.] – *Yes.* – Where does it come from? – *From the sky.* What is the shadow made of? – *Of the trees.* Shadows exist even in the night?: Look, I am making a shadow with my hand. If it were night, would it still make a shadow? – *Yes.* – Why? – *Because it is low down* [the hand is near the table.] – Would you see it? – *No.* – Why not? – *Because it would be night in the rooms.* (Piaget, 1972a: 182–3)

In the second stage, Piaget found, children discuss the cause of a shadow in relation to the object itself, and do not discuss any form of participation, such as their hand.

> Leo (7) tells us, as soon as we ask him what is a shadow: *The shadow comes from under the tree.* But this affirmation has little effect on what follows. We point out to Leo the shadow of a man walking in the street: Yes. *It's everywhere you walk, it makes the person on the ground and it makes the shadow.* – Why is it black at the back? – *Because it makes the person on the ground.* – Where does it come from? – *It comes from the steps you make.* – How is that? – *It's the person who does it on the ground. He walks and that makes the shape on the ground.* – How is that? – *It is because all the steps that you make, the person on the ground always follows your feet.* (Piaget, 1972a: 186)

The third stage is shown below through an example from Bab:

> Bab (8; 11) seems at first to be nearer the truth: How is it that there is a shadow under the tree? – *Because you can see a little bit of dark.* – Why? – *Because there are leaves, that stop you seeing the daylight.* Bab also knows, apart form a momentary mistake, how to decide on which side the shadow will appear. But he cannot explain the reason for the observed facts: Why is the shadow on this side? – *Because it ought to be on this side and not on the other. Because it can't be on the other side ... The other side makes them too ... Because it has to.* (Piaget, 1972a: 188)

Piaget interpreted Bab's responses to show evidence of the third state – that is, the child knows that the shadow will appear on the other side of the object, but the child is unable to provide a reason for this. Piaget felt this was because the child did not yet understand light, and the logic applied was that a shadow is a substance.

The fourth stage of a child's thinking about shadows is where the child gives the correct scientific definition.

What we learn from Piaget's pioneering research is that he gained insights into what children aged 3 to 12 years thought about a broad range of natural phenomena, such as the sun, moon and living creatures. He found that young children's explanations of natural phenomena tended to categorise them (in words and actions) as part of the living world. This concept, known as animism, is how children begin to categorise their world in relation to themselves and other human beings. That is, the natural phenomena are thought to hold human characteristics and their actions are attributed to what a human might do. For example, lakes act intentionally, just as a human might. While these observations were not unique to Piaget's work, the patterns he noted in relation to the ages of the children were new. Consequently, 'ages and stages' became an important dimension of his theory of child development. The work went beyond the isolated conceptions or misconceptions of children and brought attention to the systematic way of thinking at a particular age. Indeed, this is what he is still known for, along with his pioneering work in the scientific thinking of children (and mathematics, as we will see later), which together established the foundations for a theory of constructivism for education.

CHILD DEVELOPMENT REFLECTION 4.1: PIAGET IN CONTEMPORARY CONTEXTS – ANALYSING CHILDREN'S SCIENTIFIC THINKING

1   In reading through the examples on shadows, and learning about how children's logic develops, consider:
    - the questions asked by the interviewer
    - how you would respond to the questions
    - how you might respond to the questions if you had no scientific knowledge of light.

(continued)

2   Ask these same questions of children aged 5, 6 and 7. Do the children respond in the same way to those interviewed by Piaget?

3   Modify the questions. Ask your questions of another group of children of the same age:

- Are the responses the same or different?
- What patterns did you notice in children's responses?
- Do your children employ the same logic as the children interviewed by Piaget and his colleagues? Why or why not?

The studies undertaken by Piaget and his colleagues focused primarily on interviewing hundreds of children. His interest was not so much in what an individual child said – their 'misconceptions', as it later became known in science education research – but rather the similarities between children at particular ages. This orientation in his research – to look for patterns of logic in relation to children's ages – was a different approach to the one that dominated child development at the time. His early method of interview was more naturalistic than research that was more predetermined – as one might expect in formal interview contexts where precise questions are asked in a rigid sequence.

The approach that Piaget adopted was the *clinical interview*. This involved a one-to-one interview with a child, where the overall goal was known but the interview questions varied based on the circumstances of the situation, as we saw in the examples of children being interviewed about shadows. Each example had similar questions, but the questions were always formed in relation to what the child had said.

Later, Piaget adopted a cross-sectional study design in which he interviewed many children of different ages in order to gain insights into the characteristics of their thinking at a particular age. Here, he used a more formal and consistent approach, as you will see in the examples that follow on children's understanding of conservation. The patterns he found in his studies laid the foundations for his theory of child development.

CULTURALLY DIVERSE PRESCHOOL CASE STUDY

PART 1: OBSERVING AND ANALYSING CHILDREN'S DEVELOPMENT IN THE CULTURALLY DIVERSE PRESCHOOL

In the Culturally Diverse Preschool, the teachers sought to introduce specific learning concepts to the children in the play-based setting. According to Piaget, these 4-year-old children should be working with symbolic play, preparing graphical representations, making representations of what they would expect rather than what they see in their drawing, be able to produce mental images, and use language to help them think. But what sense can we make of the children from the Culturally Diverse

Preschool? In Figure 4.2, the children are using digital tools to capture their investigations – as a placeholder of what is inside the compost bin. This constitutes part of their study of microbes. Should these children be mentally able to represent microbes – something that must be imagined?

Figure 4.2 Studying the organisms in the compost bin

The children collect samples of compost and pond water so that they can examine these under a digital microscope – as shown in Figure 4.3.

Figure 4.3 Studying what is inside the pond water and the soil samples taken from the outdoor play area

These experiences provide a strong basis for studying microbes and constructing understandings about microbes.

These children are gathering data. They are predicting and representing; they are also imagining. The contexts in which they are working are meaningful – they are not decontextualised facts. The children know about the compost bin, as they put food scraps in it each day, but they have not previously studied decomposition.

Similarly, they have not studied the organisms found in the compost bin. The digital tools have made this kind of study possible. These tools clearly did not exist when Piaget developed his theory and undertook his foundational research. What is being afforded here for the children that Piaget might not have considered? Would it matter that the children are from different cultural backgrounds to the children studied by Piaget?

Much of the long-standing Western literature on learning science suggests that young children are unlikely to learn about microscopic organism until they are much older. The scope and sequence of learning science does not cover this topic for this age group in the literature or in the curriculum in Australia, where these children live. In fact, this topic has not been previously studied in this age group. Digital tools have changed how young children can and do engage in their world. What might this suggest about predetermined stages of development that Piaget theorised?

CHILD DEVELOPMENT REFLECTION 4.2: THE RESULTS OF YOUR ANALYSIS OF THE CULTURALLY DIVERSE PRESCHOOL CASE STUDY

1   What did you learn about the children's development?
2   What did you learn about using Piaget's theory?

Piaget also undertook a series of studies into children's thinking in mathematics. If you are currently studying or have studied a mathematics education unit, then undertake Child Development Reflection 4.3. Otherwise, skip over it and come back when you have finished reading this chapter.

CHILD DEVELOPMENT REFLECTION 4.3: PIAGET IN CONTEMPORARY CONTEXTS – ANALYSING THE MATHEMATICS CURRICULUM

1   Look through the scope and sequence of a program/curriculum for children learning mathematics. Examine both the EYLF and the National Curriculum for the F–6 levels. Look for the terms 'classification', 'seriation', 'correspondences', 'matrices' and 'double-entry tables' in the curriculum. Look for concepts such as one-to-one correspondence or many-to-one correspondence. At what age are these terms and concepts introduced to children?
2   As you read the next section, consider the concepts and note where they can be found in the scope and sequence of the curriculum. Consider the stage and age of a child's development at which the concept is first introduced.
3   When you look at the curriculum and at Piaget's theory, what kind of logic is being developed by the child during the different developmental periods?

Not just cognitive theory

Although Piaget is generally regarded as a cognitive theorist, according to his theory of child development, biological maturation, affective development and social interaction are all interconnected. For instance, Piaget and Inhelder (1969: 114) state that:

> The affective and social development of the child follows the same general process, since the affective, social and cognitive aspects of behavior are in fact inseparable.

Piaget and Inhelder (1967: 154) maintain that, 'Maturation is only one of many factors involved and the influence of the physical and social milieu increases in importance with the child's growth.' But less attention is given to the social and affective dimensions in their research, even though these dimensions were deemed inseparable from cognitive development.

Piaget argued that the stages of development he theorised applied to moral development, just as it did to cognitive development. However, because this aspect of Piaget's work was never taken up in education, it is not reviewed here. The key point is that Piaget himself did not consider that he was a cognitivist – his theory of development was much broader than cognitive development. However, it should be noted that Piaget used his developmental theory learned through the close study of children's thinking about their world, and his approach to studying children's development, to frame how he theorised the moral judgement of the child (Piaget, 1965). Consequently, what follows must be considered the cognitive strand of his theory of child development. The affective and moral strands of child development mirror what is presented below in terms of the stages and age periods of a child's development.

Piaget's developmental periods

Great developmental periods

Child development was conceptualised by Piaget and Inhelder in 1966 as a succession of three 'great periods' – the sensorimotor level; the concrete operations of thought and interpersonal relations; and the preadolescent and the propositional operations. Each preceding period is reconstructed in the child as part of an evolutionary process. These great periods have been variously named, and commonly known as 'sensorimotor (onset at birth)', 'preoperational (onset at about 2 years)', 'concrete operations (onset at about 6–8 years)' and 'formal operations (onset at about 11 or 12 years)'. Piaget was interested in studying how development proceeded along the evolutionary pathway he had documented as a result of a close study of children. Interestingly, many existing textbooks have placed his three great periods into four stages and sub-stages to support educators to understand children's development (see Table 4.1), even though Piaget never intended this theory to frame education (see Wadsworth, 1989).

Adaptation

Central to Piaget's theory is the concept of adaptation. Piaget (1962a: 2) said that 'every exchange between the child and his [sic] environment tends towards adaption'. He noted (1962a: 2) that, through his studies of logico-mathematical operations and intelligence, it is 'easy for me today to locate the beginning of thinking in the context of adaptation – in a more and more biological sense'. He suggested that, from infancy, the child begins a long journey of adapting to their environment. It is only by the age of 7 or 8 that the child develops a stable system of logical thought that they can use to operate in the world.

Structural integrity

Piaget referred to the characteristics of each stage as having some form of structural integrity. The term 'structure' is used to capture the patterns of behaviour observed at each stage of a child's development. A key point of Piaget's work was to explain the main patterns of behaviour he noticed. For example, in his research on children's classification, he noted that children aged between 3 and 12 years show different patterns of behaviour. For instance, children over 3 years are likely to arrange their objects according to individual similarities and differences, but also to arrange them spatially as an image or figure. Piaget named this 'figural collections'. He noted that children aged from 5.5 years begin to show rational classification – that is, they will form two groups of things that are alike and things that are different. Sub-groups might also be formed. However, when Piaget asked the children whether there were more flowers or more primroses in a grouping of flowers and sub-group of primroses, he found that the children were unable to solve this problem. Piaget found that the ability to understand this problem and to correctly answer it is established at 8 years of age. These curiosities set the stage for a great deal of empirical work in trying to understand children's thinking. Piaget and his colleagues studied many aspects of the child's development for their structural integrity – including space (Piaget & Inhelder, 1967), time (Piaget, 1969), language and thought (Piaget, 1959), logic (Inhelder & Piaget, 1964), moral reasoning (Piaget, 1965), imitation, play and dreams (Piaget, 1962b), reality (Piaget, 1954) and the world (Piaget, 1951).

Determining the mechanism

Piaget used the term 'mechanism' to capture and name the research problem he was interested in solving: 'the problem is to understand its mechanism' (Piaget & Inhelder, 1967: 153). Piaget and Inhelder (1967: 157) state that 'the central question concerns the internal mechanism of all constructivism' – that is, to find out how a child comes to construct a sense of their world, as we saw in the examples of children thinking about shadows. What might be the mechanism by which this logic develops? Piaget's research and theorisation about the psychology of the child laid the foundations for constructivism (discussed later in the chapter). This was particularly evident in science education, where his study of the child's conception of the physical world, alongside his method of studying children's thinking, changed the course of science education research and practice.

Assimilation and accommodation

Piaget introduced the concept of assimilation – borrowing the concept from biology – to capture the idea of what happens when a child meets something new. He defined assimilation as follows: 'reality data are treated or modified in such a way as to become incorporated into the structure of the subject' (Piaget & Inhelder, 1969: 5).

This means that when a child meets something for the first time, the child needs to incorporate this new object into what they already know. Piaget used the terms 'structure' and 'existing schematism' to draw attention to this process, saying that 'every newly established connection is integrated into an existing schematism' (Piaget & Inhelder, 1969: 5). He points out that how these new things are introduced is extremely important, because the child needs to become aware of the new object or item before they can assimilate it into their existing structure. Piaget makes the point that this represents a reciprocity between the object and the child. It is not a unilateral process between a stimulus (new object) and a response (child reacts). Piaget made this point in opposition to the dominant thinking at the time, which was behaviourism – see Chapter 9.

During the transition between stages, the child meets new challenges and must exercise a new form of self-regulation. In Piaget's theory, structural internal mechanisms change due to a disequilibrium. 'Disequilibrium' was a term coined by Piaget to capture those moments of mental discomfort where a child cannot make sense of what they experience or see. Disequilibrium has the effect of causing the child to reorganise their internal structures, and by so doing accommodate the new object into their new scheme of thinking. A state of equilibrium is then achieved.

Evolutionary view of child development

Piaget was interested in understanding structural differences between age periods. He divided up each great period into stages and sub-stages of development. These stages from his initial research are summarised in Table 4.1. Important for Piaget was the integration of successive structures that were laid down. The order of these structures is constant, following predictable successive stages.

Table 4.1 Piaget's stages of development (only the cognitive dimensions are shown)

1 The sensorimotor stage		
	Sensorimotor intelligence	Stimulus-response and assimilation
		Stage 1 (reflex)
		Stage 2 (first habits)
		Stage 3
		Stage 4 & 5
		Stage 6
	The construction of reality	The permanent object
		Space and time
		Causality
2 Preoperational stage		
		Deferred imitation
		Symbolic play
		Graphic representation
		Drawing
		Mental images
		Language
3 Concrete operations of thought and interpersonal relations		
	The genesis of concrete operations	Notions of conservation
		The concrete operations
		Seriation
		Classification
		Number
		Space
		Time and speed
	Representations of the universe: Causality and chance	
4 Formal operations: The preadolescent and the propositional operations		
	Formal thought and the combinatorial system	Combinatorial system
		Combination of objects
		Propositional combinations
	The two reversibilities	

(continued)

Table 4.1 Piaget's stages of development *(continued)*

	The formal operatory schemes	Proportion
		Double systems of reference
		Hydrostatic equilibrium
		Notions of probability
	The induction of laws and the dissociation of factors	Elasticity
		The pendulum

Piaget's evolutionary view of child development as summarised in Table 4.1 is now discussed further in relation to the case studies introduced in Chapter 2.

The sensorimotor stage

CHILD DEVELOPMENT REFLECTION 4.4: ANALYSING LOUISE'S DEVELOPMENT IN THE SENSORIMOTOR STAGE – RESOURCEFUL COMMUNITY CASE STUDY

In Chapter 2, you met Louise from the Peninsula family in the Resourceful Community case study, and learnt about her development at 16 months. As you read about Piaget's sensorimotor stage of development, consider Louise's development. What can you learn about Louise by using Piaget's theory?

According to Piaget, Louise would be in transition between the sensorimotor stage of development and the preoperational stage. The former period of development is characterised by both sensorimotor intelligence and the construction of reality.

Sensorimotor intelligence development begins with a stimulus–response and assimilation period that can be divided into six stages. During the first stage, Piaget argues that there is a smooth pathway for the infant from spontaneous movements and reflexive reactions with the arm or foot through to acquired habits to intelligence. For example, he suggests that when an infant initially sucks, it is a reflex action, but through association with the nipple, this leads to a recognitive assimilation during Stage 1. In Stage 2, Piaget notes that the infant begins to acquire habits, which he argues do not yet constitute intelligence. Habits are defined as acquired behaviours that he collectively terms 'habit schemes'. During the third stage, the infant begins grasping at objects, but does not yet develop a sense of causality. It is observed that the infant uses the same approach for different needs, suggesting that they are on the cusp of intelligent activity. In Stages 4 and 5, Piaget suggests that the infant now demonstrates practical intelligence – for example, moving the hand of an adult towards an object that is out of reach. By the end of this stage, the infant is observed to use knowledge of causality to act, such as pulling at a cloth with an object that is out of reach. During Stage 6, forms of insight become evident as the infant brings together previous actions to achieve a goal, such as stopping to look closely at the lid of a box in order to work out how to open it. This stage is the transition to next level of development, known as the construction of reality.

The central characteristic of the construction of reality, as noted by Piaget, is that at the beginning of this period the infant focuses on their own body and self. There is a complete lack of conscious awareness. Around 18 months, the infant progressively decentres, gaining a sense of objects existing even when they cannot be seen, and their sense of causality broadens. Could this relate to Louise's development? Cognitive egocentrism was a term that Piaget (1962a) introduced to explain and benchmark early mental development of children. This concept refers to the child's inability to differentiate between their own view and the perspective of others.

Object permanence

A defining characteristics of development in infancy is understanding the permanence of an object. Piaget notes that when an object is hidden from an infant at aged 5–7 months, such as when covering up a special object with a cloth, 'then the child simply withdraws his [sic] already extended hand or, in the case of an object of special interest (his bottle, for example), begins to cry or scream with disappointment' (Piaget & Inhelder, 1969: 14).

> Between three and six months of age ... the child begins to grasps what he [sic] sees, to bring before his eyes the objects he touches, in short to coordinate his visual universe with the tactile universe. But not until the age of 9 to 10 months does he actively search for vanished objects [by] grasping to remove solid objects that may mask or cover the desired object. This intermediate period constitutes our third stage. (Piaget, 1954: 13)
>
> OBS. 6. Laurent's reaction to falling objects still seems to be non-existent at 0;5 (24): he does not follow with his eyes any of the objects which I drop in front of him.
>
> At 0;5 (26), on the other hand, Laurent searches in front of him for a paper ball which I drop above his coverlet. He immediately looks at the coverlet after the third attempt but only in front of him, that is, where he has just grasped the ball. When I drop the object outside the bassinet Laurent does not look for it (except around my empty hand while it remains up in the air). (Piaget, 1954: 14)
>
> At 0;7 (29) he searches on the floor for everything I drop above him, if he has in the least perceived the beginning of the movement of falling. At 0;8 (I) he searches on the floor for a toy which I held in my hand and which I have just let drop without his knowledge. Not finding it, his eyes return to may hand which he examines at length, and then he again searches on the floor. (Piaget, 1954: 15)

At around 11–12 months of age, however, the infant begins to look for the object, removing the cloth.

CHILD DEVELOPMENT REFLECTION 4.5: OBJECT PERMANENCE

1   Although you do not have observations for the infancy period for Louise, when using Piaget's theory, what behaviours might you expect to see that provide evidence that Louise has object permanence?

2   What behaviours might you observe at 18 months that might be relevant for the scenario of the slide and swing set that show established object permanence?

3   Sit with an infant on the floor. Sit facing each other. Take a brightly coloured toy and hide it under a cloth to the right of the infant. Allow the infant to look for and find the toy. Then take the object and hide it under the cloth on the left side of the infant. What do you notice?

Object permanence

What is likely to have happened in your experiment is that the infant looks to the right side first, because that is where they successfully found the object. The searching action signals that the infant knows the object exists. Similarly, correct searching suggests that the infant also knows where to search for the object. The ability to understand spatial relations between the object and the hiding spot, and the order of events in which the object was hidden, was noted by Piaget in his research. This spatio-temporal observation was named by Piaget as the development of space and time structures in infancy (Table 4.1).

The final structural change that Piaget noted for the infant period was the concept of causality. During early infancy, the baby is focused on their own self, as a recipient of stroking, rubbing or swinging, and they know no other cause other than their own. There is no causal connection between things. However, as the infant gains object permanence and begins to productively search, Piaget says causality becomes objectified and spatialised. The infant can see how their action makes things happen, such as when pulling a cord and hearing the bells ring, or when physically noting a relationship between two objects, such as when a pulled cloth moves the object on which it is resting.

Preoperational stage: The semiotic or symbolic function

Towards the end of the sensorimotor period, a new function appears. The child is able to represent something – such as an object, conceptual scheme or event – through language, mental images or gestures. A form of symbolic representation is now possible at the age of around 18 months to 2 years.

CHILD DEVELOPMENT REFLECTION 4.6: ANALYSING LOUISE'S DEVELOPMENT IN THE PREOPERATIONAL STAGE

1 When you consider Louise's development, what behaviours would you expect, and how do they relate to this period of development?
2 What forms of symbolic representations might be evident?

In studying how symbolic representations develop, Piaget notes that there is deferred imitation, symbolic play, graphic representation through drawing, mental images and language. The concept of imitation is foundational to each of these because children move from using ready-made external models to using internal representations or thought. In Piaget's theory of child development, symbols are individually used, while signs are collectively understood.

Symbolic play

Piaget's theory focuses on children's adaptation to their world through acquiring the signs and symbols of the collective culture in which they live. Piaget suggests that these ready-made forms leave little room for the child's own development of symbols. However, he notes that in symbolic play, children are able to express themselves. He states:

> These symbols are borrowed from imitation as instruments, but not used to accurately picture external reality. Rather, imitation serves as a means of evocation to achieve playful assimilation. Thus, symbolic play is not merely an assimilation of reality to the self, as is play in general, but an assimilation made possible (and reinforced by a symbolic language) that is developed by the self and is capable of being modified according to its needs. (Piaget & Inhelder, 1969: 58–9)

Piaget continued to develop his research into play, outlining a theory of play, dreams and imitation in childhood (Piaget, 1962b).

CHILD DEVELOPMENT REFLECTION 4.7: LOUISE'S COMMUNICATION AND ENGAGEMENT IN SYMBOLIC PLAY AND DRAWING

In drawing upon Piaget's concept of symbolic play, and his focus on representations in drawings and language, analyse the following observations of Louise:

- *Observation 1:* Louise was given a plastic tea set for her second birthday, but she did not play with it, as might be expected later in Piaget's theory of child development. As will be shown in Chapter 6, Louise chose instead to run up and down the hallway and into the outdoor area, where she tried to bounce a ball. What might this tell you about her interest in symbolic play?

- *Observation 2:* Louise uses sounds and gestures to communicate her needs. The family members speak rapidly in short sentences because several conversations happen at the same time.
- *Observation 3:* Louise did not have access to drawing materials during the observation periods. What type of drawings might you expect Louise to produce?

Drawing

Piaget considered drawing to be halfway between symbolic play and representation through mental images (see next point). The disjunction between the real object and the graphical representation only becomes evident to the child at around the age of 8 years. Prior to this age, children intentionally draw as realistically as possible. However, they often draw what they know about a person or object rather than what they can actually see. Children's drawings of people show a developmental progression of complexity, from simple tadpole images of humans to large heads and some appendages in this preoperational period, to side views with two eyes showing, through to proportional representation when in the concrete operations period and beyond (see Figure 4.4).

Mental images

Drawing is also related to the development of spatial understandings of children, and they appear late in children's development because they are the outcome of an internalised imitation. According to Piaget, there are two types of mental images: reproductive images and anticipatory images. The former are related to things children have already seen, while the latter are related to a transformation of images or to images of things the children have not yet seen. At the preoperational level, the child's images are static and reproductive.

Language

Language gives children the capacity to consider more than what is immediately visible, to consider it quickly and to think about a range of things simultaneously. The semiotic function detaches thought from action. Language is elaborated socially in real time. When appropriated, language means a child assimilates a cognitive system, such as classification and relationships, and these are used in the service of thought for the child.

What is unique to the preoperational period, and not possible in the sensorimotor period, is how symbols and signs give a child an unlimited field of application. This is in contrast to how actions and perception make up the sensorimotor period.

Figure 4.4 'Draw a person' – Children's drawings show a developmental progression

The concrete operations of thought and interpersonal relations

Piaget explained that the characteristic of the concrete operations is direct action with objects, and not verbally stated hypotheses. It involves direct step-by-step reasoning, rather than generalisations. The operational structures include seriation, classification, number, space and time, and speed.

In the sensorimotor stage, infants decentred in relation to actions and objects, as we saw when children were able to pull an object towards them that was on a rug. During the preschool period, this decentring is at the representational level, such as when children play and consider others so that the play narrative develops. However, during the concrete operational period, decentring is in relation to operations – such as seriation, classification, number, space and time, and speed. Examples of these are discussed further below.

Decentring was explicitly examined by Piaget. He conducted a series of experiments, which he called the *mountain task*. In this task, Piaget set up a model of three mountains. Each mountain was a different colour and had some distinguishing feature: an ice cap, a house or a cross.

In this task, the child is asked to sit on one side of the table looking at the model of the three mountains. A doll is presented and placed at different points near the model. The child is presented with a problem: What does the doll see? The child is given a series of 10 pictures, each of which shows a different angle of the mountains in relation to what might be seen by the doll looking at the model. The child is asked to select the picture that shows what the doll might see. In another version of the experiment, the child is given three mountain models and asked to arrange these in relation to what the doll might see.

Piaget found that children aged 8 or 9 years were unable to take the doll's perspective. The younger children, aged 6 and 7, represented the view they could see in these mountain tasks. The research by Piaget provided evidence that children of these ages were unable to decentre, showing the difficulty young children have in taking the perspective of another. He found that the children could not imagine the perspective of the doll.

In later writing, and from others who have written about Piaget's seminal studies, the term 'egocentrism' is found to capture this idea of not being able to decentre. Simply put, this is the child's inability to see something from the perspective of another. Colloquially, this term is sometimes disparagingly applied to someone who is 'self-centred' and unable to read the situation from any other perspective than their own. Egocentrism also explains the animism discussed earlier, because children cannot explain natural phenomena without reference to themselves or others like themselves – that is, exhibiting human qualities. This term also captures how some of the children talked about the shadows during the interview.

Egocentrism

Piaget argues that a child in the concrete preoperational period is transitioning into decentring, and that this is important for being able to develop key operational structures. The operations of seriation, classification, number, space and time, and speed are examples of operations that require the child to decentre and to conserve. Examples of Piaget's conservation tasks can also be found on the companion website.

Piaget developed a series of conservation tasks that informed his theory of child development for the primary years of schooling. The operations involve progressively higher forms of logical sequencing, where new combinations of operations occur and reversible transformations are considered by the child. These characteristics of children's development of logic can be understood in relation to each of the key conservation tasks of liquid, number and length.

CHILD DEVELOPMENT REFLECTION 4.8: CONSERVATION OF LIQUIDS TASK

The adult and the child sit at a table where there are two glass beakers. The two beakers are the same size.

One of the two identical beakers is filled with milk. The child is asked to pour milk into the second identical beaker so that it is filled to exactly the same point as the first beaker. The instruction the child is given is to fill the second beaker so that it has exactly the same amount of milk as the model. The child lines up the two beakers to make sure the content is exactly the same.

The adult then introduces a third beaker, which is tall and narrow. The child is asked to pour the milk from the beaker they have just filled into the tall, narrow beaker. The child is then asked whether the tall, narrow beaker has the same amount as the original beaker. The experimenter does this by pointing to each beaker – is the amount the same in this beaker (original) to this one (tall narrow beaker)?

Try this task with children aged 6, 7 and 8. What do you notice?

Conservation tasks

Older children say that they have the same amount in each beaker. However, Piaget found that the younger children said there was more in the tall, narrow beaker. When these younger children undertake the task of pouring liquid from one container to another, they focus on the level of the liquid, not the volume of the containers. This means they say that the liquid has increased (when poured into a tall container) or decreased (when poured into a wide, low container). Reversibility is not understood – changing the form of the container but not the quantity of water being poured. After 7 or 8 years of age, the child will say that the quantity is the same, stating that nothing has been added or taken away.

Conservation was also studied by Piaget with substances other than liquids. He used a ball of plasticine, where two balls of the same size were shown, and where one of the two balls was then rolled into a sausage. When children were asked to compare the amounts, older children would say there was still the same amount, but younger children thought that the sausage-shaped plasticine had a larger amount. Conservation of number was also studied by Piaget.

CHILD DEVELOPMENT REFLECTION 4.9: CONSERVATION OF NUMBER TASK

The adult arranges a set of six sweets in a row. A child is then asked to make a similar row that will be 'the same' as the first row set up by the adult. The child is given a bowl of sweets to carry out this task. The child is then asked whether the row contains the same number of sweets. When the child responds to this question with a 'yes' then the adult rearranges the child's row of sweets by decreasing the distance between each sweet. This makes the row shorter in length. The adult invites the child to look at the row of sweets and asks, 'Are they the same now?'

Try this task with children aged 6, 7 and 8. You may wish to use counters or some other object than sweets. What do you notice?

The children in Piaget's experiments were able to conserve substances at 7 or 8 years. They knew that the change in the length of the row did not change the overall number of sweets. Prior to this age, the children believed that when spread out the number of sweets represented more sweets, and conversely that when squashed up there were fewer sweets. The children's visual perception was thought by Piaget to trick the children into thinking that there were fewer sweets in the shorter row.

Piaget undertook many different kinds of conservation tasks. His experimental approach led him to conclude that conservation occurred at the ages shown in Table 4.2.

Table 4.2 Children's ability to conserve

Conservation	Age
Number	5–6
Substance (mass)	7–8
Area	7–8
Volume (liquid)	7–8
Volume (solid)	11–12
Weight	9–10

Piaget argues that a child's capacity to conserve marks the completion of an operatory structure, and that these operations collectively move the child into the formal operations period.

Formal operations stage: The preadolescent and the propositional operations

The formal operations period begins at age 11 or 12. Propositional operations deal with hypotheses. Logical thinking and reasoning appear, and there is no longer a reliance on concrete actions and physical reality. As a more advanced way of thinking appears, more complex language emerges and children are able to separate out variables in order to test out their hypotheses, and to engage in more advanced problem-solving in mathematics. Towards the end of this period, children are able to combine ideas or hypotheses in affirmative or negative statements. They work with reversibility in mathematics. They also deal with reciprocity, where relational groupings are made. Children are liberated from the step-by-step process. The pendulum problem was designed by Piaget to determine children's logical thinking.

CHILD DEVELOPMENT REFLECTION 4.10: PENDULUM PROBLEM

This particular task involves children excluding variables in order to solve a problem – the pendulum problem.

The problem is set up by suspending a weighted object at the end of a piece of string. It is then set in motion by pushing or pulling the object that is suspended on the string. This acts as a pendulum. Children are given different weights to put on to the end of the string. The children are also given different lengths of string, to which a weight is also attached. The problem is presented to the children: they are required to explain and control the oscillations and pendulum rate of movement. The answer is that the length of the string is what determines the oscillations and pendulum rate of movement. However, as presented, the task gives many different variables of weight, string length, push/pull (force) of the weight in starting the motion of the pendulum, and the height from which the weight is dropped to start the motion.

The following responses were observed by Piaget:

- Children believe that the swing of the pendulum is dependent upon the push (force) of the weight.
- There is a relationship between the length of the string and the rate of movement. But the children also believe that the weight and push have some bearing on the rate of movement.
- Ordering the effect of one variable, such as the length of the string, on the pendulum swing rate requires some knowledge of seriation.

Piaget attributed the responses to the age of the child and their logic. Based on the stages of development discussed in Table 4.1, what age would you attribute to each of the responses observed by Piaget?

The Pendulum Experiment

The finding that young children are unable to successfully isolate variables in order to solve a problem has led some science educators to argue that only students in secondary school can form hypotheses and control variables in experiments. Do you agree with this claim? Some models of science teaching in the past, such as a process skills approach, recommended that only older children should engage in science activities that involved experiments where variables were controlled/ introduced. This recommendation has played out in science curricula. For example, in Western Australia in the 1980s, the model of science underpinning the scope and sequence of the curriculum mirrored this recommendation. The scope and sequence of content of the curriculum at that time reflected Piaget's findings. If you look at many curricula in different parts of the Western world during this period, Piaget's theory of child development provided a strong foundation from which content was shown to progress (see Chapter 9 for further discussion).

In the section that follows, you will be invited to examine the families and children from the Building Bridges Community and the Collective Inquiry School case studies, drawing upon Piaget's theory to make sense of the children's development. This is a good opportunity to engage with Table 4.1 again.

CHILD DEVELOPMENT REFLECTION 4.11: USING PIAGET'S THEORY TO ANALYSE CHILDREN'S DEVELOPMENT

As you read the case studies that follow, you are invited to use Table 4.1 to analyse the children's development.

In the Building Bridges Community case study, consider how homework is conceptualised by Aboriginal and Torres Strait Islander families, and think about how Piaget would have made sense of the children's development.

1 What stage of development do you believe the children in the Culturally Diverse Community case study have reached?
2 What evidence did you use to make this judgement?
3 What would you need to know more about to feel confident in your assessment of their development?

BUILDING BRIDGES COMMUNITY CASE STUDY
....

PART 2: BEING AWARE OF CULTURAL EXPECTATIONS

One of the defining features of constructivism is that each child constructs under- standings through active engagement in their world. In the case study, we step inside a family home as children and adults of all ages do homework as an extended family group.

The children and families from the Building Bridges Community, introduced in Chapter 3, discussed how sharing knowledge was a cultural expectation. Children are expected to work together and to assist each other. This is a valued cultural practice for the families from the Building Bridges Community. For instance:

> The children are obliged to not bring shame to their family members by being competitive. They are not to compete against each other. But they should be sharing skills, information and knowledge. This happens all the time at home when children come home with homework. The children who can draw well do the drawings for the homework; those who can write well do the writing. Homework is a collective family practice and not an individual activity. Everyone does the homework. But this is not what schools expect.

In Chapter 3, Laura explained how sharing knowledge at school was considered to be cheating. She shared that this practice in school was an individualistic conception of how children develop. Piaget's theory of child development focuses on how children construct a sense of their world. The individual and their development is central to this theory. This is a fundamentally different approach to what the families from the Building Bridges Community said about how learning and the child were conceptualised at home.

Laura also discussed how her daughter had a quiet time at school, to let others catch up – that is, Laura's daughter wanted to be with her cousins and the other children in the class. She did not wish to be above them academically. Cultural obligations of sharing and being together with others were more important than being academically competitive and individually oriented. Learning was a cultural process of being together.

Researching children individually and conceptualising their development at particular stages of development, as suggested by Piaget, did not give an accurate representation of the children's learning and development in the Building Bridges Community.

CHILD DEVELOPMENT REFLECTION 4.12: USING PIAGET'S THEORY TO UNDERSTAND THE CHILDREN FROM THE BUILDING BRIDGES COMMUNITY

1   What was made visible in the analysis of these children's development?
2   What is unique to a constructivist view of child development?
3   What does a constructivist lens make invisible?

Research by Barbara Rogoff and her colleagues (Correa-Chavez, Mejia-Arauz & Rogoff, 2015) examines how children in a number of cultures learn by observing and pitching in, and in these contexts assessment of the children's contributions is framed differently from that found in Western schools dominated by constructivist approaches (Rogoff, Mejia-Arauz & Correa-Chavez, 2015). The authors argue that children receive feedback by contributing to real-life activities, such as making tortillas, 'observing the results of their efforts and by observing whether others accept their contributions as is, fix-them' (Rogoff, Mejia-Arauz & Correa-Chavez, 2015: 10). In contrast, Western schooling sets assessment tasks that are discrete and not necessarily related to real-world problems or contexts in which the learning activity is supposed to be put into practice – for example, quizzing toddlers about things they already know the answer to, such as, 'Where is the basket?' or 'What colour is the banana?' These studies and others (Correa-Chavez, Mejia-Arauz & Rogoff, 2015) undertaken in a range of cultures show that assessment practices as they are currently understood in Western schooling are indeed cultural practices, and they collectively problematise the maturational or developmental idea that learning and development are individually constructed or co-constructed through activity. Similar challenges about the nature of assessment were also expressed by teachers in the Collective Inquiry School case study, but for older children.

COLLECTIVE INQUIRY SCHOOL CASE STUDY

PART 2: USING PIAGET'S THEORY TO DEVELOP A NEW ASSESSMENT APPROACH IN THE COLLECTIVE INQUIRY SCHOOL

The Collective Inquiry School was introduced in Chapter 2. The school was seeking to introduce a new assessment approach, but was finding this difficult (Fleer, 2015: 233). For instance, Kerri discuses how she did not like the current strategies:

> They are all horrible. We hate them. We just want to find something else. (Kerri, lunchtime forum, Year 2)

The teachers discussed the dominant approach to assessment as being skills-based and individualistically oriented. For example, Kerri noted that in discussing the Victorian Education Learning Standards (VELS), the curriculum that was being used by her school, 'Our [summative] assessment is very VELS related, and therefore very skills based. And that's what we don't like about it.' Keith noted that, 'If you were to take someone like Child X, and take his story from when he first came into prep, right up to this point now, I just don't believe that a series of VELS reports … do justice to his journey.' The skills the teachers spoke about included knowing concepts such as 'one-to-one correspondence', 'being able to seriate' and having a sense of measurement. These skills mirror those identified by Piaget for children in the concrete operational stage.

A further challenge the school was concerned about was in relation to when something should appear in a child's developmental trajectory. The teachers discussed how the curriculum that they were expected to use gave a scope and sequence to what should be learnt and what might be the expected behaviours observed. For instance, Tony said that in looking closely at the curriculum 'guidelines, we are not saying it is definitively that these are the behaviours that a child should be showing at this particular [age/time], we are saying that these are things you might look for' (Fleer, 2015: 234).

What was made visible in the analysis of children's development that was unique to a Piagetian view of child development? What was invisible?

The teachers noted that the curriculum privileged particular developmental sequences that were all centred on the age of the children, and the scope and sequence of some of the key learning areas, such as mathematics, and that this followed a clearly Piagetian pathway. This curriculum focus lent itself to producing checklists and assessment criteria for children's learning and development that was individualistic and personal in its orientation, and was always geared to what one might expect of a particular aged child. The staff felt that this was limiting and, as Keith suggested, didn't tell the whole story of the developmental journey from the first year to the final year of primary school education.

Challenges to Piaget's experiments and his interpretations

If you return to the seriation play shown in Chapter 2 (Figure 2.3) and reproduced in Figure 4.6 below, you can understand this play using Piaget's theory. Piaget (1977) found that seriation was possible at about 7 years of age, following a one-to-one serial correspondence, such as matching figures of various sizes.

Examples of seriation tasks

Further, two-dimensional seriation is also possible, such as in relation to leaves from a tree where the size and length of the leaves is considered. Evidence of his claims are shown in the examples of two observations made by Piaget:

> Various methods were used during this study. Initially, the interviewer has sets of barrels, cards, and rods, which can all be arranged in order of size: (a) six barrels (green, red, yellow, pink, blue, and orange) varying between 3.5 and 8.5 cm in

Figure 4.5 An inquiry based approach – what theory of development underpins this approach?

diameter and 2 and 5 cm in height, fitting into each other; (b) seven white rectangular cards, all the same width, but varying in length between 11 and 15.5 cm (with differences of between 5 and 12 mm) – each card having a colored spot in one corner so that the child can identify it without reference to its size; (c) six metal rods 4 cm wide and varying in length between 11 and 16 cm, with a difference of 1 cm between each. (Piaget, 1977: 301)

GUI (4,6) reaches level 1B. He arranges the barrels in a line without regard to size, then rearranges them correctly. *I've put the little one, middle-size, middle-size, middle-size, big* (the interviewer mixes up the barrels and asks GUI to do it again. Once more he starts off without regard to size, but then correctly orders them.) What's that first one like? *Big*. And the other one (and so on)? *Middle-size, middle-size as well, middle-size as well, middle-size, little*. He has the same reactions for the task with the cards, but initially describes these as *very tiny, tiny, big, big*, then reverts to the usual form of trichotomy. It is the same story with the rods: practical success and trichotomy in the verbal conceptualization. (Piaget, 1977: 303)

Yet you can see in the play of 4-year-olds (Figure 4.6) that children do spontaneously seriate in their free play at home.

Figure 4.6 One-dimensional seriation during home play

The child in Figure 4.6 is from the Resourceful Community case study. He is 4 years old, not 7 years old as in Piaget's study. According to Piaget's theory, the child is using the blocks to create a one-dimensional seriation. A child aged 4 is in the preoperational period, according to Piaget. Yet what he is doing is supposed to be part of the period of concrete operations. Many early childhood education researchers and curriculum developers in Australia believe that Piaget underestimated what children could do. They also thought that the prescribed stages were too rigid and did not reflect the learning possibilities of young children. Long-standing research has also shown the limitations of Piaget's theory with regard to preschool and primary-aged children (e.g. Donaldson, 1992; Gelman & Baillargeon, 1983; Parsonson & Naughton, 1988; Rosser, 1994), and infants and toddlers (Baillargeon, 2004; Cohen & Cashon, 2006; Ruffman, Slade & Redman, 2005; Slaughter & Boh, 2001). For example, Sylvia & Lunt (1982) ask how Piaget's theory would speak to children today. They argue that Piaget's questions to children and his approach to studying children were indeed an innovative approach at the time. But many suggest that the conclusion he reached – that children were not logical for the majority of their childhoods – was not just pessimistic but not sensible. His overall claim that children only developed logical thought later in childhood is all the more extraordinary when you consider that Piaget wrote his first scientific paper at the age of 11. However, even Piaget (1962a) later critiqued his own theory after reading Vygotsky's theory of child development.

Back in 1978, Margaret Donaldson reported on research undertaken by Martin Hughes that questioned Piaget's interpretation. Donaldson reported that when the experiments undertaken by Piaget were modified to give a social context to the tasks, children were able to do the tasks at a much earlier age than reported by Piaget. For instance, the mountain task was repeated. The children were asked to show the perspective of a doll that was hiding from two police officers. The results show that 60 per cent of children as young as 3 years were able to show the perspective of the doll. This is a very different result from that of Piaget's experiments. Subsequent research has shown that when Piaget's tasks are replicated, the results are the same. However, when the experiments are modified so that they make sense to children, such as saying, 'There is a chip on the glass so we have to pour the liquid into another container', then the results show that children do decentre much earlier than reported by Piaget.

In another critique of Piaget's experiments, McGarrigle and Donaldson (Donaldson, 1978) repeated the experiment featuring the rows of sweets. However, they contextualised the problem by introducing a 'naughty teddy' who messed up the sweets. Their research found that the children engaged with the antics of the naughty teddy, and when questioned about the rows of sweets, sensibly claimed that there was still the same number of sweets as before. They concluded that, rather than the children being deficient in their logic, they were quite capable of answering the questions when the problem was presented in a way that made sense to them.

Piaget (1962a) himself said that many criticisms directed to him centred on a belief that his theory promoted a level of individualism. For instance, in the context of egocentrism, he makes the follow rebuff:

> Cognitive egocentrism, as I have tried to make clear, stems from a lack of differentiation between one's own point of view and the other possible ones, and not at all from an individualism that precedes relations with others (as in the conception of Rousseau, which has been occasionally imputed to me, a surprising misapprehension, which Vygotsky to be sure did not share). (Piaget, 1962a: 4)

Finally, it is thought that Piaget developed a theory of education. However, Piaget developed a theory of child development that was applied by the education community. The education community used his theory to make sense of children's thinking over time. Piaget's theory formed the basis for the scope and sequence of curriculum content, and as will be discussed in the next section, informed inquiry-based learning in mathematics and science, where the term 'constructivism' captured this new way of conceptualising approaches to teaching and learning.

Constructivism

Constructivism can be theorised in a range of ways. The key point about constructivism is that it focuses teaching and learning directly on the child and their construction of reality. The conservation tasks are examples of the foundational research that was done to frame not just the scope and sequence of learning in mathematics and science, but also pedagogical approaches, including contemporary approaches such as inquiry-based learning.

Constructivism generally encompasses a series of principles of learning. They are summarised in Table 4.3.

Table 4.3 Constructivist principles of learning for mathematics and science

Principle	Description
Children have everyday understandings about a range of concepts.	Children's thinking over the years has not only been documented in mathematics, but also science. A range of conceptions have been noted, in addition to that detailed by Piaget. Key here is recognising that children have views, even alternative views or misconceptions.
Psychological structures must be in place before numerical problems or scientific challenges are introduced.	There is a need to develop logico-mathematical structures before problems become meaningful to children. Understanding concepts such as electricity is challenging, and these must be introduced to children when they can be meaningfully understood.
Teachers must understand the nature of children's alternative conceptions or their mathematical mistakes.	Mathematical errors highlight to teachers the reasoning given by children. Knowing the reasoning is key to effectively teaching children by following a constructivist approach to learning. Children's scientific reasoning – that is, the ways in which children explain their world – are important to know because they help teachers to organise learning experiences in ways that challenge children's misconceptions. For instance, thinking that light emanates from the eyes, rather than eyes being light receptors, is important to know when setting up science experiences.
Children must have opportunities to invent mathematical or scientific relations.	Giving children possibilities to construct their own working models in mathematics or science to explain the relations observed between things/problems is key to a constructivist approach to teaching children.

Conclusion

In this chapter, you examined Piaget's theory of child development. You considered how Piaget's theory explained an evolutionary view of development, where ages and stages were important. The cognitive dimension of children's development was foregrounded, even though Piaget argued that the social and affective dimensions were inseparable. He noted that affect was also a part of the stages and sub-stages he put forward for explaining the great periods of development. Piaget (1965) also wrote about moral development.

The limitations of Piaget's theory were also considered in the contemporary context of children and families from the case studies. You considered the scope and sequence of mathematics through Piaget's careful study of children's thinking, noting how the structures in the concrete operational period mirror the mathematical concepts in many mathematics curricula.

Using theory to understand children's development is important in education. Piaget's theory has been significant for early childhood and primary education. It is the basis of constructivism, a theory still widely used in primary schools. Even Piaget himself critiqued his own work, coming to refine earlier conclusions in light of further research and critique by Vygotsky and others. In the next chapter, you will consider Bronfenbrenner's bioecological theory to inform thinking about children's development. Here, the lens moves from the individual and interpersonal to a nested view of the individual in the family, community and society as a bioecological model of human development.

References

Baillareon, R 2004, 'Infants' physical worlds', *Current Directions in Psychological Science*, 13, 89–94.

Cohen, LB & Cashon, CH 2006, 'Infant cognition', in W Damon & RM Lerner (eds in chief) and D Kuhn & RS Siegler (eds), *Handbook of child psychology: Vol 2, Cognition perception and language* (6th ed.), Hoboken, NJ: Wiley, pp. 214–51.

Correa-Chavez, M, Mejia-Arauz, R & Rogoff, B (eds) 2015, *Advances in child development and behaviour: Children learning by observing and contributing to family and community endeavors: A cultural paradigm*, Amsterdam: Elsevier.

Donaldson, M 1978, *Children's minds*, Glasgow: William Collins Sons and Co.

—— 1992, *Human minds: An exploration*, Harmondsworth: Penguin.

Fleer, M 2015, 'Developing an assessment pedagogy: The tensions and struggles in re-theorising assessment from a cultural-historical perspective', *Assessment in Education: Principles, Policy and Practice*, 22(2), 224–46.

Gelman, R & Baillareon, R 1983, 'A review of some Piagetian concepts', in JH Flavell & EM Markman (eds), *Handbook of child psychology: Vol. 3 – cognitive development*, New York: Wiley.

Inhelder, B & Piaget, J 1964, *The early growth of logic in the child: Classification and Seriation*, H. Weaver (trans.), London: Routledge and Kegan Paul.

Parsonson, B & Naughton, K 1988, 'Training generalized conservation in 5-year-old children', *Journal of Experimental Child Psychology*, 46(3), 372–90.

Piaget, J 1951, *The child's conception of the world*, J Tomlinson & A Tomlinson (trans.), London: Routledge & Kegan Paul.

—— 1952, *The origins of intelligence in children*, New York: International Universities Press.

—— 1954, *The construction of reality in the child*, M Cook (trans.), New York: Basic Books.

—— 1959, *The language and thought of the child*, 3rd ed., M Gabain & R Gabain (trans.), London: Routledge & Kegan Paul.

—— 1962a, *Comments on Vygotsky's critical remarks concerning the language and thought of the child, and judgements and reasoning in the child*, Cambridge, MA: MIT Press.

—— 1962b, *Play, dreams and imitation in childhood*, C Gattegno & FM Hodgson (trans.), New York: WW Norton.

—— 1965, *The moral judgement of the child*, New York: The Free Press.

—— 1969, *The child's conception of time*, AJ Pomerans (trans.), London: Routledge.

—— 1972a [1930], *The child's conception of physical causality*, M Gabain (trans.), New York: Littlefield, Adams & Co.

—— 1972b, *The principles of genetic epistemology*, W Mays (trans.), London: Routledge Kegan & Paul.

—— 1977, *The grasp of consciousness: Action and concept in the young child*, S Wedgwood (trans.), London: Routledge & Kegan Paul.

Piaget, J & Inhelder, B 1967 [1956], *The child's conception of space*, FJ Langdon & JL Lunzer (trans.), New York: WW Norton.

—— 1969, *The psychology of the child*, H Weaver (trans.), London: Routledge & Kegan Paul.

Rogoff, B, Mejia-Arauz, R & Correa-Chavez, M 2015, 'A cultural paradigm: Learning by observing and pitching in', in M Correa-Chavez, R Mejia-Arauz & B Rogoff (eds), *Advances in child development and behaviour: Children learning by observing and contributing to family and community endeavors – a cultural paradigm*), Amsterdam: Elsevier, pp. 1–22.

Rosser, BR 1994, *Cognitive development: Psychological and biological perspectives*, Boston: Allyn and Bacon.

Ruffman, T, Slade, L & Redman, J 2005, 'Young infants' expectations about hidden objects', *Cognition*, 97(2), B35–B43.

Slaugher, V & Boh, W 2001, 'Decalage in infants' search for mothers versus toys demonstrated with a delayed response task', *Infancy*, 2(3), 405–13.

Sylva, K & Lunt, I 1982, *Child development: A first course*, Oxford: Basil Blackwell.

Wadsworth, BJ 1989, *Piaget's theory of cognitive and affective development*, 4th ed., New York: Longman.

CHAPTER 5

Using a bioecological model to analyse learning and development

Introduction

The work of Uri Bronfenbrenner has been used by many in the field of early childhood and primary education over the years. Even now, researchers draw upon both his original and contemporary model of human development (e.g. Ballam, Perry & Garpeln, 2016; Hayes, O'Toole & Halpenny, 2017). It is still an important part of the New Zealand Curriculum (Te Whāriki), which explicitly mentions the bioecological model (Ministry of Education New Zealand, 2017). Consequently, it is important to examine what Bronfenbrenner's theory affords for the field, and how his model informs what we understand about young children's development. This chapter seeks to give a detailed account of his original ecological model (Bronfenbrenner, 1979) and to discuss and critique his latest work – a bioecological model (Bronfenbrenner & Morris, 2006).

Through engaging with the content of this chapter, it is anticipated that you will:

- consider child development in relation to Bronfenbrenner's original and most recent theory
- think about the importance of conceptualising child development in relation to the future
- learn that theories determine what you see and how you act
- understand the importance of using theory to inform your analysis of children's development.

In this chapter you will also return to the Culturally Diverse Preschool and Resourceful Community case studies, where you will use Bronfenbrenner's

original and most recent model of child development to understand the conditions that are created
to support children's development. However, before
you learn about Bronfenbrenner's theory of child
development, it is important to meet the person
behind the ideas.

Researchers say that before Bronfenbrenner,
child psychologists studied the child, sociologists
examined the family, anthropologists the society,
economists the economic framework of the times
and political scientists the structure. As the result
of Bronfenbrenner's groundbreaking concept of
the ecology of human development, these
environments – from the family to economic and
political structures – were viewed as part of the life
course, embracing both childhood and adulthood (Lang, 2005).

Figure 5.1 Urie Bronfenbrenner pushed against decontexualised research that saw a carving up of the human being into variables.

Source: Wikimedia Commons/ Marco Vicente González

Biography of Urie Bronfenbrenner

Urie Bronfenbrenner was born in 1917 and died in 2005. He was born in Russia and
immigrated to the United States when he was 6 years old. When he was a young
child, Bronfenbrenner's father frequently drew attention to the interdependence
between the environment and living things. These early beginnings laid the foundations for a very different approach to the study of human development in
psychology.

Bronfenbrenner studied psychology at Cornell University, and later studied for a
Masters degree at Harvard University and completed his PhD at the University of
Michigan. After 1942, he worked as a psychologist for the army, followed by a
position as an academic at the University of Michigan, and in 1948 took on an
academic position at Cornell University. Bronfenbrenner's research focused on
human development, family studies and psychology.

In addition to his theory of human development, Bronfenbrenner is also
known for his role as the co-founder of the famous US Head Start program,
which was designed to support the wellbeing and education of children and
families from poor communities. His focus on trying to understand the 'forces
acting on children', meant that a generation of researchers became concerned
with building a 'more accurate picture of human development' and drawing
upon this knowledge to improve the life conditions of children from disadvan-
taged communities.

Bronfenbrenner received many accolades and awards over his lifetime, including the James McKeen Catell Award for dedication to research and an award for his
lifetime contribution to developmental psychology, bestowed by the American

Psychological Society. In 1970, he held the prestigious position of the chair of the White House Conference on Children.

Bronfenbrenner's theory of child development also grew out of cross-cultural research. He undertook research in different parts of Europe, the former Soviet Union, Israel and China. It is probable that his cross-cultural research, and his early experiences with his father of looking at organisms in relation to their environment, led his theory of human development to focus on the relations between children, families and environments. He published over 300 articles and chapters, as well as 14 books. As a prominent and original thinker, 'His writings were widely translated, and his students and colleagues number among today's most internationally influential developmental psychologists' (Lang, 2005).

A reciprocity between person and environment underpins Bronfenbrenner's theory of human development. Consequently, it is not surprising that his work on public policy for improving the life conditions of families and children was also celebrated as an important contribution to society.

Bronfenbrenner continued to develop his theory over his lifetime (Bronfenbrenner, 2005), later naming it the *bioecological model of human development* (Bronfenbrenner & Morris, 2006).

Bronfenbrenner's biographical information

Bronfenbrenner's approach to researching human development

Given that Bronfenbrenner was interested in making a difference to the lives of children and families, it is not surprising that he was concerned by laboratory-based research and the model of research in which dyads became the central focus for gathering data. He suggested that although psychologists at the time talked about the relations between the dyads, in reality the research really focused on the development of one member of the dyad: the child. He said:

> In keeping with the traditional focus of the laboratory procedure on a single experi-mental subject, data are typically collected about only one person at a time, for instance, about either the mother or the child but rarely for both simultaneously. (Bronfenbrenner, 1979: 5)

The legacy of this original thinker has allowed for different research contexts to emerge, in which the reciprocity between the environment of the child can be studied and new ways of conceptualising human development can be considered. For example, it is noted in publicly available material on Bronfen-brenner that:

His theoretical model transformed the way many social and behavioral scientists approached the study of human beings and their environments. It led to new directions in basic research and to applications in the design of programs and policies affecting the well-being of children and families both in the United States and abroad. (New World Encyclopedia, 2015)

It is important to know about the context of Bronfenbrenner's research, because how evidence is generated impacts on how findings are reported, and also how theory is developed. As will become evident in the next chapter, Bronfenbrenner – like Vygotsky – did not do a lot of research to support all the dimensions of his model. A lot of his research was theoretically driven. For example, Bronfenbrenner was not 'greatly involved in the collection of empirical data that could serve to support (or case doubt on)' his theory, but he has 'commented on the research of others that approximates the types of studies that he believes should be conducted' (Tudge, 2008: 71).

In reading and critiquing the works of others, Bronfenbrenner often came to different conclusions. For instance, he argued that:

Much of contemporary developmental psychology is the science of the strange behavior of children in strange situations with strange adults for the briefest possible periods of time. (Bronfenbrenner, 1977: 513)

The final model of development that he conceptualized and wrote about in 1995 was never researched – as Bronfenbrenner noted when he said that his model represented an 'integration, within each projected research design, of conceptual elements successively introduced [in his ecological original model]' (Bronfenbrenner, 1977: 620) and 'Propositions 1 and 2 [final bioecological model], when expressed in the form of concrete hypotheses, are subject to empirical test' (Bronfenbrenner, 1977: 621).

Jonathan Tudge (2008: 71), drawing upon Bronfenbrenner's model of development to frame his own research and subsequent theorisation, states that 'Bronfenbrenner's theory is also, in my mind, far easier to apply in research'. Like many others, Tudge (2008) does not use Bronfenbrenner's model of development without considering the strengths and limitations of the theoretical research and modelling done. You will explore aspects of the strengths and weakness later in this chapter, after you have gained an understanding of his original and revised model of human development.

What worried Bronfenbrenner

Bronfenbrenner noted problems with the methods of study at the time, and this alerted him to consider how behaviour was being documented in research. For instance, he wrote:

the behavior of the individual is classified without regard to its relation to the behavior of other persons present in the situation. In short, activities are not viewed in their interpersonal context. Third, consistent with this orientation, the setting is conceived in purely behavioral terms without reference to social structure either in the immediate or the more remote environment. Finally, there is no attempt to examine molar activity from a developmental perspective, to view its complexity and content as reflecting the level of the person's psychological growth. In sum, neither the properties of the person nor the environment are conceptualized in systems terms. (Bronfenbrenner, 1979: 49)

There was also the problem of the neglect of research into play, fantasy and games in the United States at that time. Bronfenbrenner (1979: 51) argues that:

> This neglect is particularly marked for play, fantasy, and games. Although the importance of such activities to developmental processes has been stressed in the theoretical writings and clinical observation of Piaget (1962), the translation of these into research and practice has been minimal, at least in the United States.

Bronfenbrenner (1979: 51) points out that in many societies, play and games are considered important 'topics of extended scientific study, and the results serve as the basis of recommended practice in homes, preschools, and school curricula'. Because Bronfenbrenner understood the Russian context, he knew that researchers there were very interested in the study of children's play. Yet most of the Western scientific community had not considered this area to be of great value to study. Even now, there are fewer researchers in psychology interested in this area than in other topics of research. However, there is a great deal of research into play in the field of early childhood education (see Fleer, 2017 for an overview). There are many scholars, such as Bert van Oers, who have spent their lives researching children's play, not just in terms of opportunities for children's development, but also as a vehicle for learning. Interestingly, Bronfenbrenner cites the work and theories of scholars studying play from Russia. For example, he references the following: 'Elkonin, 1978; Leontiev, 1965; Vygotsky, 1962, 1978; Zaparozhets and Elkonin, 1971 ... Venger, 1973; Zaporozhets and Elkonin, 1971; Zaporozhets and Markova, 1976; Zhukovskaya, 1976)' (Bronfenbrenner, 1979: 51–2). What is surprising is that Bronfenbrenner does not include play in his theory of child development.

Bronfenbrenner's ecological model

Back in 1979, Urie Bronfenbrenner theorised a new perspective on human development that focused on not just the developing child, but also the environment and 'especially ... the evolving interaction between the two' (Bronfenbrenner, 1979: 3). For Bronfenbrenner, one important aspect was a theoretical integration that took into account the immediate and remote environment and theorised human development over the child's lifespan. Bronfenbrenner's theoretical exposition was derived from both a deductive approach through analysing existing research (as a set of hypotheses and propositions) and the application of his developmental framework to empirical investigation. The propositions he put forward constitute the axioms of his theory, while the hypotheses present the processes and relationships.

Bronfenbrenner was influenced by Kurt Lewin's writing (e.g. Lewin, 1935), especially his emphasis on the close interconnections and isomorphism between the situation and the person. He was also influenced by Piaget's (Chapter 4) conception of the construction of reality by the child. The difference, Bronfenbrenner argued, was that Piaget decontextualised the person, and did not go far enough in recognising the mesosystem of the child (see below).

Figure 5.2 Urie Bronfenbrenner's model of human development is conceptualised as a system, and was shown through the metaphor of nested Russian Babushka dolls

Through careful synthesis and critique of the research at that time, Bronfenbrenner conceived his original systems theory through the metaphor of a 'set of nested structures, each inside the next, like a set of Russian dolls' (Bronfenbrenner, 1979: 3). He conceptualised his original theory through a series of propositions, and named his theory 'an ecological model of human development'.

Bronfenbrenner's (1979) model brings together the developing person in their immediate setting as the inner Russian doll. The inner circle of his model also captures the home and classroom, but also the laboratory. This second circle also includes the relations between these settings, which create the developmental conditions for the child. The third circle captures how the 'person's development is profoundly affected by events occurring in settings in which the person is not even present' (Bronfenbrenner, 1979: 3), such as parents' employment, changes in maternity ward practices, or an economic crisis. Bronfenbrenner (1979: 4) put forward the view that:

> there is a striking phenomenon pertaining to settings at all three levels of the ecological environment … within any culture or subculture, settings of a given kind – such as homes, streets, or offices – tend to be very much alike, whereas between cultures they are distinctly different. It is as if within each society or subculture there existed a blueprint for the organization of every type of setting.

It is only through the use of a theoretical model that is designed to make visible these wide-ranging developmental influences that it becomes possible to take account of all that affects the developing child – this captures the outermost circle or nested Russian doll.

The four Russian dolls or circles in Bronfenbrenner's model were named by Bronfenbrenner as the microsystem, the mesosystem, the exosystem and the macrosystem.

Ecological model

RESOURCEFUL COMMUNITY CASE STUDY

PART 2: USING THE ORIGINAL ECOLOGICAL MODEL TO ANALYSE THE ACTIVITIES OF ANDREW FROM THE PENINSULA FAMILY

The configuration of the dimensions of the whole system, as metaphorically presented through a series of four nested Russian dolls, are now discussed in the context of Andrew from the Peninsula family.

Microsystem

A 'microsystem is a complex of interrelations within the immediate setting' (Bronfenbrenner, 1979: 7), such as the object and the people. The focus is on the nature of the links with others – first hand and personal, or indirect. If we return to Andrew from the Peninsula family, it is possible to examine the context in which Andrew was developing in the family home. Andrew was part of the family. He had access to a slide and swing set in the second year of the study (see Chapter 6 for more details). In the first moments of playing on the slide and swing set, Andrew was able to competently swing, slide and balance. As time passed, and he gained more confidence and competence in playing on the slide and swing set, a qualitative change was observed. Andrew began to climb onto the seat of the swing and challenge himself – balancing and swinging. In the final period of the study, Andrew was observed climbing not just onto the swing but to the very top of the A-frame that supported the swing. He was able to hang upside down, swinging his arms. He was able to pirouette over and over the bar that was at the top of the A-frame. He was also able to do each of these physical movements with great speed, rocking the A-frame dangerously, with laugher and with great confidence and physical competence. But Andrew's activities were not done alone. He performed these feats of physical activity in conjunction with his two brothers, JJ and Nick. Nick and Andrew had to coordinate their actions, as there was not enough space at the top of the A-frame for both children to be hanging upside down and swinging. This relation between the objects and the family members constituted the microsystem of Andrew's developmental conditions in the family home.

Mesosystem

The mesosystem was introduced by Bronfenbrenner as a concept to capture the links between settings that have an immediate impact upon the child. It is probable that a child participates across settings, such as being at school, but also through other settings, such as when attending scouts or some other club activity. In the Peninsula family, it was found that the context of the home was very different from the context of the school. The family pedagogy of continually moving about the home was different to the school context, where Andrew had to seek permission to move from one point to another. Further, Andrew was expected to sit still for long periods of time. The transition between home and school each day afforded very different conditions for Andrew's development. This meant that Andrew devoted a lot of time working out how to sit still, while also seeing what each child was doing in the classroom and engaging in the content of the school curriculum. This presented new possibilities for his development. Considering the transitions Andrew was experiencing between the settings he encountered, this provided a possibility to analyse the shared (or not) culture, language, beliefs and pedagogy in order to see how these affected Andrew's development. The concept of the mesosystem seeks to capture these different microsystems and to study their relations when examining children's development.

Exosystem

Bronfenbrenner noted that children also participate in settings that are connected in some way to another setting. Even though the child does not participate in that setting, its effect is felt. For instance, school conditions are determined by the policies of education departments. The ratio and qualifications of the staff who teach children like Andrew is set in the state of Victoria, Australia. The policy determines whether the person teaching has university qualifications. In childcare centres, the rules are different, and this means that Andrew's siblings may or may not have a qualified teacher teaching them. It is known from longitudinal research that a qualified teacher who engages in shared sustained conversations with children as the dominant pedagogical approach (Siraj-Blatchford et al, 2008) enriches the educational experiences of the children, and this in turn increases the life chances of the children later in life (Heckman & Masterov, 2007).

Macrosystem

The complex of nested and interconnected systems is brought together – that is, the microsystem, mesosystem and exosystem. These are conceptualised together by Bronfenbrenner as the macrosystem. The macrosystem is evident when we think about Andrew and the contexts within which he is developing. Through his interactions at home among the family, he engages in free flow and active exploration of his environment. Through going to school, he engages in new school practices – something he has never experienced before. He has to work out how to conform to the new behavioural expectations, while also being able to bring into the school context his interest in other children – what they are doing, paying attention to, talking about and so on. The way Andrew has to behave is determined by the teacher, through what is expected of schools – to educate children in an orderly and, in the case of Andrew's school, traditional way and to be seated for long periods of time.

The additional classroom support provided in this particular school, in the form of speech pathologists, social workers and others, was made possible because of the way the school was classified. Andrew's school is located in a low SES community, and has been classified as in need of additional support, as determined by the assessment of the children by the teachers in the school. As discussed in Chapter 2, the teachers in the schools in this particular community had low expectations of the children. The macrosystem appeared to be supporting a deficit view of the community and the school community and, as will become increasingly evident in this book, of Andrew's development. This is a macrosystem view of Andrew's development as analysed through Bronfenbrenner's model of child development. As Bronfenbrenner (1979: 8) argues,

> by analyzing and comparing the micro-, meso-, and exosystem characterizing different social classes, ethnic and religious groups, or entire societies, it becomes possible to describe systematically and to distinguish the ecological properties of these larger social contexts as environments for human development.

Tudge (2008) suggests that Bronfenbrenner's model, like many other models of development, does have some shortcomings in relation to explaining the cultural nature of human development. Even though Bronfenbrenner went beyond explaining culture as one variable among a series of variables that made up the person (social class, ethic and religious groups etc), his model was never researched by him in relation to culture. Bronfenbrenner's lack of focus on the cultural nature of human development was also a concern of Barbara Rogoff (2003) and, to some extent, Jonathon Tudge (2008). These points will be taken up later.

Bronfenbrenner (1979) also drew upon constructs such as *molar activity, dyad, role, setting, social network, institution, subculture* and *culture*. However, he brought these constructs together in ways that were different from how other psychologists at the time used these terms. These terms were used within a theoretical framing that focused on the interconnections between them, as well as their impact on the psychological growth of the child.

Ecological transitions

Throughout a person's life, there are continual shifts in a person's role and the settings they inhabit. For example, the arrival of a new sibling changes the role a child has in the family into a brother or sister. Other role transitions are caused by entry into preschool or school; graduating and starting work; getting married; moving house/country; and retirement.

Molar activity

Different expectations emerge when a person takes on a new role or position in society. The person's behaviour changes. How that person is treated, how they act, what they do, and possibly how they think and feel also change. But it is not just the person whose behaviour changes – the behaviours of the people around them also change. For example,

> A three-year-old is more likely to learn to talk if others around her are talking and especially if they speak to her directly. Once the child herself begins to talk, it constitutes evidence that development has actually taken place in the form of a newly acquired *molar activity* (as opposed to molecular behavior, which is momentary and typically devoid of learning or intent). (Bronfenbrenner, 1979: 6, emphasis in original)

Bronfenbrenner suggests that the concept of molar activity captures what the child brings – that is, the internal mechanisms – while at the same time it considers the external manifestations of the psychological growth.

CHILD DEVELOPMENT REFLECTION 5.1: BRONFENBRENNER'S ORIGINAL MODEL OF CHILD DEVELOPMENT

1   What is unique to Bronfenbrenner's original model of child development?
2   What does his model focus on that is of interest to you?

....

What is unique to Bronfenbrenner's original model of child development?

....

   Bronfenbrenner (1979: 9) defines development as 'the person's evolving conception of the ecological environment, and his [sic.] relation to it, as well as the person's growing capacity to discover, sustain, or alter its properties'. Rather than focusing on perception, motivation, thinking and learning, Bronfenbrenner's model of development is more concerned with content – how children think about something, how knowledge is acquired, what children are oriented towards and, finally, 'how the nature of this psychological material changes as a function of a person's exposure to and interaction with the environment' Bronfenbrenner (1979: 9).

One key characteristic of Bronfenbrenner's theory is that he pays attention to aspects of the individual person, while examining the person's interactions with objects, people and so on; however, he simultaneously considers the broader context. (Later, he further takes into account the spatial and temporal dimensions.) This is a much broader conceptualisation of a child's development than looking just at an individual child and the way the environment influences their development.

Another key characteristic of Bronfenbrenner's theory is that he takes a much more 'variegated view of context' (Tudge, 2008: 67) than had been discussed in the literature at the time. The four systems (microsystem, mesosystem, exosystem and macrosystem) show how 'context' can be better theorised to provide more detail and more possibilities for studying children. What is important here is that someone who, in studying a child's development in a laboratory setting or studying children's development more broadly in a group setting, has a much more nuanced understanding of context. The microsystem, mesosystem, exosystem and macrosystem help us to think in very different ways about the context of a child's development.

Figure 5.3 Including the child's contexts as part of studying human development

Bronfenbrenner's model also allows researchers, educators and policy writers to think about the transitions between differing contexts, and how this affects a child's development. As a child moves between child care and preschool, where different dynamics might be afforded, one service having a higher ratio of qualified staff in the setting potentially affects a child's development in different ways. Further, how a child transitions between these settings during one week as they move between two types of group care situation, such as family day care and child care, might also affect the child's development in different ways. As noted by Bronfenbrenner (1989: 205):

> Prior studies of development in day care and preschool environments have concentrated almost exclusively on events within the setting rather than on the interconnections between that setting and others in which the child spends her time.

Bronfenbrenner's model of child development helped educators and researchers to consider these transitions across settings as an important contributor to a child's development. This point is also taken up in Chapter 6, where we examine the theory of child development put forward by Mariane Hedegaard.

Another key contribution of Bronfenbrenner's theory is the *interrelatedness* that he seeks to capture in his systems approach. For instance, Bronfenbrenner theorised the various connections and interrelations within a microsystem, as we see in the family home, and with peer groups, as well as the places where individuals spend a lot of time, such as preschools, schools, outside school hours care and clubs, and the relations between these microsystems are captured as the mesosystem. Here, the interactions are embedded within a peer group, for instance, but at the same time are located in a particular setting, such as a club, and together this is a form of interrelatedness. This is an example of a nested interaction between peers (microsystem), but also within a particular setting and between particular settings, as captured in the mesosystem. Interrelatedness is also made visible through the exosystem because this concept captures influences that are not present, but where the child's development is affected through the macrosystems, such as local government by-laws about transport routes and timetables, or insurance costs skyrocketing, resulting in reductions to services to poorer communities.

Finally, Bronfenbrenner's model of child development is a *systems theory*, which speaks directly to policy work by organisations and governments. The nested model makes visible the exosystem that is affecting a child's development, even though the child might not directly experience the changed laws or situation. This concept, as nested, allows researchers to examine the consequences of indirect policy changes to a child's life conditions and therefore to their development. Similarly, when all the nested systems are considered as an interacting system, this macrosystem allows researchers to speak more broadly about how a whole community might be working productively, or not, to support children's development in that particular community.

Bronfenbrenner's model of human development spoke directly to policy. Changes were made to social policies in the United States, and funding was directed to supporting low-income families to improve the conditions of their children's development. The result was the development of Head Start in 1965.

Head Start

CHILD DEVELOPMENT REFLECTION 5.2: USING BRONFENBRENNER'S ORIGINAL MODEL OF DEVELOPMENT – PART 1

1   How does Bronfenbrenner's original model help you to analyse children's development?
2   As you read Part 2 of the Culturally Diverse Preschool case study (below), use Bronfenbrenner's original model to analyse the children's development. Focus on one child and take notes on your focus child:
    a   What happens to the child?
    b   Who are all the people with whom the child makes contact?
3   Draw a model of your focus child's development:
    a   Who is in the child's microsystem?
    b   What are the interactions in the child's mesosystem?
    c   Who is in the child's exosystem?
    d   Who is in the child's macrosystem?
4   Record your analysis in the model you have drawn.

CULTURALLY DIVERSE PRESCHOOL CASE STUDY

PART 2: ANALYSING CHILDREN'S DEVELOPMENT

It is outdoor play time at the Culturally Diverse Preschool. The outdoor area is large compared with other preschools in Australia. There are many very old and large trees shading the play area. The preschool building is made up of two preschool rooms, a generous entry hall, a small office near the entry and a small room adjacent to the entry that is used by families (and occasionally the children and teachers). The centre has a director, two qualified university-educated teachers and two assistant teachers. One of the assistants is of Vietnamese heritage, having arrived as a refugee in Australia 20 years ago. She is currently upgrading her qualifications to a degree at a university. Another assistant is of Chinese heritage. She has vocational qualification. The teachers speak predominantly English to the children, but also speak Vietnamese and Chinese in specific contexts.

The centre has been in the community for a long time. The community is close to the city, on a tram line, and within a short commute to a train station. The community has many newly arrived refugees from Vietnam, China and different parts of Africa. There are also families of Chinese and European heritage in the community whose children attend this preschool. Families are encouraged to be involved in the centre, and the teachers are welcoming of them in their program. The centre equipment and furnishings are mostly made of wood, and have been used by many children over the years.

All the children can be seen moving about freely in the outdoor area, but there is a lot of activity in three different parts of the outdoor play area. In one corner of the outdoor area, under a very large tree, are four children: Yijun, Hugh, Samantha and Andrea are playing together. They are involved in a camping game (see Chapter 3). Hugh is standing and observing the three children who are busily collecting sticks and leaves that have fallen from the tree and placing them in a pretend campfire. Hugh is observing what is going on, appearing to be following the play narrative that is developing. He stands for a long time observing. Yijun says to Andrea, 'This fire is going to be really hot.' Hugh takes a stick and offers it to Yijun, saying, 'This can go in too. It will help make it hotter.'

In another part of the outdoor area, five children are actively lifting up logs and other objects. They use their iPads and magnifying lenses to observe the organisms living under these objects. The teacher who is present is encouraging the children to lift the logs to see what might be there. A conversation between the teacher and the children emerges:

> **Teacher:** Malcolm, you go and choose the log you want us to look under. Today might be a really good day for findings things . . . because the grounds been made very wet with the rain.
>
> **Malcolm:** Bugs love the rain.
>
> **Teacher:** Bugs love rain, do they?
>
> **Malcolm:** Yeah, because I watched it on television.
>
> **Teacher:** I am going to have to use all of my muscles here (the teacher is lifting a log, and the children immediately help).
>
> **Malcolm:** I had *Bugs Life*, and they're so funny . . .
>
> The children and the teacher find worms and imagine all the colours of the worms, then count them, then ask about what else they can see. They find a slug.
>
> **Teacher:** I wish I had a magnifying glass with me so we could see it a bit more clearly.
>
> **Malcolm:** I can see it clearly, but you can't, but you can't see its face because they are so tiny.

Further discussions about the slugs takes place, and the children retrieve magnifiers and digital devices to study the organisms more closely. Eventually one child says, 'It's trying to camouflage itself.' . . . 'That one is trying to camouflage itself for other people.' (Fleer, 2017)

Some of the children have been sitting at a table that is under the preschool verandah. The children and a teacher have been preparing the fruit for morning tea. The children have collected all the scraps from the fruit and have taken them over to the compost bin. As they lift the lid of the bin, they become excited and scream. The teacher has taken magnifying glasses and an iPad with her. Before placing all the scraps into the compost bin, the teacher asks the children to look into the bin, giving them hand-held magnifying glasses. This causes the children to cry out. The children are also encouraged by the teacher to take photographs of what they see – worms. Some of the children wander off and take photographs of other things in the environment. The children who remain tip the food scraps into the compost bin. However, as they do so they begin to look at the difference between the fresh scraps just deposited and the ones that were put into the compost bin the week before – when they also saw worms. A curiosity arises, and a problem is articulated: how does composting actually happen? (Fleer, 2017)

Figure 5.4 The problem arises – how does composting actually happen?

The children begin discussing compost bins – who has one, what do they put into it, and what they think happens. Some of the children talk about how they just throw the scraps into their regular bin. Other children say they do not know. One child says, 'It is a bit smelly!' One of the assistant teachers comes over to find out what is going on. She asks, 'What are you all doing here?' She then speaks in Vietnamese to the children, discussing the compost bin and talking about decomposition.

Later, the teacher talks to the research assistants about the community, saying that there are a lot of families in the community who live in the high-rise building behind the preschool. She says the children have mostly been introduced to composting through the routine of the preschool.

The Culturally Diverse Preschool has a membership of Early Childhood Australia (ECA). ECA is the major professional association for educators in Australia – regardless of the classroom or centre in which they are working. ECA is partly funded by government and actively supports its membership through publications, a bi-annual conference, a newsletter, a website, a magazine, professional development and more. ECA has made a commitment to supporting sustainability. Policy statements and resources, plus regular updates on sustainability and environmental events, are posted on the website, but also through the e-newsletter that all members receive. Australia has made a commitment to supporting recycling through the introduction by local councils of supplying recycling bins to every household. Australia has not met its agreed targets for sustainability. In 2016 it was ranked 20th in the world according to the United Nations (Thwaites, 2016).

CHILD DEVELOPMENT REFLECTION 5.3 USING BRONFENBRENNER'S ORIGINAL MODEL OF DEVELOPMENT – PART 2

1   What did Bronfenbrenner's original model of child development help you to notice about the children's development? Record your results.
2   What aspects of culture were made visible in the case study? How did the model explain culture?
3   Did you notice any limitations in using Bronfenbrenner's original model?
4   Consider how you might overcome some of the challenges you found when analysing the development of the children from the culturally diverse preschool.
    a   What do you need to add to Bronfenbrenner's model?
    b   Create your own model, using Bronfenbrenner's model as the basis for studying children's development.
5   Now examine some of the limitations of his original theory shown in the section below.

Critiques of the ecological model

Over a period of 27 years (1979–2006), Bronfenbrenner progressively critiqued his own model of child development. In this section, you are introduced to aspects of his critique. As you read, document the main points, and consider why he chose to revise his model of development.

Self-critiques

In the literature, you will see that Bronfenbrenner continued to redevelop his model of human development. It is probable that he did this as part of his ongoing work, and also in response to the critiques he received from others.

Over time, Bronfenbrenner noted some dimensions of his model that needed to be changed. The direct quotes from a series of publications are provided to show how he engaged in the ongoing process of self-critique:

- Bronfenbrenner (1989: 188) wrote: 'Existing developmental studies sub-scribing to an ecological model have provided far more knowledge about the nature of developmentally relevant environments, near and far, than about the characteristics of developing individuals, then and now ... the criticism I just made also applies to my own writings ... Nowhere in the 1979 monograph, nor elsewhere until today, does one find a parallel set of structures for conceptualizing the characteristics of the developing person.'
- Bronfenbrenner and Morris (2006: 796) wrote: 'These formulations of qualities of the person that shape his or her future development have had the unantici-pated effect of further differentiating, expanding, and integrating the original 1979 conceptualization of the environment in terms of nested systems ranging from *micro* to *macro* ...' (emphasis in original)
- Bronfenbrenner and Morris (2006: 796): 'The 1979 Volume scarcely mentions the term [time], whereas in the current formulation, it has a prominent place at three successive levels ...'

These critiques and ongoing work of Bronfenbrenner led to him retheorising and renaming his model as a bioecological model of human development. His revised model is discussed further below.

Critiques from others

Rogoff (2003) also discussed the ecological model of Bronfenbrenner in the context of how her model of the cultural nature of human development is different from Bronfenbrenner's ecological model. In drawing attention to the nested dolls, Rogoff (2003) notes how Bronfenbrenner's model and theorisation explicitly question treating individual and cultural processes as separate variables. She foregrounds the strength of the model in examining the cultural contexts and relations between the different environments that a child experiences, such as home, the workplace and school. In her critique, she argues that although Bronfenbrenner states that the person and the environment are interrelated, his writing does position children as products of their immediate setting and larger contexts. She also notes that the relations between the four systems (micro-, meso-, exo- and macrosystems) are not so well theorised. She says:

> Bronfenbrenner's approach makes several key contributions. In particular, it emphasizes studying the relations among multiple settings in which child and their families are directly and indirectly involved the idea of examining how children and families make transitions among their different ecological settings is also extremely important. Nonetheless, the separation into nested systems constrains ideas of the relations between individual and cultural processes. (Rogoff, 2003: 48)

Tudge (2008: 71) discusses a series of weaknesses of Bronfenbrenner's theory. He argues that a rigorous conceptualisation of Bronfenbrenner's model from a contextualist perspective would see each nested system interacting – that is, 'from cultural to genetic'. Tudge says that his theory falls short of its promise at the genetic level. Bronfenbrenner's own writings spoke about how genes determine the range of reactions, which are then, in turn, influenced by the environment. This positioning of genes being influenced by the environment suggests that the environment has an influential effect, which is one-way or uni-directional, and not a reciprocal relation as his bi-directional arrows suggest. This is a genuine problem in his model, but at that time Bronfenbrenner did not have access to the research that was to come about how certain genes switch on and off dynamically in relation to the environmental conditions of the person. This research led to new ways of thinking in genetics, and allowed for new theoretical paradigms that helped make sense of the ground-breaking work that was done by Barbara McClintock on jumping genes (Fox Keller, 1983).

The macrosystem, and later the expansion of this theory to include proximal processes (see further below), were theorised in relation to large-scale research, such as longitudinal studies, which do not actually allow for a systems analysis. Tudge (2008) notes that there were many ethnographic studies available at the time (and since), which Bronfenbrenner could have drawn upon to support macro-systems and proximal processes in the further development of his theory. However, for whatever reason, he did not draw upon this expansive body of research, with its thick descriptions of variegated contexts. This adds further evidence to the claim that Bronfenbrenner's model did not come out of evidence garnered from his own research. This is both remarkable and also problematic, as the model proposed by him was not based on research specific to the development of the model.

Tudge (2008) suggests that a further problem with Bronfenbrenner's model relates to the dimension of policy. Bronfenbrenner wanted to make a difference to the way children and families lived their lives. Being the co-founder of Head Start is evidence of this lifelong ambition.

According to Tudge (2008: 72), Bronfenbrenner was focused primarily on the positive outcomes for children and families, and therefore the focus of his work was always on 'what needs to happen'. Tudge suggests that this is problematic. As discussed in Chapter 8, much of the research into Aboriginal and Torres Strait Islander education has focused primarily on the poverty and low outcomes noted for Aboriginal and Torres Strait Islander children, with the slogan of 'Closing the Gap'. The focus is on what is wrong with the system, and the system needing to be fixed. It is argued by some that this leads to a strong association between poverty and Aboriginal and Torres Strait Islander people. Less attention is directed to what works, and positive images of Aboriginal and Torres Strait Islander children and families, as also discussed in Chapter 3 in relation to the the Building Bridges Community case study.

Tudge (2008: 72) points out that in line with many psychologists at the time (and today), Bronfenbrenner 'clearly viewed positive development from a Western (primarily North American) and middle-class perspective'. This point was also discussed in Chapter 3 in relation to the Building Bridges Community case study, and is explored further in relation to the pioneering work of Barbara Rogoff (2003) and her colleagues in subsequent chapters. Without a theory of child development that makes a broad range of cultural practices visible, certain forms of development are invisible – or worse, completely misunderstood in the context of the family and community conditions created to support valued forms of development for their children. Tudge (2008: 72) states categorically that Bronfenbrenner's theory does 'not deal adequately with issue of culture'. Tudge (2008: 72–3) goes on to say:

> I'm not bothered by the fact that the term 'culture' rarely appears within Bronfenbrenner's writings because his definition of macrosystem encompasses culture ... What is missing is that there is no sense in his writings that cultural groups with values, beliefs, lifestyles, and patterns of social interchange different from those found in North American middle-class communities would necessarily value different types of proximal process [see Child Development Reflection 5.4] or that what counts as more complex to one group might be viewed as less complex by another.

Tudge cites the example of family research used by Bronfenbrenner to discuss the impact of parenting styles on children's development. What Tudge insightfully notes is how Bronfenbrenner discussed the findings in relation to a mesosystem effect. In other words, he discussed the findings in relation to the links between the home and school. Bronfenbrenner did not discuss the research from the perspective of different macrosystems or subcultures within the North American context – of which there are many, and increasingly more. This alone shows how a theory can be used in a completely racist way, because the invisible assumption here is that family upbringing and practices are normed against the school – and in this case, this means a North American middle-class framing.

CHILD DEVELOPMENT REFLECTION 5.4: IMAGES OF THE CHILD

Read the following quotation:

> Bronfenbrenner's theory, with its emphasis on the powerful influence of multiple contexts on the child, both directly and indirectly through his/her parents, has had a profound effect on how others view a child who has difficulties in school. It is no longer sufficient to simply blame the parents or conclude that the child has a low aptitude for learning. In fact, Bronfenbrenner explicitly argued that it is the cumulative effect of the specific, enduring, supportive interactions children have with all of the individuals in their lives that allows them to live up to their biological potential. He called these interactions 'proximal processes' and asserted that others share responsibility for both directly providing such interactions to children and creating social conditions that allow their parents to do so.

(continued)

1 Do you believe Bronfenbrenner's theory had a profound effect on how others view a child who has difficulties in school?
2 What is the dominant image of the child that is presented in Bronfenbrenner's theory?

Re-consider these questions again as you learn about his bioecological model of human development. You will come back to these questions later.

Since the publication of Bronfenbrenner's seminal model in 1979, and the series of papers that reflected how his thinking changed over time, we note that Bronfenbrenner developed a new model. This new model is discussed in the next section. However, his original models are shown in Figures 5.5 and 5.6.

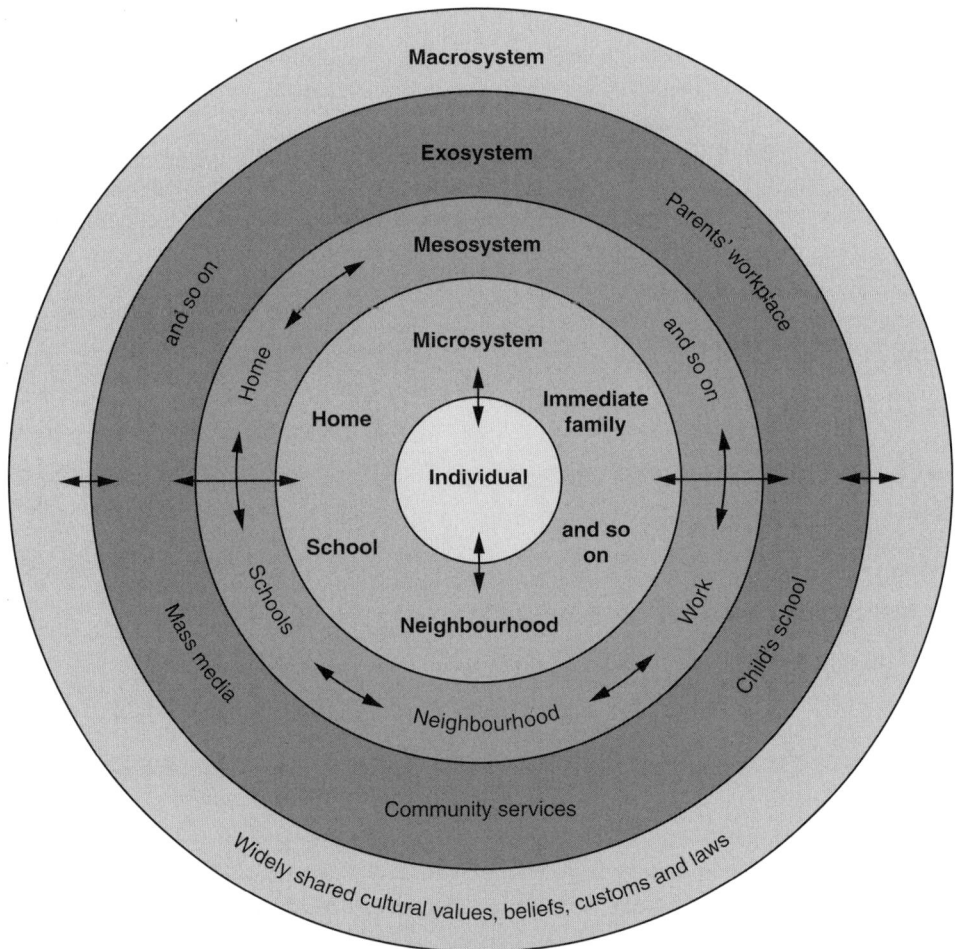

Figure 5.5 Bronfenbrenner's original 1979 model

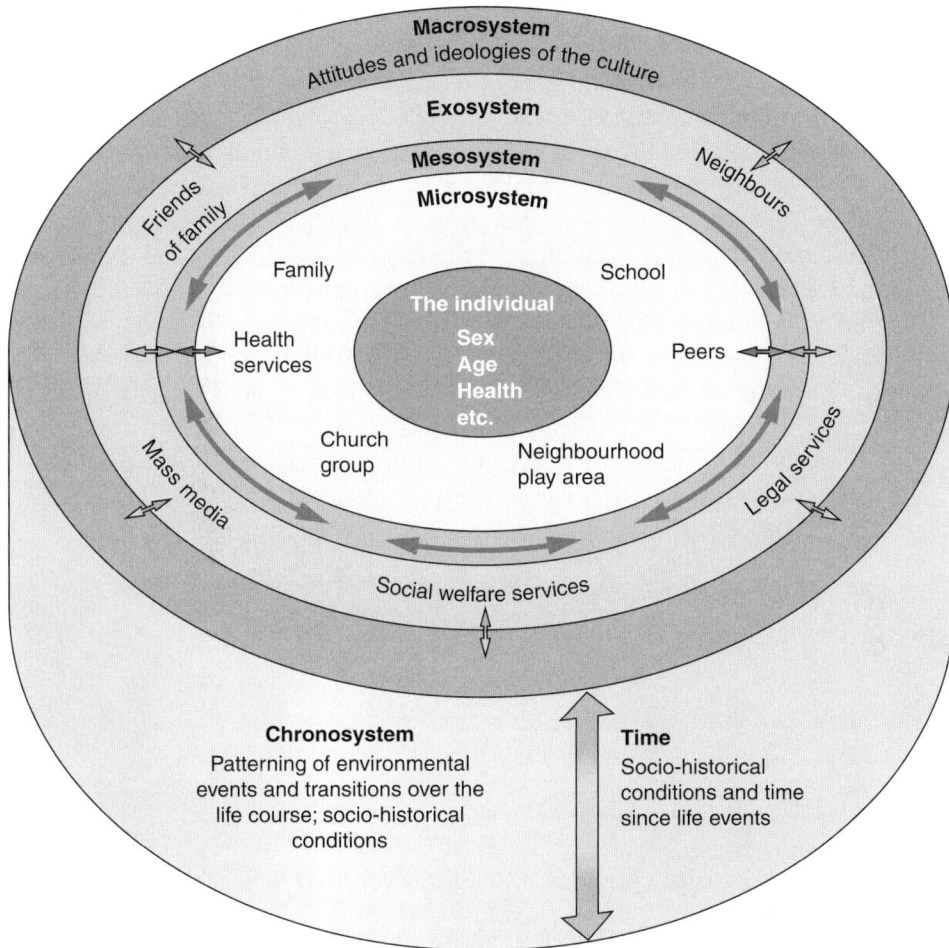

Figure 5.6 Bronfenbrenner's revised model (to include time)

Bronfenbrenner's bioecological model of human development

In 1994, Bronfenbrenner introduced into the literature his new bioecological model of human development (see Bronfenbrenner & Ceci, 1994). In this section, you will explore the characteristics of his most recent model. As you read, consider what is unique about the bioecological model versus the ecological model.

You will find in the field of education that many have used Bronfenbrenner's model of human development to support their work. However, it is important to pay close attention to which model of development is being used. Many do not realise that Bronfenbrenner revised his model and so continue to draw upon his older model. As you are now aware, even Bronfenbrenner critiqued his original model.

Tudge (2008: 67) draws attention to the shift in Bronfenbrenner's thinking when he says that 'those who cite his work for the most part continue to write as though he is a theorist of contextual influences on development, rather than a theorist working within the contextualist paradigm'. The term 'ecology' was used to signal that Bronfenbrenner tried to capture the interrelatedness of individual and context. Moving from ecology to bioecology marked another important and new dimension of this work. However, there was a step in between, where Bronfenbrenner noted that he had not paid enough attention to the future – that is, the time dimension. He introduced the terms 'chronosystem' and 'time' to capture this new dimension of his thinking, expanding his original 1994 model (Bronfenbrenner, 1994) with this in mind. In Child Development Reflection 5.4, you will consider how the model has changed – there is a visual difference in the model that reflects his new thinking. The chronosystem captured the transitions and patterns of environmental events over a person's life-course. These became known as socio-historical conditions. They were time related and they were future oriented, and of course these dimensions were further developed in the final model he conceptualised.

CHILD DEVELOPMENT REFLECTION 5.5: MOVING FROM ECOLOGY TO BIOECOLOGY AS A MODEL OF DEVELOPMENT

A bioecological model

Go back to the model you prepared in Child Development Reflection 5.2.

1   What might you add to your model in analysing your focus child from the Culturally Diverse Preschool case study?
2   What similarities do you notice between the models? What differences do you see? Does it matter?

The content that follows will help you to prepare a new model that takes into account the process-person-context-time (PPCT) model described below. Keep this in mind as you continue reading.

The two key propositions in Bronfenbrenner's work were discussed by him in 1995. Consider these propositions.

• *Proposition 1:* Especially in its early phases, and to a great extent throughout the life-course, human development takes place through processes of progressively more complex reciprocal interaction between an active, evolving biopsychological human organism and the persons, objects and symbols in its immediate environment. To be effective, the interaction must occur on a fairly regular basis over extended periods of time. Such enduring forms of interaction in the immediate environment are referred to as *proximal processes* ... (Bronfenbrenner, 1995: 620)

- *Proposition 2:* The form, power, content and direction of the proximal processes effecting development vary systematically as a joint function of the bio-psychological characteristics of the developing person; of the environment, both immediate and more remote, in which the process are taking place; and the nature of the developmental outcomes under consideration. (Bronfenbrenner, 1995: 621)

Bronfenbrenner revised his original model through a series of propositions to develop his new model. To achieve this, he used a process-person-context-time (PPCT) model to permit him to do the necessary theoretical work on the introduced propositions – which he said were specific hypotheses that needed to be tested.

The defining properties of the bioecological model

The PPCT model of development is based upon the interrelations between the four dimensions of *process, person, context* and *time*. They are discussed in relation to Bronfenbrenner's more recent writings and propositions – all of which feature below as the key theoretical or propositional characteristics of his new model.

The structure of bioecological model as an integrated system

First of all, it is worth noting that Bronfenbrenner (1995: 622) said the key dimensions of the bioecological model were

> not to be found in the original exposition of the ecological systems theory ... and when it did first see the light of day 4 years later, it appeared in truncated form as a 'person-process-context model with the critical component of 'time' still missing.

Bronfenbrenner's work highlights how a person's development is more than their biography; it includes all of the biopsychological characteristics – both as an individual and a member of the human race or species. This is a broad conceptualisation of a person's development because it captures the development of the species as a whole – that is, the development of the person includes more than just the person. It has 'as much to do with their development' as with the environments in which that person lives (Bronfenbrenner, 1995: 623). This interrelation of person and environment over time captures the integrated system of Bronfenbrenner's bioecological model of human development. In this model, the person cannot be divided into the components of physical, social and emotional, cognitive and language development (as we saw in Chapter 3 for a maturational theory of development). Development is not defined within the person, but rather takes into account time, the human condition or race, and the environments in which the person is located. This is a dynamic, interrelated and integrated system view of human development.

A critical defining element in the bioecological model is experience. This includes both the objective and subjective dimensions of experience. Bronfenbrenner and Morris (2006) argue that, in opposition to behaviourism (see Chapter 9), not all experiences can be defined objectively as observable behaviours, and there is a need to include subjective experiences in any model of child development. Experience captures many of the subjective processes involved in being human, such as hopes, doubts and personal beliefs. Together, the objective and subjective experiences are part of the course of human development.

Bronfenbrenner and Ceci (1994: 572) state that, in the process of development:

> The external becomes internal and becomes transformed in the process. However, because from the very beginning the organism begins to change its environment, the internal becomes external and becomes transformed in the process.

This bidirectional relation is central to Bronfenbrenner's model. Bronfenbrenner wished to make a difference to the lives of children through informing policy. Consequently, his theorising of development focused on, 'The realization of human potentials', which 'requires intervening mechanisms that connect the inner with the outer in a two-way process that occurs not instantly, but over time'. Development over time is conceptualised as 'moving from the more general to the more differentiated and complex' (Bronfenbrenner & Ceci, 1994: 572).

The components of the model function together in the system as a whole

The characteristics of the person in the PPCT model appear twice: first as influencing the form, power, content and direction of the actual proximal process; and

Figure 5.7 Studying human development is a complex process involving the dimensions of proximal processes, resource characteristics, force characteristics and time

second as the developmental outcomes – that is, as qualities of the developing person. The person is both the producer and the product of the process of development.

To understand the development of the person from within a bioecological framework, the mechanisms by which development occurs through the PPCT model can be captured through the proximal processes, the resource characteristics, the force characteristics, and the time dimension. These are now discussed in relation to the four elements of the PPCT model.

Proximal processes

In the context of the two propositions introduced above, proximal processes are the mechanism by which the potential of the person can be realised. Bronfenbrenner and Ceci (1994) link this concept with that of Vygotsky's zone of proximal development (ZPD) (see Chapter 6). Proximal processes act as the engine for development. As the basis of Proposition 1 (see above), proximal processes foreground development through progressively more complex interactions, such as those that we see between infants and parents over time, where 'children increasingly become agents of their own development' (Bronfenbrenner & Morris, 2006: 797).

The distinctive properties of the proximal processes are as follows:

- The child is engaged in some form of activity.
- The activity must occur regularly.
- Activities must occur over time so that they can become increasingly more complex.
- A reciprocity of exchange in the interactions takes place – it is not just the child receiving but also the child contributing to the activity that is important for development.
- More than interaction with people, the processes include interactions with objects and symbols – but interaction that affords being noticed, engaging the child in exploration and manipulation, and offering possibilities for elaboration and imagination.
- The criteria detailed in Proposition 2 (above), but where:
  - over time the proximal processes become increasingly complex so as to mirror and be ahead of the increasingly developmental capabilities of the child
  - the circle of significant others increases and actively contributes to the child's development.

Without these proximal processes, Bronfenbrenner and Morris (2006) argue that the child's potential remains unactualised. However, as can be seen, these proximal processes are content-free simply because they are processes. Consequently, this component of proximal processes needs to be related to the other components in Bronfenbrenner's model.

Resource characteristics influencing later development

Rather than considering the child as simply being in the environment, where others react to the child because of their age, skin colour, gender, level of education and so on, Bronfenbrenner foregrounded in his model a rich role for the child in their environment. A child changes their environment based on the resources they have available to them. The child draws upon their physical, mental and emotional resources to engage and change their environment. But how effective they are is also dependent upon their motivation. Bronfenbrenner and Morris (2006) argue that two children in the same situation may bring a different level of motivation to their environment. Children with the same resource characteristics may have a different developmental trajectory if their motivation levels are different. Force characteristics in Bronfenbrenner's model include differences in the child's temperament and their level of persistence, but also their motivation. These aspects of the development of the person are elaborated below.

Force characteristics as shapers of development

Bronfenbrenner and Morris (2006) suggest that there are two forces that shape development. The first force is generative and includes characteristics such as curiosity, the child's initiative, levels of engagement with others or alone, and the ability to defer self-gratification. The second is disruptive, and includes impulsiveness, distractibility, lack of self-regulation and aggression. At the other extreme are characteristics such as apathy, insecurity, lack of responsiveness, shyness and a tendency to withdraw from activity.

The generative characteristics are described below:

- *Developmentally generative dispositions in life-course perspective.* The generative characteristics take the form of selective responsiveness to the social and physical world – as we might see when an infant is soothed by being held vertically in order to participate in mutual gazing (early development), or actively engages with and rearranges objects (further development), or as the infant grows older is increasingly able to conceptualise their experiences – affecting their beliefs about themselves as capable and confident.
- *Resource characteristics of the person as shapers of development.* Resource characteristics refer to those dimensions of a child's life that act as emotional and mental resources – for example, access to healthy food, adequate housing, a caring family and quality educational experiences over the life-course. Resources available to the child during one time period will impact the child's development at another time period. For example, breastfeeding will promote the development of a healthy baby who engages in their world, which in turn lays the foundations for later development.
- *Demand characteristics of the person as developmental influences.* This person characteristic is related to the positive or negative affordances provided by the social environment. For example, a smiling baby is likely to elicit positive

responses from those around them. A healthy baby is more likely to engage socially and physically with others, which in turn potentially engages more social and physical interactions from others. The disruptive characteristics of the person can best be described as the inverted mirror image of those discussed above, such as being a fussy baby, being inattentive, being difficult to soothe or comfort, not having access to quality food, rest and care, or not having consistent and positive social relations with those around the infant or child.

The role of focus of attention in proximal processes

This characteristic of proximal processes in child development studies focuses on the bi-directional nature of attention. An understanding of, or observance for, looking at the other's focus of attention is needed. For example, there is always a bi-directional relationship between a parent and an infant. How the parent responds to the infant's initiative – or not – has a direct impact on the infant. Similarly, how the infant responds to the parent affects how the parent will respond to the infant in the future. An example of this is the way adults hold a baby. When an infant has always been held in a particular way from birth – such as facing out to the community to engage with all those around them, or facing inwards to mostly a parent's gaze – they will respond with discomfort if held differently. The baby's response affects the adult at that moment in time, but also potentially in the future. The focus of attention is always bi-directional.

Proximal process in solo activities with object and symbols

The focus here is not on the social interactions, but rather the interactions between the person and the physical world. Further, Bronfenbrenner and Morris (2006) argue that age, gender and ethnicity define a person in their community or even the society in which they live. This means focusing on more than just the developing person: the structure and substance of the environmental contexts must also be considered, which in turn affects the personal outcomes of the developing child.

The microsystem magnified: Activities, relationships and roles

The different dimensions of the environment as contexts for development are discussed in this section. Bronfenbrenner and Morris (2006) state that the centre of the original nested model is still the same in the bioecological model – that is, the microsystem of interactions as the central structure of the model is still featured. In examining the physical contexts of the child's development, Bronfenbrenner foregrounds the effects of the physical environment on the psychological development of the child. Positive environments for development are described by Bronfenbrenner and Morris (2006) as:

- a physically responsive environment
- sheltered areas
- set-up of the environment so that it promotes exploration
- low levels of noise and confusion
- temporal regularity
- predictable structure and organisation
- stability.

The social contexts of the child's development highlighted by Bronfenbrenner in his model to support children's development focus on the quality of the relationships formed early in life. The dimensions of this relationship, as discussed by Bronfenbrenner and Morris (2006), include:

- an emotional attachment between mother and child that becomes increasingly more complex over time
- a complementary sense of self through a responsive caregiver
- the infant building an internalised model of interaction between self and caregiver, which forms the foundations on which future interactions are formed/based
- participation in increasingly complex and regular reciprocal activity over extended time periods.

Time in the bioecological model: Micro-, meso-, and macrochronological systems

The time dimension of Bronfenbrenner's model (see Bronfenbrenner & Morris, 2006) returned to the original naming of the nested systems of micro, meso and macro, but in the context of time – that is, microchronological, mesochronological and macrochronological systems:

- *Microchronological system:* This examines the time periods within an activity or during the course of an interaction.
- *Mesochronological system:* The progressively more complex reciprocal interactions that are plotted as particular micro-time points form part of the mesochronologial system – for example, steadiness versus unsteadiness in family life conditions, where the frequency of transitions are measured, such as the number of times the family moved house or countries, the number of child-care arrangements in a week, such as preschool attendance, child-care centre attendance and family day care attendance, or incidences of absences of a primary carer.
- *Macrochronological systems:* This time period captures both the life-course of the person, and the historical time period and context in which the individual is developing or has lived.

A child growing up in a war-torn area is an example of an historical time and place. In addition, the following points are relevant:

- Patterns in child-rearing practices change over the generations. This is an example of the historical period that has an impact on the life-course of a developing person.
- The timing of particular events in someone's life or a succession of life transitions can also influence a person's life-course.
- Lives are lived through interdependent and social and historical moments and events. These shared relationships and networks influence a person's development over their life-course.

Environmental changes, such as changes in child-rearing practices or changes in the role of women in society, can produce significant developmental changes in direction or the timing of life-course events. For example, there is evidence that educating girls has produced significant changes in the life conditions of extended families, communities and even societies.

CHILD DEVELOPMENT REFLECTION 5.6: BRONFENBRENNER'S BIOECOLOGICAL MODEL

1 What was unique to Bronfenbrenner's bioecological model of child development? How was this different from his original ecological model of human development?
2 Re-analyse the material from the Culturally Diverse Preschool case study using Bronfenbrenner's bioecological model:
   a Is your re-analysis very different?
   b What does Bronfenbrenner's revised model allow you to see in relation to the children's development that his original model did not make visible?
   c Compare what you learnt through using Bronfenbrenner's model of child development in relation to what you learnt when you used his most recent model of child development.
3 Debate the following statement with a colleague, arguing the key point: 'The theory has helped tease out what is needed for the understanding of what makes human beings human.'

Bronfenbrenner's 'bioecological' approach to human development shattered barriers among the social sciences and forged bridges among the disciplines. This has allowed findings to emerge about which key elements in the larger social structure and across societies are vital for developing the potential of human nature. The theory has helped tease out what is needed for the understanding of what makes human beings human (Lang, 2005).

CHILD DEVELOPMENT REFLECTION 5.7: THE DOMINANT IMAGE OF THE CHILD IN BRONFENBRENNER'S BIOECOLOGICAL MODEL

Now return to Child Development Reflection 5.4:

1 What is your view about the images of the child presented in Bronfenbrenner's bioecological model of development?
2 Do you still believe his theory had a profound effect on how others view a child who has difficulties in school?
3 What is the dominant image of the child presented in Bronfenbrenner's bioecological model?
4 Have your views changed?

Conclusion

In this chapter, you examined Bronfenbrenner's original and final model of child development. You considered what each model offered. You were also invited to use both models to analyse children's development from the Culturally Diverse Preschool case study. As part of learning about the different concepts in each model, you also revisited the development of Andrew from the Peninsula family. In Chapter 6, you will have the opportunity to consider context in a different way from that presented by Bronfenbrenner in his models of child development.

References

Ballam, N, Perry, B & Garpelin, A 2016, *Pedagogies of educational transitions: European and Antipodean research*, Dordrecht: Springer.

Bronfenbrenner, U 1977, 'Toward an experimental ecology of human development', *American Psychologist*, 32, 513–31.

——— 1979, *The ecology of human development*, Cambridge, MA: Harvard University Press.

——— 1989, 'Ecological systems theory', in R Vasta (ed.), *Six theories of child development*, Greenwich, CT: JAI Press, pp. 185–246.

——— 1994, 'Ecological models of human development', in *International Encyclopedia of Education, vol. 3*, 2nd ed., Oxford: Elsevier, pp. 1643–7.

——— 1995, 'The bioecological model from a life course perspective: Reflections of a participant observer', in P Moen, GH Elder, Jr & K Luschur (eds), *Examining lives*

Chapter 5: Using a bioecological model   127

in context: Perspectives on the ecology of human development, Washington, DC: American Psychological Association, pp. 599–618.

—— 2005, *Making human beings human: Bioecological perspectives on human development*, Thousand Oaks, CA: Sage.

Bronfenbrenner, U & Ceci, S 1994, 'Nature–nurture reconceptualised in developmental perspective: A bioecological model', *Psychological Review*, 101, 4, 568–86.

Bronfenbrenner, U & Morris, PA 2006, 'The bioecological model of human development', in *Handbook of child psychology, vol. 1*, 6th ed., Hoboken, NJ: John Wiley & Sons, pp. 793–828.

Fleer, M 2017, 'Digital playworlds in an Australia context', in T Bruce, M Bredikyte & P Hakkarainen (eds), *Routledge handbook of play in early childhood*, London: Routledge.

Fox Keller, E 1983, *A feeling for the organism: Life and work of Barbara McClintock*, New York: Freeman.

Hayes, N, O'Toole, L & Halpenny, AM 2017, *Introducing Bronfenbrenner: A guide for practitioners and students in early years education*. London: Routledge.

Heckman, JJ & Masterov, DV 2007, *The productivity argument for investing in young children*, Bonn: Institute for Labour Study.

Lang, S 2005, 'Urie Bronfenbrenner: Father of Head Start program and pre-eminent "human ecologist", dies at age 88', *Cornell Chronicle*, September. Available at: http://news.cornell.edu/stories/2005/09/head-start-founder-urie-bronfen brenner-dies-88 [Accessed 20 April 2017].

Lewin, K 1935, *A dynamic theory of personality*, New York: McGraw-Hill.

Ministry of Education New Zealand 2017, *Te Whāriki: He whāriki mātauranga mōngā mokopuna o Aotearoa: Early childhood curriculum*, Wellington: New Zealand Government.

New World Encyclopedia 2015, 'Urie Bronfenbrenner'. Available at: http://www .newworldencyclopedia.org/entry/Urie_Bronfenbrenner [Accessed 19 August 2017].

Rogoff, B 2003, *The cultural nature of human development*, Oxford: Oxford University Press.

Siraj-Blatchford, I, Taggart, B, Sylva, K, Sammons, P & Melhuish, M 2008, 'Towards the transformation of practice in early childhood education: The effective provision of pre-school education (EPPE) project', *Cambridge Journal of Education*, 38(1), 23–36.

Thwaites, J 2016, 'Australia ranks 20th on progress towards the Sustainable Development Goals', *The Conversation*, 21 July. Available at: https://the conversation.com/australia-ranks-20th-on-progress-towards-the-sustainable-development-goals-62820?sa=pg1&sq=australia+ranks+20th+on&sr=1 [Accessed 20 August 2017].

Tudge, J 2008, *The everyday lives of young children: Culture, class, and child rearing in diverse societies*, Cambridge: Cambridge University Press.

CHAPTER 6

Using cultural-historical theory to analyse learning and development

Introduction

In this chapter, you will study the central concepts of a cultural-historical theory of child development. The chapter will detail Vygotsky's theory of child development, as well as introduce key contemporary concepts by theorists such as Mariane Hedegaard and Elena Kravtsova. The specific cultural-historical concepts to be discussed are:

- periodisation
- crisis
- the social situation of development
- the relations between the ideal and real form
- the zone of actual and proximal development
- motives
- leading activity
- leading motives – the play motive and the learning motive.

Through engaging with the content of this chapter, it is anticipated that you will:

- meet the ideas of contemporary child development theorists working in education, such as Mariane Hedegaard and Elena Kravtsova (Vygotsky's granddaughter), and long-standing theorists Lev Vygotsky, Daniil Borisovich Elkonin and Lidya Ilyinichna Bozhovich
- be oriented to a cultural-historical theory of child development for informing educational practice
- become aware of those concepts that make up a cultural-historical view of child development.

Cultural-historical theory is complex because it captures and theorises children's development while it is taking place. This means that many concepts are needed to explain the complexity of children's development. The system of concepts that will be discussed, and that make up Vygotsky's theory, goes beyond what is traditionally associated with his work.

Figure 6.1 Understanding 'learning to walk' from a cultural-historical perspective

In this chapter, you will build upon the sociocultural concepts introduced in Chapter 2 and the case study material presented thus far in the Resourceful Community case study.

This chapter begins with an expansion of the two families already introduced in the Resourceful Community case study – the Peninsula and Westernport families. Through analysing the stories of the teachers, children and families, key concepts from a cultural-historical conception of child development can be better understood. However, before the details of a cultural-historical conception of child development are given, you will meet the giants who began and developed the theoretical concepts, and those who took the concepts further for use in contemporary contexts.

The biographies of Vygotsky, Kravtsova and Hedegaard

Lev (LS) Vygotsky is known as the founder of cultural-historical theory. He was born in 1896 and died in 1934. During his short life, he changed the course of research in many fields – particularly education and psychology. He became known as an original thinker who contributed a new theory of child development. The arguments and theorisation he put forward in support of this new theory of child development pushed against the dominant behaviourist thinking of the time (see Chapter 9 for details of behaviourism). As a Jewish child growing up in Gomel, Belorussia in pre-revolutionary Russia, his opportunities for education were limited. However, he did study law at the Moscow State University and at the same time also studied humanities at the unofficial Shanyavsky University. In 1925, he completed his doctoral dissertation, 'The Psychology of Art'. Unfortunately, he suffered an attack of tuberculosis in 1934, a crippling disease that plagued his life, resulting in his premature death in 1934.

The Vygotsky story

Professor Elena Kravstova, formerly from the Russian State University for the Humanities, is the grand-daughter of LS Vygotsky. As former head of the Vygotsky Institute, and course leader for an innovative program of training for psychologists known as 'psychological theatre', she has made a major contribution to thinking in child development in Russia and internationally. Elena Kravstova has published widely on child development and is internationally recognised for her research on pedagogy, having introduced the Golden Key Schools in Russia. This is an approach to education that draws directly from cultural-historical theory (see Kravtsov & Kravtsova, 2011), the theory that was originally developed by her grandfather.

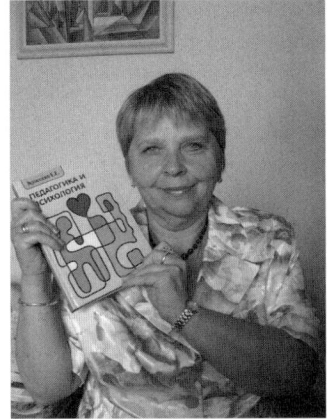

Figure 6.2 Elena Kravtsova, grand-daughter of LS Vygotsky

Professor Mariane Hedegaard, from the University of Copenhagen, is a recognised international researcher in child development. Her research into children focuses on the everyday lives of children across different institutions, and her theoretical model of child development (see later in this chapter) focuses directly on the personal, institutional and societal conditions of children's development.

In following the intentions of children as they participate in activities within the different institutional practices of the home, school and after-school activities, she has put forward a cultural-historical theory of child development. In addition, she has theorised a cultural-historical methodology for studying children's development in everyday settings. Her research and methods of studying children have drawn upon the cultural-historical approach of LS Vygotsky and the phenomenology approach of Alfred Schutz.

Figure 6.3 Professor Mariane Hedegaard

A cultural-historical conception of child development

In this section of the chapter, you will visit the Peninsula family's home over a period of time as Louise learns to climb and run. In Chapter 2, you were introduced to the Peninsula family and you learnt that the children in the family were very active – except for Louise. Observations made of Louise over three observation periods spanning eight months are detailed below (Fleer, 2010). We discuss these observations from a cultural-historical perspective, which is different from the perspective presented in Chapters 3 (observing from the perspective of a maturational theory of development) and 4 (Piaget's stages of development).

CHILD DEVELOPMENT REFLECTION 6.1: UNDERSTANDING 'LEARNING TO WALK' FROM A CULTURAL-HISTORICAL PERSPECTIVE

Before you begin to read the observations and the cultural-historical analysis of Louise, go back to your responses to Child Development Reflection 2.1. You were asked to analyse the Peninsula family. Did you comment on why Louise was not yet walking? Did you have an opinion about the concern of the social worker? As you read each observation below, record what you notice about both the social and material context and about what Louise is showing a motivation towards.

RESOURCEFUL COMMUNITY CASE STUDY

PART 3: DEVELOPING MOTIVES – FOLLOWING LOUISE IN THE PENINSULA FAMILY

We return to Observation Period 1 when Louise is 16 months old. As outlined in Chapters 2, 3 and 4, on the first visit to the Peninsula family home, the mother explained about the concerns of the social workers who visited regularly and advised her that Louise should be walking by now. Over the month of observing Louise, a summary of family life became possible:

The routine in Louise's family is, for the adults and the older children, to rise and dress ready for the 10 km walk. At the last moment in the morning, Louise is woken and taken from her enclosed cot and placed in the stroller, which is parked in the hallway near the front door. Final arrangements, such as lunches, are made by the mother, while Louise drinks a bottle of milk in the stroller and the older children assemble at the doorway. The walk is repeated on the return trip in the late afternoon. Louise is usually placed in a high-chair as dinner is prepared, and is held while the adults perform later afternoon chores or supervised outside while the older children play with their bikes or with balls. Louise is often placed in the high-chair when the children are outside, or held and moved about as the carer [either the mother or the father] moves about doing things inside or outside the house. (Field notes, Family Observations, Louise at 16 months, Period 1, Visits 1–4) (Fleer, 2010: 175)

From the observations of Louise's development over this brief one-month period, it is possible to notice that at 16 months Louise does not need to walk. Her siblings return within seconds to wherever she is seated or held. Even when Louise is in her mother's arms, the children will run back and forth and circle the mother and Louise. When Louise is in the high-chair near the kitchen table, the siblings will run from room to room, but always returning to Louise or running past her. Louise is able to observe all the activity from the vantage point of the stroller, the high-chair or the arms of her mother. Louise has a dynamic view of all the activities of the Peninsula family.

During Observation Period 2, Visit 1, Louise is 19 months old. The researchers find that the Peninsula family has received a Christmas gift of a slide and swing set. This addition to the backyard has presented a challenge for Louise. She cannot walk, and therefore cannot use the swing and slide set without adult support. Her siblings are not strong enough to lift her and they cannot place her in the seat of the swing. She must rely upon the adults to do so.

Figure 6.4 The introduction of the slide and swing is a crisis for Louise

The introduction of the slide and swing set appears to have developed a new need for Louise to independently get on to the swing and slide. The swing and slide set has changed the conditions in the family and created new possibilities for the children's development. For Louise in particular, there has been a change in motivation: she must learn to walk if she is to access the slide and swing set. This new situation has caused a crisis for Louise.

Vygotsky (1998) explains transition points that occur in children's development by explaining these dynamic moments as 'crises'. The crisis as a scientific concept was introduced by Vygotsky to explain how changes in development take place over time. He explains (1998: 191) that crisis appears as

> abrupt and major shifts and displacements, changes, and discontinuities in the child's personality are concentrated in a relatively short time (several months, a year or at most, two) ... Development takes a stormy, impetuous, and sometimes catastrophic character that resembles a revolutionary course of events in both rate of the changes that are occurring and in the sense of the alternations that are made. These are turning points in the child's development that sometime take the form of a severe crisis.

Not being able to access the slide and swing set constitutes a critical period in Louise's development at 19 months. The researchers have not visited for three months and the family appears to be keen to show them that Louise can take steps with the assistance of an adult.

> Louise is seated on a swing. She is holding on to the metal bars that support the swing as the father gently moves the swing back and forth. The father explains to the researchers, who have not visited the house for three months, 'She won't go and walk by herself'. The father takes Louise from the swing and places her on her feet. He continues to hold one hand and walks with Louise, saying, 'She will walk around everywhere doing this.' Louise looks to the researchers and smiles as they show appreciation of her walking. The father then explains that if he lets go of her hand, Louise immediately sits down and won't continue to walk. (Fleer, 2010: 176)

What has changed for Louise is that she now has a motive orientation for learning to walk. The concept of motives is not something that is biologically inherent in the child. A cultural-historical reading of motives suggests that families, schools/preschools and society create the conditions for orienting people and children to certain activities and events, and even to particular valued cultural practices. A motive develops through social relations. This conception of motives is not the commonly understood one, however: this scientific conception of motives underpins an important dimension of a cultural-historical conception of child development.

El'konin (1971), a contemporary of Vygotsky, explains that a 'self-reflective awareness on the part of the child' is a form of self-consciousness that emerges, as we saw with Louise becoming aware that she could not walk (emergence of a new self-awareness) because she wanted to be on the slide and swing set. A form of social consciousness is diverted inwards and, consequently, it 'permits the emergence of new motives and objectives that direct the child's own activity toward the future', which was also evident in the observations of Louise. El'konin (1971: 558) states that developments in motives are reflected throughout the life-course of children and adults, as we see when a child's own activity becomes directed to the future in terms 'of education and career' or learning to walk – in this case, to access the slide and swing set. The ways in which children's development changes over time constituted a central problem for Vygotsky. Observing what children are oriented towards provides an indication of children's motive orientation, and this helps us to better understand children's actual development. We return to this later when we discuss the zone of proximal development in the context of periodisation.

In subsequent visits to Louise's house, it was observed that Louise could walk independently. She was regularly observed walking to the slide and swing set. She was also able to crawl into the swing seat. Once in the seat, her siblings could push her. Louise could also walk to the ladder of the slide. However, the rungs of the ladder were challenging, as was observed during Observation Period 2, Visit 3 when Louise was 20 months old:

> Louise toddles over to the ladder of the slide. She attempts to lift one leg onto the rung of the ladder – she makes eye contact with an adult who is close by. The adult is visiting the family and notices Louise's repeated attempts to step onto the ladder. The adult lifts Louise to the top of the slide. He then supports her body all the way down the slide. He steps back. Louise walks around from the slide to the ladder and again attempts to step onto the rung. After two attempts, she looks to the adult, who steps forward and lifts her to the top of the slide and once again supports her down the slide. This process continues, with the adult each time giving less support on the slide. Eventually, the adult invites the father to observe Louise going down the slide without adult support, saying, 'She can now do it on her own.' (Fleer, 2010: 177)

In Observation Period 2, Visit 3, Louise could not manage the ladder or the slide. However, in Observation Period 2, Visit 5, which was two weeks later, she was able to negotiate the ladder and independently slide, albeit clumsily and dangerously:

> Louise has climbed to the top of the slide. She is seated on the slide holding onto the rails at the top. She calls to her mother. Her mother is inside and responds with a call, but does not come out to Louise. Louise pushes herself from the top of the slide, sliding down awkwardly, jolting from side to side. She arrives at the bottom of the slide and drops to the ground, knocking herself back as she falls. She rubs her back with her hand and cries. Both Nick and JJ look to her as she cries. (Fleer, 2010: 177)

The concept of motives helps to explain Louise's development. Louise has observed her siblings enjoying the swing and slide set, and this was motivating. She also observed how they each challenged themselves by using the swing and slide set in ways that went beyond its original design, such as climbing to the top of the frame, and pirouetting and hanging upside down. The feats of physicality by Louise's brothers became more and more daring over the 12 months of observations. The models of activity that they were constructing and demonstrating provided an ideal form of activity for Louise about what was done in the Peninsula family. Vygotsky (1994: 346) defines this as the relation between the ideal and real form of development:

> The greatest characteristic feature of child development is that this development is achieved under particular conditions of interaction with the environment, where this

ideal and final form (that form which is going to appear only at the end of the process of development) is not only already there in the environment and from the very start in contact with the child, but actually interacts and exerts a real influence on the primary form, on the first steps of the child's development.

In line with this, the observations made of Louise showed that she used the equipment to challenge herself, despite having limited adult support for managing the ladder and slide. The concept of the relations between ideal or final form and the rudimentary or real form of development helps to explain what is going on. Louise's rudimentary form of development was different from her brothers' development. But it is this relation or interaction between her rudimentary form of development and the ideal form of development of her brothers that created a motive orientation for wanting to learn to walk and to climb up the ladder of the slide and slide down the slide as her brothers did. Learning to walk was a means to an end – that is, her interest was in the swing and slide set, and to use it as her brothers did. To do this, she needed to be able to walk.

Figure 6.5 From walking to climbing and sliding

During Observation Period 3, Visit 1, when Louise was 24 months old, the researchers returned and found that she was running with great dexterity, just as her brothers did:

Louise has just had her birthday. She was given a plastic tea set and a small number of other play items. These items are in her bedroom on the floor. While the researchers visit, Nick, Andrew and JJ play with these new toys in Louise's bedroom. Louise does not appear interested in the toys. Rather, she runs up and down the hallway, back and forth to the researchers. She smiles and calls as she runs, looking back to the researchers, appearing to check that they are noticing her running. She then makes some sounds while pointing to the back door, which leads to the backyard. The mother interprets and says she is talking about the dog. The door is opened and Louise runs outside and then back again to the researchers. She smiles and giggles as she meets the researchers in the hallway. She appears to be pleased about showing the researchers her running skills, as she moves about the house and backyard in a similar way to her siblings. Later she tries to tap a flat ball, as though trying to make it bounce, something she has observed her brothers do on many occasions. (Field Notes, Family Observations, Period 3, Visit 1)

Although the social workers had worried about Louise's development, the concerns they expressed about her physical development of 'not walking' did not take into account that Louise's brothers and parents were physically active, and modelled many ways of walking, running and climbing. This was an important family practice. In summary, Louise did not have a need to learn to walk because everyone came to her. The family had a long way to walk each day to school, and this demanded that Louise be in a pram for extended periods of time. Finally, we can see that the development of a motive for walking resulted because of the crisis of not being able to independently go on to the swing and slide set when she wanted to. The crisis moved forward Louise's development in a context of the relations between her actual activity and the ideal form of activeness that she continually observed around her.

It would appear that those who visited the Peninsula family home had a view of child development that reflected a maturational or developmental view of development (as introduced in Chapter 3). However, when a cultural-historical conception of development is adopted, the same observations of Louise can be interpreted very differently. The concepts of crisis, the relations between the ideal and rudimentary form of development and motives, are important for analysing and understanding Louise's development. These concepts point to important moments or transitions in a child's life where development is actively noticed. Together, they help to explain Louise's development – development that did not follow a 'normal' developmental trajectory associated with age. A developmental or maturational view of development foregrounds age as the central criterion of child development. This conception of age is also used by theorists such as Piaget to explain the different stages of development, which are linked to a child's age (Chapter 4). Vygotsky (1998: 190) suggests that the single trait of age does not explain how development takes place:

> development is nothing other than realization, modification, and combination of deposits. Nothing new develops here – only a growth, branching, and regrouping of those factors that were already present at the very beginning ... But this alone is not enough for dividing child development into periods scientifically.

Rather than ages and stages of development as an evolutionary process, Vygotsky's cultural-historical conception of development refers to a revolutionary process of stable periods and crisis periods that are not linear but rather iterative. Biology is not ignored in a cultural-historical conception of development, but it does not take a front seat in framing or leading children's development. Learning to walk for Louise was about her motives for walking, rather than her physical development. But her physical capacity cannot be ignored in analysing the observations. Louise's development can best be explained as a stable period of no visible development. However, during the stable periods development is also taking place, even though we might not see her trying to walk. Louise is observing the new social situation of the slide and swing set over time, as well as growing in strength and size.

The critical period as described by Vygotsky can be seen in Observation Period 2 in the form of a crisis because of the introduction of the swing and slide set. However, this critical period where Louise develops a motive for walking is not always visible. It is only in the post-critical period that we observe Louise's motive development through her actually walking. Vygotsky (1998) says that the critical period constitutes a new self-awareness, which he names as a new psychological formation (sometimes translated as a neoformation), and which only becomes evident in the post-critical period. Louise developed a new relationship with her social and material environment because she could walk, and this new relationship is considered to be a new psychological formation or neoformation.

Elena Kravtsova (2006), the granddaughter of Lev Vygotsky, has taken forward a cultural-historical conception of child development through her empirical and theoretical work by explaining the iterative relations between stable periods and critical periods (crisis or dramatic periods). She states (2006: 13–14)

> In both crisis formation and formations emerging during a stable period, the child first realizes this formation in communication with those around him [sic.], and then with the help of an adult, learns to use it in daily life. Admittedly, in the first case, incorporation of the new formation does not presume any change in the children's activity. The adult helps the child endow familiar actions with a new meaning. The lytic-age [neoformation] formation emerges as a result of this help.

You may have noticed in the case study of the Peninsula family that Louise did develop mentally and physically. It is not possible to separate Louise's development into just physicality or just cognitive development (the latter is incorrectly ascribed to Vygotsky). Her development must be understood as both physical and cognitive development (as a new self-awareness or consciousness), and as dependent on her social and material environment. Her worldview changed through developing a motive towards walking, and later towards physicality – being as active as her brothers – when she ran and climbed with great dexterity, stability and speed. Physicality is an important family practice for the Peninsula family. Although this practice is particular to the Peninsula family, there are other dominant activities that children engage with that have been noted by cultural-historical theorists. Vygotsky (1966), and later Leontiev (1978), named a dominant orientation as a *leading activity*. These leading activities have been described as beginning with the newborn focused on communicating and building relationships, followed by developing a play motive, then developing a learning motive on entering school, and finally communication and relationships when entering the teenage years (see Chapter 7 for a further elaboration).

Kravtsova (2006: 14) discusses development as a change from one leading activity to another. She notes the importance of the development in a child's leading activity through the relations between these stable periods and critical periods (crises):

> by the end of the stable period, a child becomes the subject of his [sic.] own leading activity. This means that he has mastered all its components and can externalize it individually, that he is able to voluntarily realize this activity under any conditions, and that he reflects its process.

In the Peninsula family, both the siblings and the parents supported Louise's development. Prior to the arrival of the swing and slide set, Louise's relationship with her family was in terms of being embedded passively in the activity that surrounded her. During the crisis period when Louise wanted to be on the swing and slide set, her relationship with her siblings changed. She was no longer content with sitting and being helped by being moved from place to place. In the post-critical period, Louise's relationship with her family changed because she could independently walk to where she wanted to go. As noted by Kravtsova (2006: 15–16),

> the child's new communication with the adult during the post-critical period, realized as everyday actions, are endowed with new meaning, leading to the appearance of new attitudes toward reality (the lytic-period formation) on the part of the subject.

Louise was now walking and her motive orientation was to physically engage with her social and material environment. Kravtsova (2006: 17) says that 'new psychological formations [which] express the special features of a subject's consciousness and self-awareness' become evident. Vygotsky introduced the concept of central and peripheral lines of development to capture the changes in the child's motives.

> The process of development that are more or less directly connected with the basic neoformation we shall call *central lines of development* … and all other partial processes and changes occurring at the given age, we shall call *peripheral lines of development*. (Vygotsky, 1998: 197, emphasis in original)

The dynamic of a cultural-historical theory of child development is about capturing the process of development, and many other dimensions of Louise's development will be happening simultaneously, such as language development. Central and peripheral lines of development are always in motion. However, Vygotsky did not develop this dimension of his theory, thus leaving the door open for others to theoretically and empirically solve the problem of how motives change when 'the dynamics of age is to understand that the relations between the personality of the child and his [sic] social environment at each age level are mobile' (Vygotsky, 1998: 198). Vygotsky always refers to the cultural age of the child, rather than the biological age of the child.

Cultural-historical theory draws attention to changes in the leading activity of the child during the process of development. A change in the child's leading activity means a change in the child's relationship with those around them, and this change in relationships is evidence of a child's development. However, this also means that the adults surrounding the child must build a new relationship with the child, as the child has new competencies and motives, and the support given will need to be different. Common examples of this change in a child's development have been strongly felt when toddlers and adolescents wish to do things themselves and resist the support of the adults around them – 'I can do it!' or 'Me do it'. Such statements are heard when adults have not changed the nature of their interactions in recognition of the toddler's or adolescent's newly developed competencies.

CHILD DEVELOPMENT REFLECTION 6.2: THE CONCEPT OF LEADING ACTIVITY

In the cultural-historical literature, there are leading activities that vary in the way they are named by theorists. Examples are shown below. These reflect particular time periods and cultural communities. As you read these examples, consider how they reflect the cultural community in which you grew up or in which you are likely to be teaching. Record your views. We will return to these ideas.

Please note that some quotations have used the term 'stages'. This is a translation from Russian to English. However, the translation of the term 'periodisation' is more accurate, as this footnote in El'konin's theory of child development shows:

> The Russian term used here may be translated literally as 'periodization'. The term 'stage' is used because it is more consistent with current Western European and American usage. – Ed. (El'konin, 1971: 538)

Translation challenges have made interpretation of Vygotsky's original texts difficult for those not able to read the original volumes in Russian. For consistency, the quotations below use the term 'periodisation' rather than stages.

Vygotsky's (1998) conception of periodisation includes the following:

- crisis of the newborn
- infancy (2 months to 2 years)
- crisis at age 1
- early childhood (1 to 3 years)
- crisis at age 3
- preschool age (3 to 7 years)
- crisis at age 7
- school age (8 to 12 years)
- crisis at age 13

(continued)

- age of puberty (14 to 18 years)
- crisis at age 17.

El'konin's (1971) conception of periodisation of child development also includes two phases at each period of development: early childhood (infancy, early childhood); childhood (preschool, early school); and adolescence (early adolescence, late adolescence).

Bozhovich (2009: 60) says:

> But even as we divide schoolchildren's development into these three periods – young, middle, and older school age – we must point out that these periods have no precise boundaries; their boundaries are fluid and can change depending on the specific circumstances of life and activity and the demands placed on children by those around them.

Bozhovich (2009: 82) goes on to state that

> the formation of children's personality is determined by the relationships between the place that they occupy within the system of human relationships available to them (and, consequently, the corresponding demands placed on them) and the psychological features that have formed in them as a result of their previous experience. It is out of this relationship that children's internal position emerges, that is, the system of their needs and impulses (subjectively represented by the emotional experiences that correspond to them) that, refracting and mediating the effects of the environment, become the immediate force driving the development of new mental qualities in them.

What is the same across these conceptions of periodisation? What is unique? What might be central and what might be peripheral to these periodisations?

The concept of motives seems to be common across these conceptions of periodisation by Russian scholars of child development. Crisis is another key dimension of child development discussed by these theorists, where crisis is the force or dynamic that brings about a change in the leading activity or leading motives of the child during the different periods of development (periodisation). El'konin (1971: 545) asks, 'With what particular aspect of reality does the child interact – and, consequently, toward which aspect does he [sic] become oriented – in performing this or that activity?' As noted previously, the leading motive for preschool children in the cultural-historical literature is play. This does not mean that a child does not have other motives – on the contrary, it is expected that a child *will* have other motives. El'konin (1971: 559) argues that:

> In each period, a child's life is many-sided, and the activities of which his [sic.] life is composed are varied. New sorts of activity appear; the child forms new relations with his surroundings. When a new activity becomes dominant, it does not cancel all previously existing activities: it merely alters their status within the overall

system of relations between the child and his surrounding, which thereby become increasingly richer.

The question for analysis concerns what the leading motive of the child is at different points in their development. This question underpinned the theoretical work of Vygotsky, El'konin and Kravtsova during the process of formulating both their conceptualisation of periodisation (Child Development Reflection 6.2) and their theory of child development.

El'konin (1971: 543) states that, 'Blonsky and Vygotsky were never able to put their principles of developmental periods to work, owing to the absence of conditions for solving the problem of motive forces of children's mental development.' El'konin also worried about the linearity of child development, as is promoted by both ages and stages of development. He suggested a periodic scheme involving three principles (Elkonin, 1971: 561–2):

> First of all, the principal theoretical significance of our hypothesis lies in the fact that it permits us to overcome the dichotomy in child psychology between the development of the need-motivational aspect and the intellectual and cognitive aspect of the personality; it permits us to show their dialectical unity in opposition. Second, our hypothesis enables us to view the process of mental development as an ascending spiral rather than linearly. Third, it opens the way for studying the links between individual phases, for explaining how each 'sets the stage' fictionally for the following one. Further our hypothesis breaks down development into periods and phases in a way that corresponds to the inner laws of that development, not for mere external factors.

It is clear is that both Vygotsky and El'konin sought to go beyond the linearity of an evolutionary view of child development that had dominated psychology, and that historically underpins the maturational theory of child development used in early childhood education (see Chapter 3). However, maturational (Chapter 3) and stage-based (Chapter 4) theories of child development were the philosophies most widely available to many Western European heritage communities until Vygotsky's (1998) theory of child development was translated – offering another perspective on children's development.

In the next section, you will further explore motives through considering how a motive for learning develops for Jason and for Alex in the Westernport family in the Resourceful Community case study (Fleer, 2013).

RESOURCEFUL COMMUNITY CASE STUDY

PART 4: WESTERNPORT FAMILY – DEVELOPING A MOTIVE ORIENTATION FOR LEARNING

The Westernport family was introduced in Chapter 2, where it was shown that Jason had just commenced school and the family was actively establishing a homework routine. The case study is further elaborated in this chapter. Figure 6.6 shows the

Westernport family establishing a homework routine. You will recall that Jason was not happy about leaving his play in the lounge room in order to sit at the kitchen table to do homework. Return to Child Development Reflection 2.2 and note your responses to this moment in the Westernport family's life.

Figure 6.6 Establishing a homework routine in the Westernport family

Before and during Jason's homework time, Mandy and Cam throw and catch a yellow ball round the kitchen. The father participates in this activity as Jason moves to the 'homework seat' – as shown in Figure 6.6. Uncle Martin is shown behind the mother in Figure 6.6. He is playing on the computer and discussing with the grandmother [out of the photo] what he is doing across the table as the mother places the school reader in front of Jason to read. Gran and Mandy throw the ball to each other, and later to Uncle Martin, but he declines to join in the play. In the meantime, Jason is sitting and trying to read word by word what is in the reader, as the mother is pointing. Mandy throws the ball and it goes in the direction of Jason. The grandmother says in a kind voice, 'You can't give it to Jason – he is busy reading.'

What we notice here is that Jason has a new social position of being a school child, and this is foregrounded by the grandmother when she says, 'You can't give it to Jason, he is busy reading.' As noted by Bozhovich (2009: 76):

Starting school inaugurates a breaking point in children's lives, characterized for and foremost by the fact that, by becoming schoolchildren, they receive new rights and responsibilities and for the first time enter into serious, socially significant activity, their level of achievement in which will determine their place among and their relationship with those around them.

As the observation continues, we notice that Alex is very interested in the new social position of Jason as a school child:

> As Jason vacates the homework chair, the second eldest child Alex, immediately sits in the 'school homework chair' and insists on putting away the cards. The father allows this. (Field Notes, Family Observations, Period 3, Visit 2)

In the Westernport family, the practices of the school are being brought into the family home. A new practice tradition has to be established: doing homework. Homework is a different practice from what the children have previously known. Homework is an explicit presentation of school knowledge. Through doing homework, with the new social position of being a school child, Jason has acquired a new status in the family home. The school practices that are brought into the family home are keenly observed by the other children, as their behaviours suggest that the new practice is valued by them, as can be seen in relation to Alex. Hedegaard (2002: 11) argues that:

> School learning is conceptualized as a special kind of cultural practice where children through participation in this practice appropriate subject-matter concepts that can qualify their everyday concepts so they become able to function on a higher theoretical level. This process of theoretical qualification of children's everyday concepts depends on how children in the class activity are supported in acquiring a learning motive.

The process of acquiring a learning motive was supported in the family home, as shown by the way the mother created a central homework space, the father used Jason's motive for card playing to engage him in reading the sight words on the cards, and the grandmother acknowledged Jason's new status as someone learning to read, but also gently joined the homework activity to make it fun and playful (see also Chapter 2 for further details of the case study).

CHILD DEVELOPMENT REFLECTION 6.3: DEVELOPING A HOMEWORK ROUTINE – DEVELOPING A MOTIVE FOR LEARNING

Expanding on Child Development Reflection 2.2, consider the different perspectives of all the children in this same activity setting of establishing a homework routine:

- What is Jason's perspective?
- What is Alex's perspective?
- What is Cam's perspective?
- What is Mandy's perspective?
- What is your perspective on how Jason is developing a motive for learning at home through the establishment of a homework routine?

Hedegaard and Chaiklin (2005: 80) observe that:

> During school age the child's motives are dominated by the learning motive which both lets the child orient himself [sic.] to knowledge about the world in general, and to specific skills appreciated in his community. The schoolchild becomes oriented to topics that are valued by his parents, by the community, or that the child finds new and exciting to explore. The schoolchild's social motive and play motive are still important.

What you have probably noticed about the Westernport family is that the same activity setting of doing homework was being experienced differently by each child. To understand why children interact differently in the same activity setting, we need another cultural-historical concept: the social situation of development. This important concept is explained in the next section.

RESOURCEFUL COMMUNITY CASE STUDY

PART 5: PENINSULA FAMILY – SOCIAL SITUATION OF DEVELOPMENT OF THE CHILDREN IN THE EARLY MORNING

Another key concept for understanding a cultural-historical conception of child development is the social situation of development. To understand this important concept, you are introduced to the following observations made in the early morning period in the family home (Hedegaard & Fleer, 2013). This is followed by an analysis of the observation using this concept.

It is the early morning period in the Peninsula family. Louise is still in her cot asleep. JJ, Andrew and Nick are getting dressed. The mother is helping JJ. Andrew is dressed, with his back-pack on his back. He walks into the kitchen. His mother goes between the kitchen and JJ. The mother begins preparing Andrew's school lunch, and later Louise's bottle of milk.

Andrew anticipates each step of the process, and goes to the fridge to retrieve things his mother will need. However, the mother misreads this and says to Andrew in a gruff voice, 'Don't get in my way, please.' Nevertheless, Andrew persists.

Nick, who is now dressed, joins Andrew and his mother in the kitchen. He immediately opens the fridge door and stands looking into the fridge for an extended period. He moves his body up and down as he surveys the shelves of the fridge (Figure 6.7). There is very little food in the fridge.

Nick says in a soft whine as he looks into the fridge, 'I'm hungry.' His mother responds immediately by pointing her finger at him, yelling, 'Go away!' Nick repeats more loudly, 'I'm hungry.' The mother says, 'Don't start that now.' Nick drops to the floor and cries. Andrew and his mother continue to pack his lunchbox, putting in a sandwich and a muesli bar. Nick notices and asks for a muesli bar.

JJ, who is now dressed, runs up and down the hallway between his bedroom and the kitchen. He stops as Nick asks for the muesli bar. The mother complains as she goes into

Figure 6.7 Morning routine in the Peninsula family

her bedroom and takes three muesli bars from a cupboard and gives one to each child. Nick eats the bar. JJ takes a few bites and throws it on the floor. The family dog finds the bar and eats it. The mother yells, 'There isn't any more!', referring to not having any muesli bars available for Andrew's lunchbox until government living expenses are made available to the family again.

With the help of Andrew, the mother prepares Louise's bottle. Louise is taken from her cot, dressed and placed in the stroller. Andrew gives her the bottle while JJ continues to run up and down the hall. Nick is leaning his head against the wall of the hallway, still upset. The mother leads the children out of the door of the house, and together they walk to the child-care centre to drop off JJ and Louise, and then on to the school where Nick, Andrew and the mother participate in the School Breakfast Program (Period 1, Visit 3).

CHILD DEVELOPMENT REFLECTION 6.4: SOCIAL SITUATION OF DEVELOPMENT AS CENTRAL FOR UNDERSTANDING CHILDREN'S DEVELOPMENT

How do you interpret this observation of the early morning period? Document what is going on from the perspective of:

- Nick
- Andrew
- JJ
- Louise
- the mother.

Social situation of development

Vygotsky (1994) introduced the concept of the social situation of development in order to explain how three children from the same family could experience exactly the same situation quite differently. His famous example is recounted here. The family on which he reports is made up of the mother, who has a substance abuse problem, and three children. The eldest child is between 10 and 11 years of age. The family circumstances mean that the children's upbringing has experienced many moments of physical and mental abuse. In the example, the youngest child responds by developing neurotic symptoms, such as being defensive. He is overwhelmed by the horror of his situation and responds in a helpless manner. The second child has developed an agonising condition, where he responds by wanting to show love and fear of his mother at the same time. The eldest child, in contrast, shows a precocious level of maturity, wanting to help the situation by taking care of his siblings and calming his mother when needed. In analysing this same situation, and how the children experienced it, Vygotsky (1994: 339) states that:

> The emotional experience [*perezhivanie*] arising from any situation or from any aspect of his [sic.] environment, determines what kind of influence this situation or this environment will have on the child. Therefore, it is not any of the factors in themselves (if taken without reference to the child) which determines how they will influence the future course of development, but the same factors refracted through the prism of the child's emotional experience [*perezhivanie*].

Key here is the way the same situation is experienced differently because of each child's social situation of development. Vygotsky (1998: 199) states that 'the social situation of development is nothing other than a system of relations between the child of a given age and social reality. And if the child changed in a radical way, it is inevitable that these relations must be reconstructed.'

The concept of *perezhivanie*

In the observation of the Peninsula family, it is possible to see that the mother was very stressed by the situation in which she found herself during the early morning period. There was no food for breakfast. The available food was precious and had to be saved for the lunches that were prepared each morning for Andrew. The muesli bars were kept out of reach in the mother's bedroom, signalling how precious they were. But the children were hungry – especially Nick, who stood for a long time searching the fridge for something to eat. We can see that the same situation of not having food for breakfast was experienced differently by each child. Nick was distressed, and unable to wait for his breakfast. He wanted food right away. He could not wait for the breakfast program at the school. JJ did not appear concerned by the events. He ran up and down the hallway while he waited for everyone to be ready to walk to school. He did not appear to understand how precious the muesli bar was to the mother, tossing it to the floor after taking only a small bite. Louise was asleep and was only woken and placed in the stroller near the front door when her milk bottle was ready and the family was ready to walk to school. Andrew, like the eldest child in the family described by Vygotsky (1994), took on a responsible position, helping his mother. Andrew predicted the routine, retrieving the milk from the fridge and looking for the wrapping paper to put around the sandwich his mother was making for his lunch. He was also ready first, dressed for school with his back-pack on his back.

Each child experiences the early morning routine through their own social situation of development. Bozhovich (2009: 81) argues that the 'internal position conditions the structure of their attitude toward reality ... every moment, the effects coming from the environment are refracted through this internal position'. For instance, Andrew was helpful, predicting what needed to be done; Nick was distressed, not being able to manage his hunger; JJ was happy running about, not noticing the conflict; and Louise only joined the routine when her milk was ready.

This example of using the social situation of development to understand how children in the same situation experience it differently can also be used in educational settings for understanding children's development. The developmental conditions provided to children, whether at home, preschool or school, are also experienced differently (Fleer, 2016). How groups of children experience the same teaching–learning situation set up by a teacher will be based on each child's social situation of development. The concept of the social situation of development is helpful for analysing and explaining variability in children's development – not only in families, but also in group settings, such as child-care centres, preschools and schools. However, Vygotsky also introduced another phenomenon known as *perezhivanie* (see special issue of *Mind, Culture and Activity*, 2016), which is translated in the work of Bozhovich (2009) as *experience*. Bozhovich (2009: 66) suggests that in studying the social situation of development of children, 'the nature of children's experience must be understood' and the 'nature of their affective relationship to the environment' should be foregrounded. She states that *experience*, from a Vygotskian perspective,

> is a 'unit' that, in indissoluble unity, represents, on the one hand, the environment, that is what the child experiences and on the other, the subject, that is, what introduces the child into this experience and, in turn, is defined by the level of mental development of the child has already achieved.

Unfortunately, in educational settings where a maturational view of children's development is foregrounded, children's actual development – rather than their social situation of development – is often used to assess children's development. This is in opposition to looking at the process of development, the affective relations and refractions of the activity setting and their relations with others who are supporting their development, where the dynamics between the ideal and real form of development are considered. A maturational view examines what children can do on their own, influenced by their environment. Vygotsky (1998) suggests that in a maturational view, the fruits of the children's development are measured – that is, what has already matured, rather than what is the process of development. A cultural-historical conception of development captures the cooperative role of the adult in children's development – that is, the proximal rather than the actual development of the child.

The zone of proximal development (ZPD) is one of the most cited but misunder-stood concepts of Vygotsky's theory of child development. First, it is a concept of development, not of learning (Chaiklin, 2003). It is not a zone of proximal learning. Vygotsky (1998) does acknowledge the practical benefit of this concept for teaching, arguing that a key dimension of teaching is determining the actual and proximal development of children.

The concept of the ZPD foregrounds the relationship or cooperation between a child and an adult or expert other (teacher). The zone is about making visible the maturing functions that are in the process of development, which are being supported by the adult. Kravtsova and Fleer, at different times, have added to Vygotsky's original conception of the ZPD by introducing the idea of the zone of potential development (Fleer, 2010) in order to capture the ideal form of develop-ment that needs to be in the environment of the child, but that is not yet even in the process of developing. These are the motivating conditions, as we saw in the Westernport family in terms of introducing a homework routine, and through using Jason's motive for play to engage him in homework – that is, shuffling the cards and the grandmother turning the sight-reading activity into a game between herself and Jason. Learning to read was not something to which Jason was oriented, but through the cooperation of the adults with Jason in a partnership, it could be argued that the activity setting was providing a potential zone of development for Jason. Over time, the motivating activity by the family of using his play motive through their ongoing cooperation created the conditions for the development of a learning motive – that is, Jason was then in the process of developing a learning motive for learning to read, but with the cooperation of the adults. Jason's ZPD had been broadened from play to learning. As Vygotsky (1998: 204) states:

> The process of teaching is always done in the form of the child's cooperation with adults and represents a partial case of the interaction of the ideal and present form ... by applying the principle of cooperation for establishing in the zone of proximal development, we make it possible to study directly what determines most precisely the mental maturation that must be realized in the proximal and subse-quent period of his [sic.] stage of development.

The concept of the zone of proximal development

In summary, the relations between the actual and proximal zones of development foreground the maturing functions that are in the process of development. This is captured through the relations between the ideal and real form of development that is present in the child's environment. Further, there are stable periods, crises and post-critical periods, which explain the child's social situation of development and their motive orientation. This motive change is suggestive of a change in a child's leading activity. Together, these concepts explain the dynamic nature of Vygotsky's cultural-historical theory of child development.

Hedegaard's cultural-historical model of child development: Societal, institutional and personal perspectives

Hedegaard (2012) has introduced a theory of child development that takes into account the perspectives of society, the institution and the child. Her model of child development emerged from research within Denmark (Hedegaard, 2002; 2012), as well as the United States (Hedegaard & Chaiklin, 2005). She has conceptualised a holistic model of child development, as shown in Figure 6.8.

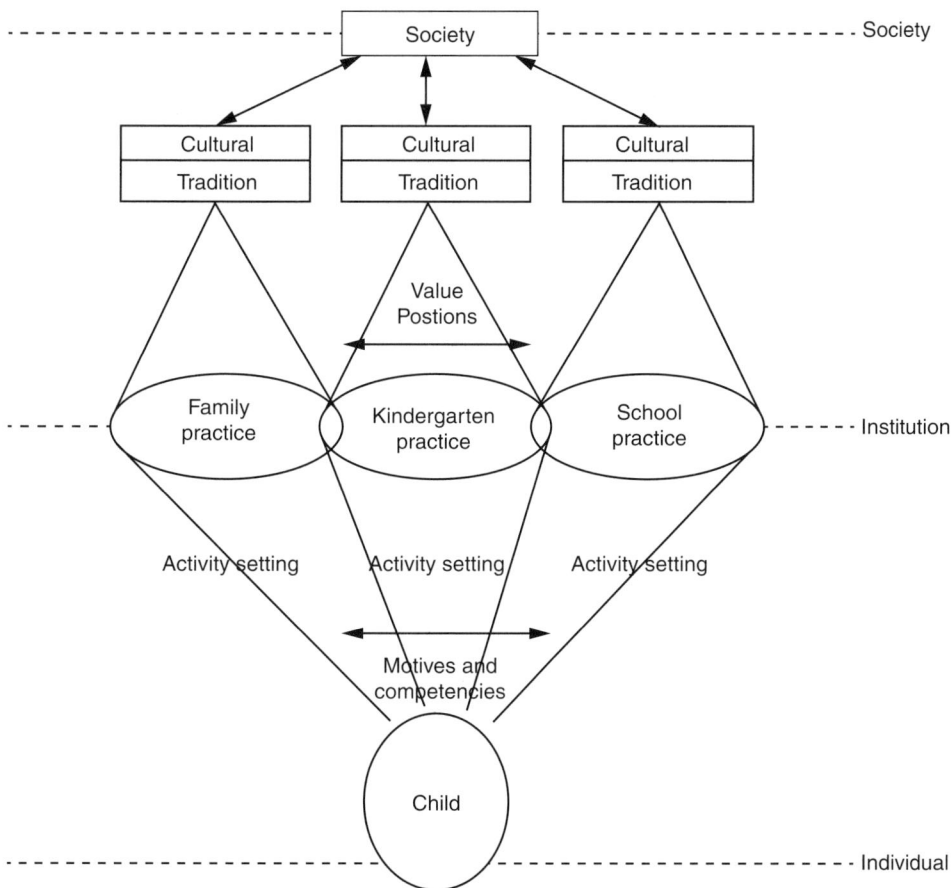

Figure 6.8 Hedegaard's model of child development

This holistic model of child development captures how the child transitions through the different institutions that they attend, such as school, after-school care and clubs.

The goals a society has for schooling determine what practices take place in schools. Even though teachers will each create their own learning experiences for children, the rules and regulations set by the institution shape what might be possible. For example, the teacher-to-child ratio is set by Departments of Education, and this determines how an individual child may experience teaching and learning in school. Being a member of a group of 50 children is a very different experience from being part of a group of 18 children.

How a child transitions from home to school each morning, or when first starting school or changing classrooms, can bring with it many crises because the forms of knowledge they encounter may be very different from what they have known:

> Societal knowledge refers to collective knowledge within different institutions. Subject-matter knowledge is a kind of societal knowledge and the most relevant form of school-based collective knowledge to consider here. Explicit or shared knowledge of community and family practices is another kind of societal knowledge. (Hedegaard, 2002: 23)

But most societies have some form of schooling, even though a child begins school in different ways and at different times. Starting school is an important life experience for a child. It is even celebrated in some communities, and often photographed to capture this important moment in a child's life.

Hedegaard's work points to the importance of the institution – whether it is the institution of the family home, the preschool or the school. How that institution is experienced will shape how the child relates to, or in turn shapes, that particular institution. How the child moves in and out of different institutions is also an important dimension of studying children's development. For instance, Hedegaard (2002: 17) says that:

> When practice in an institution changes or when a child goes from one social institution to the next (e.g. kindergarten, school, professional education and work) the child develops new psychic capacities and progresses to a new period or stage in development.

This holistic view of development is different from those models of development discussed previously (Chapters 2, 3 and 4), where age was key to benchmarking and paying attention to the child's development. It is, however, close to Bronfenbrenner's ecological model in name, because it draws attention to the societal, institutional and personal nested system (Chapter 5). Yet there are key conceptual differences, as noted by Rogoff (2003) (see Chapter 5).

Hedegaard has introduced her model of child development in order to fill a gap in Vygotsky's theory. She argues that he did not take account of the societal perspective in his holistic view of child development:

> Forms of school practice are anchored in societal and cultural traditions which give content to these practices (i.e. the activities of the school). If we want to understand child development we have to conceptualise it in connection with the activities that are practised in the school as an institution. (Hedegaard, 2002: 14)

However, the question that Hedegaard asks is how a societal goal can become a personal activity for a child. She suggests (Hedegaard, 2002: 19) that:

It is important to understand that cultural practice and meaning systems are not only acquired by the child; the child is also a co-creator or co-producer of practice and meaning systems.

That is, the child has agency: they can take the initiative and assume responsibility for their actions in these institutions. Hedegaard (2002) draws attention to capturing or noticing how a child contributes to, or experiences, the institution of the school or home – that is, in studying a child's development, you must also try to follow and understand the child's intentions and motives.

This holistic model of child development, which includes three interacting perspectives, gives a broad conception of the many dimensions that shape and are shaped in the process of a child's lived experience. To appreciate the power of this theory of child development, you are invited to draw upon the observations made in the Resourceful Community case study, and in particular to analyse the development of Jason (Westernport family) and Louise (Peninsula family).

CHILD DEVELOPMENT REFLECTION 6.5: THE DEVELOPMENT OF PLAY AND DEVELOPING CHILDREN

Using the Resourceful Community case study presented above and in previous chapters, analyse the data in relation to Hedegaard's model of child development.

1   Focus on the three interacting levels:
     a   What is the child's perspective?
     b   What is the perspective of the family?
     c   What is the perspective of the school?
2   What is the societal perspective? What particular values are being promoted in this particular Australian community?
3   What are the demands being made by the children in each of the families? What demands are being made by the school? What demands do the parents/grandparent make upon the children?
4   How do each of these perspectives intersect, inform and shape, and how are they shaped by, each other?

Transitioning to school

5   Practise using Hedegaard's model by analysing Andrew's transition to school.
6   Using the information from the Collective Inquiry School case study from previous chapters, prepare a digital animation or poster of the key cultural-historical concepts that are used in the school. Examine child development from a 'personal', 'institutional' and 'societal' perspective for the Collective Inquiry School.

In Chapter 7, Hedegaard's central concept of motives will be used to understand children's development in the context of through their participation in school. We now return to Vygotsky's theory of child development to discuss the two families that have been reported in this chapter: the Westernport family and the Peninsula family. First,

> cultural development of the child represents a special type of development, in other words, the process of the child's growing into a culture cannot be equated, on the one hand, with the process of organic maturation and on the other, it cannot be reduced to a simple mechanical assimilation of certain external habits (Vygotsky, 1997: 231).

Second, Vygotsky argues that a change in children's development does not follow a linear and evolutionary pathway; rather, it is a revolutionary process. He used the example of a metamorphosis whereby a caterpillar is qualitatively changed or transformed into a chrysalis and from a chrysalis into a butterfly.

The case studies discussed in this chapter characterise the process of qualitative change, as we saw in the Westernport family, where Jason's new social position gave him high status in the family. Beginning school has brought new responsibilities, such as homework and learning to read. The establishment of a homework routine supported the development of a learning motive in the family. It required the whole family's participation, whereby Jason was being oriented to activities that showed, through his behaviours, maturing functions in the process of developing. The ZPD captures this concept (Chaiklin, 2003).

This was also evident for Louise, who was in the process of developing a motive orientation to physical activity in relation not just to the swing and slide set, but as a collectively motivating activity with her siblings as the ideal form of development in her family. A learning motive for schoolwork or language development was not a valued family practice, and did not constitute the dominant or ideal form of development in this family: 'Something which is only supposed to take shape at the vey end of development, somehow influences the very first steps in this development' (Vygotsky, 1994: 346).

Vygotsky (1998) argues that child development is also characterised by a unique consciousness or a new relationship between the child and the child's environment. How a child relates to the environment can only be understood in relation to their motive orientation. A change in their motives means that the child's engagement with the same environment will be different, as we saw when we discussed the unique social situation of development of the children from the Peninsula family during the early morning period.

Vygotsky sought to understand how the social situation of development of the child framed how the social and physical environment was experienced. This experience, he maintains (Vygotsky, 1998), is refracted by the child through their social situation of development. As we saw, the four children from the Peninsula family understood their unique circumstances of the early morning routine of going to school without breakfast differently. How they – consciously or not – understood this experience determined whether or how they could generalise the experience. Andrew knew he would have breakfast when he got to school. He could bring this to the experience, and not only self-regulate his demand of food but also, through understanding the situation, help his mother, thereby alleviating her stress and arriving at school faster in the morning. Vygotsky foregrounded this affective relationship with the environment when discussing the social situation of children's development.

....

Collective Inquiry School

....

Conclusion

In this chapter, we have examined the cultural-historical conception of child development, particularly the concepts of the social situation of development, the relations between the ideal and real form of development, the zone of proximal development, dynamic crises and stable periods. These concepts make up the system of concepts for understanding children's development.

We have also looked at contemporary child development theorists, such as Mariane Hedegaard and Elena Kravtsova. Hedegaard introduced the concepts of the societal, institutional and personal perspectives to build on Vygotsky's original conception of child development by theorising the societal dimensions absent in his theory. Elena Kravtsova has shown how one leading activity changes into another leading activity in the early childhood period. When there is a change in leading activity, this signals development.

See the companion website for activities associated with examining different cultural-historical child development concepts and how they can be used by teachers in schools.

Finally, the concept of leading motives was introduced in relation to institutional practices and the full suite of Vygotskian concepts in order to study children's development. In the next chapter, the concept of motives is expanded further when studying Australian children.

References

Bozhovich, LI 2009, 'The social situation of development', *Journal of Russian and East European Psychology*, 47, 59–86.

Chaiklin, S 2003, 'The zone of proximal development in Vygotsky's analysis of learning and instruction', in A Kozulin, B Gindis, VS Ageyev & SM Miller (eds), *Vygotsky's educational theory in cultural context*, New York: Cambridge University Press, pp. 39–64.

El'konin, DB 1971, 'Toward the problem of stages in the mental development of the child', *Voprosy psikhologii*, 4, 538–63.

Fleer, M 2010, *Early learning and development: Cultural-historical concepts in play*, Melbourne: Cambridge University Press.

——2013, 'Examining the relations between a play motive and a learning motive for enhancing school achievement', in K Ku & S Phillipson (eds), *Constructing achievement: A sociocultural perspective*, London: Routledge, pp. 105–17.

——2016, 'Digital playworlds in an Australian context', in T Bruce, M Bredikyte & P Hakkarainen (eds), *Routledge handbook of play in early childhood*, London: Routledge, Chapter 21.

Hedegaard, M 2002, *Learning and child development: A cultural-historical study*, Aarhus: Aarhus University Press.

——2012, 'The dynamic aspects in children's learning and development', in M Hedegaard, A Edwards & M Fleer (eds), *Children's development of motives: A cultural-historical approach*, Cambridge: Cambridge University Press, pp. 9–27.

Hedegaard, M & Chaiklin, S 2005, *Radical-local teaching and learning: A cultural-historical approach*, Aarhus: Aarhus University Press.

Hedegaard, M & Fleer, M 2013, *Play, learning and children's development: Everyday life in families and transition to school*, New York: Cambridge University Press.

Kravtsova, EE 2006, 'The concept of age-specific new psychological formations in contemporary developmental psychology', *Journal of Russian and East European Psychology*, 44(6), 6–18.

Kravtsov, GG & Kravtsova, EE 2011, 'The cultural-historical basis of the "Golden Key" program', *International Journal of Early Years Education*, 19(1), 27–34.

Leontiev, AN 1978, *Activity, consciousness and personality*, Englewood Cliffs, NJ: Prentice Hall.

Mind Culture and Activity 2016, Special issue: Symposium on Perezhivanie, 23(4).

Rogoff, B 2003, *The cultural nature of human development*, New York: Oxford University Press.

Vygotsky, LS 1966, 'Play and its role in the mental development of the child', *Voprosy Psikhologii*, 12(6), 62–76.

——1994, 'The problem of the environment', in R van der Veer & J Valsiner (eds), *The Vygotsky reader*, Cambridge: Blackwell, pp. 338–54.

——1997, *The history of the development of higher mental functions: The collected works of LS Vygotsky, vol. 4*, RW Rieber (ed.), MH Hall (trans.), New York: Plenum Press.

——1998, *Child psychology: The collected works of LS Vygotsky, vol. 5*, RW Rieber (ed.), MH Hall (trans.), New York: Kluwer Academic and Plenum Press.

CHAPTER 7

Children and families in Australia as agents of their own development

Introduction

In this chapter, you will think about child development in relation to Australian children, families, communities and educational settings. The conditions created in child-care centres, preschools and primary schools to support children's development will be foregrounded. This chapter draws upon the content of Chapter 6, but takes a step forward by examining the contexts of Australian children and families rather than the countries in which the dominant theories were developed (Russia, Denmark, Switzerland, the United States). Through introducing the concept of motives to explore the contexts of development, this chapter draws attention to a new way of thinking about child development and learning for Australian children. This chapter and Chapter 8 are designed for you to read, analyse and consider what might be unique about child development for Australian children from birth to 12 years.

Through engaging with the content of this chapter, it is anticipated that you will:

- be oriented to the child's perspective when theorising about children's development
- learn how a theory of motives affords a new view of child development that positions Australian children and families with agency
- be aware of the motives of a selected group of Australian children from birth to 12 years
- analyse children's development in relation to dominant motives, meaning-making motives and stimulating motives.

Analysing children's motives

Examine Figure 7.1 and record your views on the following:

1 When you think about your own childhood, growing up in Australia or another country, what things did you like doing? What experiences did you have that were memorable?
2 What things do you believe children aged from birth to 12 years of age like to do, know and learn?
3 What do you think Australian children are oriented to in the twenty-first century?
4 What is their perspective about what they like to do, and what are the contexts in which they play, learn and live?

By thinking about the contexts in which Australian children play, learn and live, you will begin to think about what they are drawn to, what interests them and how those around them shape their development through the rich experiences that are created for them.

Figure 7.1 What do young Australian children like to do?

CHILD DEVELOPMENT REFLECTION 7.2: WHAT ARE THE CONTEXTS THAT DEVELOP CHILDREN'S MOTIVES?

Consider the contexts that develop motive orientations – at home, at school or in early childhood settings.

Where are the children?

Barbara Rogoff (2003) suggests that in middle-class families, children do not like helping at home. But she says there is a puzzle. Little children everywhere appear to want to pitch in and help in valued community and family activities. But in middle-class families they stop wanting to do jobs. However, in Mexican families everyone helps and wants to help, and this does not change. Why might this be?

In considering what children are interested in, we can begin to better understand their motive orientation.

Motives: Defining children's development

In Chapter 6, we considered the development of children's motives from a cultural-historical perspective. In particular, that chapter foregrounded the view that motives are developed through the interactions children have with their social and material environments. It was suggested that a change in motives – from play to learning, for example – showed that a child had developed. The term 'leading activity' was discussed, and this term oriented you to think about the contexts of children's development, rather than just the child's biology for determining a stage of development. In Child Development Reflection 6.2, you explored a range of leading activities, as well as ways in which theorists such as Vygotsky, El'konin and Bozhovich framed children's development – not as stages associated with the age of a child, but rather as the intertwining of the child's context, biology and social situation of development – as a dynamic where the child contributed to their own developmental conditions. The case studies presented in Chapter 6 provided examples of how the contexts of children in families draw attention to the conditions that shape children's development. However, these examples were very different to how the families were interpreted when drawing upon Piagetian stages of development:

> The changes taking place in the course of education and upbringing reveal that the 'pedagogical division of stages' lacks a sufficiently firm theoretical foundation and is unable to answer a number of essential practical questions (for example, when

school education should begin, what special features education should exhibit at the time of transition to a new stage, and so forth). (El'konin, 1971: 539)

The conditions of starting school and other major transitions in a child's life were also discussed in Chapter 6 as key moments that afforded opportunities for children's development. The contexts of child development matter, and how a society organises the way children experience life, through attending child care, preschool and school, has an impact on children's development. Like stages of development, contexts should also not be considered the only driving force for children's development.

Central to the work of Hedegaard, and underpinning the early work of Vygotsky, is the concept of motives. A cultural-historical conception of motives captures the dynamics between the social situation of a child's development and the social and material environment or context in which the child is developing. Hedegaard (2002: 19) draws attention to the fact that:

> The child's intentions and reflections are influenced by, but at the same time also influence, the activities the child is part of in the family, at day-care centres, at school, in a peer group, etc. It is therefore important when describing child development that the child's intentions and motives are included together with describing societal and cultural practices as conditions for development.

The major institutions and curricula orientation for Australian children are shown in Table 7.1.

Table 7.1 A framework of the leading motives for educational institutions in Australia

Institution	Child care/ family	Kindergarten	Primary school	Secondary school	Study or work related
Leading motive	Relationships motive	Play motive	Learning motive	Relationships motive	Being an adult motive
Social position	Social position of being a family members	Social position of a friend	Social position of a school child	Social position of a secondary school student	Social position of an adult doing work-related activities (or studying/practising to do these)

The framework in Table 7.1 seeks to support the important work of educators in determining what might be the leading motives of children in their particular community, and the particular societal configuration of the educational institutions that children attend, where motivating conditions are created to support the development of children. This framework used for determining the leading motives, rather than using milestones associated with age (see Chapter 4), provides a tool for educators to analyse the contexts of children's development.

Leading motives as a concept allows educators to go from ages (maturational developmental model) and stages (Piaget's stages of cognitive development) to characterising how institutions create specific conditions for children's development (Hedegaard, 2012). How do teachers create motivating conditions for children's development in ways that connect with the leading motives of children during the different moments inside the different institutions?

Play as a leading motive

Play creates conditions for children's development during the early childhood period. The institutions that preschool children attend generally privilege a leading motive for play. It has been shown that in play, children explore the rules and roles of society by creating an imaginary situation where they can come to understand how their environment works (Vygotsky, 1966). Children select for play those themes that surround them (El'konin, 1971), such as pretending to go to school or pretending to be a mother or father cooking dinner. Children also play with those themes that are experienced vicariously through television, books and movies, and through games and web-based content (Sutton-Smith, 1997). Play is like a window into what matters for children. Observing children's play gives teachers insights into children's motives, and also offers insights into what is characterising child development at that moment.

Learning as a leading motive

The institutions that a child attends frame what is possible, and introduce new content and experiences for children that afford new and different opportunities for their development. Schools are set up to support the development of children's learning. Through making these learning experiences motivating, children develop a motive for learning particular content, but also when they are successful, a general motive for learning – that is, the leading motive changes from play to learning when the institutions foreground this developmental change in a child's motives. While a motive orientation reflects the child's developmental period, as their leading motive orientation, teachers are charged with the task of creating conditions to support children's development. This means conceptualising learning experiences in ways that are meaningful to children (meaningful motives) and that engage children, and capture or generate new interest (stimulating motives). These three concepts introduced by Hedegaard are useful for analysing the contexts experienced by children, but also for deliberately creating new conditions for children's development.

Dominant or leading motive

'Dominant motives are associated with the types of activities that are central and important for a person's life' (Hedegaard, 2002: 63). In preschools in Australia, play is the leading motive of early childhood education. Teachers plan play-based programs to support the leading motive of play for Australian children. The EYLF supports this approach and all Department of Education in Australia expect teachers to allow time for and allocate resources to children's play.

Stimulating motives

In both early childhood settings and schools, teachers are expected to plan learning experiences for children. Hedegaard (2002) argues that teachers can work with children's leading or dominant motives in order for children to become oriented to something they wish to teach. She states, 'Dominant motives can be used as a stimulating motive in a teaching situation to stimulate activities which in themselves are not at first motivating' (Hedegaard, 2002: 65). In early childhood settings, this means creating learning experiences that feature play.

Meaning-giving motives

This term was introduced by Hedegaard (2002) to capture the idea that children show what they are oriented towards in their activity and their intentions. Children engage with their environment in relation to their motives, as these meaning-giving motives guide how a child attends to something. We see this in preschools when a child picks up an object, such as the characters from a fairy tale of *Goldilocks and the Three Bears*, and plays with these object to recreate the fairy tale. The child is oriented to play, and the child expresses their personality through their meaning-giving motive. However, another child might pick up the same objects and work with these in order to learn about how to successfully make a digital animation. The objects are used by the child for expression through learning with the objects. This child's intentions are oriented to learning, while the other child's intentions are oriented to play (Fleer, 2014).

As discussed in Chapter 6, the concept of the social situation of development helps to explain how the institution and its content is being experienced differently by the children. The concept of the relations between the ideal and rudimentary form of development helps teachers to conceptualise what might be the motivating conditions and create the pedagogical structures for developing a new motive orientation (Hedegaard, 2002; Hedegaard & Chaiklin, 2005).

A change in the leading motive of a child from play to learning is central to the work of early childhood and primary teachers. The institutional structures across many countries organise children into preschools where play is the leading motive orientation, and schools where learning becomes the leading motive for children. This change in motives is a central goal for most teachers who work in education systems. This conceptualisation of child development is characterised by profiling the leading motives of children attending particular institutional settings, where societal values and institutional practices create the developmental conditions for the child. This is shown in Table 7.1. However, as Bozhovich (2009: 71) notes, it is difficult to analyse the entire complex system of a child's motivational sphere. Yet it is possible to use Table 7.1 as a tool for beginning discussions with educators in early childhood centres, and between staff in schools, in order to map the leading motives of children that characterise that particular community. Some communities, as noted by Wong and Fleer (2012) (Hong Kong immigrant families), orient children to a learning motive rather than a play motive from birth. This creates a very different developmental condition for children in those families, and it is known that cultural variations are important to understand – especially when children start preschool or school (see Correa-Chavez, Mejia-Arauz & Rogoff, 2015).

By drawing together the key concepts developed by Vygotsky and Hedegaard's model of child development, it becomes possible to put a framework in place for documenting the leading motives that characterise children's development as they attend different institutions. This is reflected in Table 7.1. This framework not only moves beyond age as the central criterion for describing how development changes, but seeks to examine the developmental conditions to which children are oriented in the institutions they attend at different times in their lives. The institutional naming requires those using the framework to consider how the institutions are configured in a particular society. The pedagogical practices that are promoted for orienting children to the goals of that institution constitute the simulating motive (and are later expected to become their leading motive). Finally, the social position adopted by the child will be dependent upon both the pedagogical practices and the particular institution that an individual child from a particular community is attending. As with Hedegaard's model, children experience more than one institution at time, but some institutions will dominate a child's life (either because they spend long hours there or because they are highly valued in the community, such as music or horse riding clubs), and these become the leading practice tradition that children experience.

Analysing children's motives

The motive orientations shown in the literature were based on theorisation by scholars from countries such as Denmark and Russia. But what might children growing up in Australia express as their meaning-giving motives? In order to gain the child's perspective, children from the Collective Inquiry School case study were invited to draw pictures of what they liked doing at school and at home. The children shared their drawings with each other and their teacher through a focus group discussion. An example from each of the neighbourhood communities is shown in Figures 7.2 to 7.6.

CHILD DEVELOPMENT REFLECTION 7.3: ANALYSING CHILDREN'S DRAWINGS

1　In looking at the drawings of children shown in Figures 7.2 to 7.6, what might be the meaning-making motive that is being expressed by the children?

2　If you were the teacher, how might you use this understanding of their motives for supporting their learning and development? Record one idea for each drawing.

Figure 7.2 Motive orientation in the first year of school

First year in school

Figure 7.2 shows examples of what this child does at home (left side) and at school (right side). The child talks about playing with his sister at home, and creating a space on the top of his bunk, out of the reach of his sister, so that he can do 'his work' without her interrupting or spoiling what he is doing. It is a private space. The images on the right reflect the things he likes doing at school, and these (plus the focus group interview) show the dominant activities of schooling, such as drawing, writing, reading and playing on the school swings. *His motive orientation appears to be 'being a successful school child'* (see also Fleer & Hedegaard, 2010).

Figure 7.3 shows an example of a drawing from the children who were in the Year 1 and 2 class at the Collective Inquiry School. The children discussed enjoying doing science at school, playing and watching science fiction games and movies, and using construction materials to build elaborate fantasy narratives (with others and alone). *The children appeared to be oriented to fantasy – especially science fiction.*

The children in the neighbourhood community also discussed enjoying reading – both in and out of school. However, the children primarily mentioned how the books allowed them to imagine. They spoke about reading every night. They also discussed how much they enjoyed playing with friends (as shown in Figure 7.3) and their love of pets. Interestingly, some of the children spoke about how much they enjoyed maths at school. Those children said they enjoyed maths because it felt satisfying to figure out difficult problems. *The children's motive orientation appeared to capture a range of things, but primarily the children's motive orientation was to fantasy and imagination.*

The children who had been at school for four to five years spoke a lot about organised sport and gymnastics. What emerged during the focus group discussions

Figure 7.3 Motive orientation after two to three years of schooling

Figure 7.4 Motive orientation after three to four years of schooling

was an orientation towards competition – that is, the children appeared to enjoy excelling at their chosen physical activity, and in winning against themselves or others (depending upon the sport or physical activity). *The children's motive orientation was to competition.*

After six and seven years of schooling, it appeared that the children had two kinds of interest. The children drew pictures of a range of activities, both in and out of school, that focused on friendship. They spoke about the difficulties of friendship, how to not upset others and how to be a good friend. Friendships and activities associated with this featured in both school work and home life. *The overall motive orientation appeared to be in relation to friendship.*

Figure 7.5 Motive orientation after four to five years of schooling

However, a further motive orientation also emerged, and this was in relation to the children's competence in school work. During the focus group sessions with the children, they mentioned that they also enjoyed doing school work, especially mathematics and chess. However, it should be mentioned that in the context of the neighbourhood community, the teachers had specialist mathematical knowledge (female teacher) and skills in chess (male teacher). This expertise appeared to have generated a motive for successful mathematics competence, and this seemed to dominate some of the girls' comments. This example highlights how teachers create motivating conditions for children – as stimulating motives – and, through this, orient children to different things. The example also highlights how context matters in children's development. A change in motive orientation from one leading motive to another suggests children have developed.

What emerges from the drawings are different motive orientations across the years of schooling. The images and the interviews are summarised in Table 7.2.

Table 7.2 Children's motive orientation across years of schooling

Years of schooling	Motive orientation	Figure
1 year	Motive orientation to being a successful school child	7.2
2–3 years	Motive orientation to fantasy and science fiction	7.3
3–4 years	Motive orientation to fantasy and imagination through reading	7.4
4–5 years	Motive orientation to competition	7.5
6–7 years	Motive orientation to friendship and academic competence	7.6 and 7.7

Figure 7.6 Motive orientation after six to seven years of schooling

Examine your response to *Child Development Reflection 7.3* in relation to the content of the table. Did you come up with similar motives?

Table 7.2 is specific to the Collective Inquiry School – a school within an urban community where there is a broad range of children (discussed in Chapter 1). It is

What I like to do at school

Figure 7.7 What I like doing at school

not typical of all children and all schooling experiences. However, it is possible to see that the motive orientation of the children can be linked with that discussed in Chapter 6. Children entering school transition from a leading motive for play to a leading motive for learning. This is evident in the new social position they have as a school child – this is their role at school and is recognised in the family, as shown in Figure 7.2, where the child had created a special space at home to do 'school work' free of his siblings. We see this leading motive for learning still in place after three years, where there is a relationship between fantasy and science fiction in children's preferred activities. Children's play has not disappeared as a motive, but it is not the children's leading motive. After more years of schooling, it would appear that competence becomes increasingly important, as noted in Figures 7.5 and 7.6. Through competition – either with self or others – children begin to focus on how well they can do things. This appears through sport and school achievement because the institutions the child attends focus on these characteristics. However, the motives for competition, competence and friendship (how to be a good friend) appear to become increasingly important as schooling progresses.

Rather than biology determining children's motives, the drawings suggest that the institutions the child attends (clubs, sporting activities, school) orient the child to what is valued in the particular institution and in society as a whole. Australians appear to value sport and the competition associated with this national pastime and activity. Families and schools also appear to value competition (in terms of grades and physical activity). Additionally, Australian society expects that schools will support academic achievement and good citizenship. Both of these attributes appear in the motives of the children who drew pictures of what they liked doing.

Children growing up in different countries may well value different things. Even within Australia, different communities (rural and urban) and different families will value different things. The point is to capture what it is that children like doing, so that it becomes possible to identify their motive orientation and to use this knowledge for creating the conditions for their development. This can be done in ways that are motivating for children – for example, a stimulating motive – so educators can meet the societal and/or community expectations of valued educational practices and outcomes. In taking the child's perspective (Table 7.2), it becomes possible to create your own framework for children's development in the community in which you will be teaching – that is, modify Table 7.1 so that it reflects the children in your preschool or school.

Motives: From the perspective of families, communities and schools

In this section of the chapter, you are invited to read each of the two case studies and to analyse their content for how teachers create motivating conditions, and how children change their motive orientation. Draw upon Tables 7.1 and 7.2 to develop your own table of children's development for children who attend preschools and then for children who attend school. Together, this will allow you to create your own framework for children's development. Alternatively, study the children in your preschool/school, inviting them to draw pictures of what they like doing at school/preschool and at home. Interview the children – gain their perspective. Then interview the families and your teaching peers. This expands what is presented in this chapter, and provides insights from the perspective of children, families, preschools and schools about child development for your community.

CHILD DEVELOPMENT REFLECTION 7.4: MOTIVES AS TOOLS FOR ANALYSING CHILDREN'S DEVELOPMENT

Consider the concept of motives in relation to the three dimensions discussed previously: dominant or leading motives, stimulating motives, and meaning-making motives. Use these dimensions of motives to analyse the two case studies reported below. As you read each case study, think about the following questions:

- What might be the leading or dominant motive of the children in each of the settings described in the case studies?
- Do the teachers use the children's possible leading motive to orient the children to new learning?

(continued)

- How are the educators and teachers creating the conditions for a stimulating motive?
- What evidence is there of a meaning-making motive?

Prepare your own framework of child development, drawing upon the content of Tables 7.1 and 7.2 to guide you.

CULTURALLY DIVERSE PRESCHOOL CASE STUDY

PART 3: USING HEDEGAARD'S LEADING MOTIVES THEORY TO UNDERSTAND THE CULTURALLY DIVERSE PRESCHOOL

Play is the leading activity for the children in the Culturally Diverse Preschool. In Figure 7.8, the children are looking at the play they have captured on the iPad. The teacher and the children look intently at photos and video clips taken by the children of the camping play introduced in Chapter 3. In line with Vygotsky's theory of play, the children have used the digital tool as a placeholder of their play. The play was captured and replayed to the child who was absent from preschool – a child who would normally be part of the camping play. The children had wanted to capture their play on that day so that the missing child could see how the play narrative had developed. As a digital placeholder, the digitally captured play could be revisited by all the children involved. It was through viewing and replaying the play that the digital play acted as a pivot to take the play forward. Digital play is a new type of activity that is found increasingly in preschools and family homes. If you return to Chapter 3 and examine the play conditions set up in the preschool, it is also possible to better understand the possibilities for play and learning from the personal, institutional and societal perspectives featured through the three-lens analysis shown there.

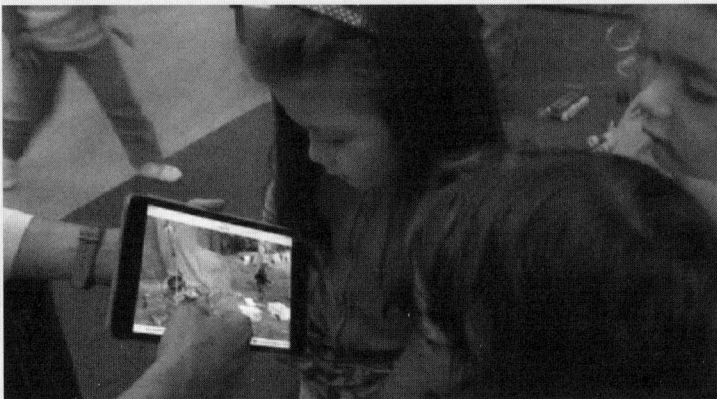

Figure 7.8 Digital placeholders and virtual pivots

Is it possible that the children will develop a digital play motive? The relations between play and learning are problematised in this case study. How do institutions like preschools, which have free play settings, allow for a motive for play and a motive for learning?

CHILD DEVELOPMENT REFLECTION 7.5: ANALYSING THE LEADING MOTIVE ORIENTATIONS OF CHILDREN IN THE CULTURALLY DIVERSE PRESCHOOL CASE STUDY

Using the content of Table 7.2, you are invited to consider the Culturally Diverse Preschool case study. As you read the observations and analysis, consider the following:

1　What social position do the preschool children have? Document what you believe their social position to be.
2　What is the leading motive of the preschool children? Document what you believe their motive orientation to be.
3　To what is the teacher orienting the children (for example, see Figure 7.9)? Document the range of activity settings in which the children are located and record what you believe are the evident orienting motives.

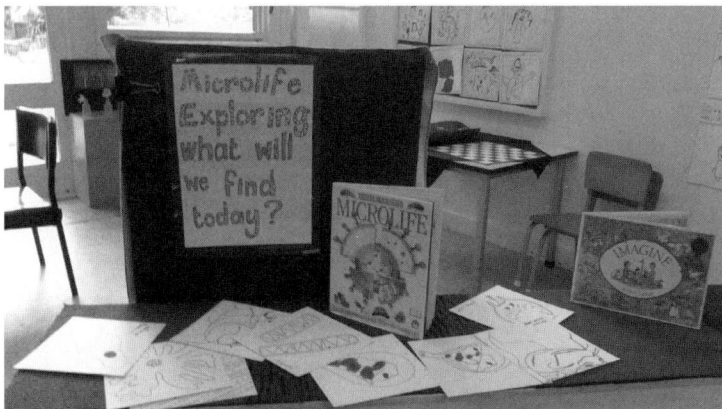

Figure 7.9 Finding out more about the microscopic environment

In Figure 7.10, the children from the Culturally Diverse Preschool imagine being microscopic. The children have experienced the magnification process through using hand lenses and digital devices, as well as a digital microscope. This gives a rich context of preschool experiences in which to imagine. The children enter into an inflated plastic bubble, where they pretend to be inside a drop of water (Figure 7.11). The children imagine being the creatures they see inside a water drop; they also imagine the organisms they have found inside the compost bin. Imagining being microscopic supports the children to understand magnification.

Figure 7.10 Getting ready to enter into the playworlds – imagining the microscopic life

Figure 7.11 Playworlds – imagining being inside a drop of water

Relations between play and learning in the Culturally Diverse Preschool

What did you notice about the relations between play and learning in the Culturally Diverse Preschool?

Leading motive

You would have noticed that the children were experiencing a learning program in which they were investigating their outdoor environment. However, they were also involved in role-play, imagining being inside a drop of water. Both learning and play are featured in this program.

Motivating conditions

In your analysis you would have found that a motive for play was drawn upon by the teacher to support the children to better understand the complex science they were experiencing. The investigations were challenging for the children. The play supported their learning, and the investigations appeared to support the children's development. The children were being oriented to a learning motive through the investigations – something that would dominate their lives once at school. It would appear that the children's active engagement and willingness to undertake the investigations set up by the teachers would suggest that a learning motive was in the process of development. The learning motive was therefore in the stable period of the children's development. The preschool teachers oriented the children to learning through the investigations. But they also used play to support the learning. In this way, preschool institutions create conditions for children's development, in anticipation of the change in the leading activity from play to learning on entering school.

Social position

In the Culturally Diverse Preschool, the children still hold the social position of being preschool children at play – even though the children engage in leaning situations throughout the day.

COLLECTIVE INQUIRY SCHOOL CASE STUDY

PART 3: USING HEDEGAARD'S LEADING MOTIVES THEORY TO UNDERSTAND THE COLLECTIVE INQUIRY SCHOOL

Margie is in her final year at the Collective Inquiry School. She has been appointed by Tim, her Year 5/6 neighbourhood teacher, to be the theatre director of the play *Alice in Wonderland.* At the end of the year, Margie reflects on her experiences at her school, and also speaks about her role that year, and her own development through the approach to teaching and learning in the school, known as inquiry time (see Chapter 2 for more details):

> Everyone learns the basic maths and English. But you also have a really good opportunity
> to find where your strengths are, and where your weaknesses are, and find things you
> didn't know you were good at. For example, up until Grade 4, I was involved in singing
> and performing. But I had never thought about being a director, and then I discovered
> this world of directing, and the way you can have this vision and really bring it to life. You

can think about what happens and then see it happen. One of my learning experiences in this learning inquiry was that there are all these different roles, and you can work together to create the thing you want, and I learned how to work with lots of different people and how to coordinate everything into one big production.

How was this level of reflection possible for Margie? What school conditions supported her development?

You will now read about the reflections of Margie's school principal, Esme (Context 1), and then those of Margie's teacher, Tim (Context 2) to learn how this might be possible. How did Margie's motive for theatre and being a theatre director develop in this school? Context 3 captures how Tim brings together Contexts 1 and 2.

The concept of motives as used by teachers

Context 1: Reflections of Margie's school principal

The teachers in the Collective Inquiry School meet periodically during lunch breaks and in the evenings over dinner for professional discussions about the child development concepts that informed their pedagogical practices. This first example is related to thinking about children's development over the course of primary schooling – the children's motive development. Esme, the principal of the school, discusses with her senior leadership team the problem of children's motives for learning across the year levels. Esme reflects on how children's motives change over the course of their primary schooling:

> [We have asked] what are the motives of 5-year-olds, and as we know, how do those motives change for 12- and 13-year-olds? Both groups have very different motives to engage in the school context. How do we bring the learning to that, to their motive orientation? (Esme, two-day staff conference) (Fleer, 2015: 239)

Esme discusses the concept of the *social situation of development* and the concept of *motives.* Like Hedegaard (2012), Esme talks about *motives* as not being inside a person – that is, biologically determined and linked to age. Rather, the theory upon which Esme is drawing argues that teachers create the conditions to inspire and motivate children, making the learning activities motivating. It is through children's changes in *motives,* from play leading their thinking and actions to learning leading their activities, that development is said to take place in this *cultural-historical theory of child development.*

The *social situation of development* she mentions recognises that both the child and the environment together act as a source of development for the child. She argues that it is not just the biology of the child or the environment that develops the child, but both. What the child brings to the social situation in the school – their experiences, interests and motives – determines how they respond to a particular learning environment. For Esme, the *social situation of development* helps to explain how different children in each neighbourhood community experience the same environment differently. This concept also helps to explain how one child's relationship with the same environment might be different when they have a different level of development. For instance, Esme refers to the different year levels in the school and the different motives the children may have for engaging with the learning contexts the teachers create. In taking a cultural-historical perspective on development, she uses two key concepts: *motives* and the *social situation of development.*

As mentioned above, according to a cultural-historical theory of child development, a child who has just entered school has the motive to be a successful school child and to take seriously their social position of being a school child. In taking this position, the child will want to do school activities, to learn to read, and to feel and have others respond to them in relation to the new social position of no longer being a child, but a *school* child. Being a school child is the social position, and learning in this new social position is the child's leading motive. In contrast, a child in the final year of primary school may predominantly wish to focus on socialising with their peers – to practise socialising with others, to want to take more responsibility for their own projects, but also to be with others, focusing on being a good friend. The leading motive is socialising and communicating with their peers. The child just starting school has a very different motive from the child who is at the end of primary school and transitioning into secondary school – for example, Margie.

Context 2: Dance group pedagogy

In the second example, Tim analyses the pedagogy of a dance group that came into the school to teach hip-hop songs to the children in his group. Tim used a concept from cultural-historical theory of child development to analyse the pedagogical practices of the dance group. He contrasts this with his own practice of staging *Alice in Wonderland* as a theatrical production with the 5/6 Neighbourhood Community – for which Margie was the stage director.

Tim used the concept of the relations between the ideal and real form of development to make sense of why what he observed didn't seem to work. He noticed that the company broke down the steps to the song (behaviourism – see Chapter 9) and taught them in isolation; as a result, the experience did not connect with the children. In using the concept of the ideal and real form of development, Tim reconceptualised a better pedagogical approach for the same activity of learning a hip-hop song:

> When we had people come in to teach 'hip-hop' song . . . I thought a better way to go was to do the hip-hop song first [ideal form], and then break it up, but they didn't, they broke it up first and the kids didn't know where they were going. (Tim, lunchtime forum) (Fleer, 2015: 241).

Here Tim discusses the relationship between the ideal form of development (being able to perform a hip-hop song) and the real form of development of the children (not engaged in the silly movements). The relational concept helps Tim to bring together his knowledge of the children's development and the appropriate pedagogical practice that will develop them further. Tim takes this a step further by stating,

We are thinking about that now, the relations between the ideal form of development we want the children to have, and the actual form of development of the children when we are conceptualising all our projects, and this means bringing the outside world into the school. (adapted from Fleer, 2015: 239)

Context 3: The relations between ideal and real/rudimentary forms of development

In the next statement, Tim shows how he used Vygotsky's concept of the relations between the ideal and real form to analyse the *Alice in Wonderland Project*. He had brought the outside world into the school. The children visited the theatre (Malt House) and went backstage to see all the departments – the make-up department, the costume department, the lighting department and the stage management department, but also the accounts department, the ticket office for making bookings, and so on. The activities observed constituted the ideal form of development. The children went back to the school and re-created each of these departments, so that they could eventually success-fully stage *Alice in Wonderland.* Tim reflects on this:

We set ourselves up in different project groups [in the classroom], ... [the classrooms across the Year 5/6 neighbourhood] as a theatre company. Part of that experience was going out to a theatre company. We went out to a theatre company for a day ... and got to see behind the production, the sets, went into the costume department, the dressing rooms, backstage, we went and looked at the sets ... (Tim, teacher–child interviews) (Fleer, 2015: 241)

Figure 7.12 is the stage model made by Margie's team. They had visited the theatre in their local community, talking with all the members of the production to gain insights into the different roles and functions of putting on a theatre production.

Figure 7.12 Developing the relations between the ideal and real form in the Collective Inquiry School – the stage design

Figure 7.13 shows the mock-up designs for costumes. The children worked together with a parent to design the costumes. Tim had set up the costume department so it was like the one the children had seen at the theatre they had visited. The children went through the same process of designing, selecting fabric, producing patterns and finally making the actual costumes (see Figure 7.14). The costume department was responsible for this important production goal.

Tim reflects upon the concept that underpins the approach to teaching that was used in the production of *Alice in Wonderland*:

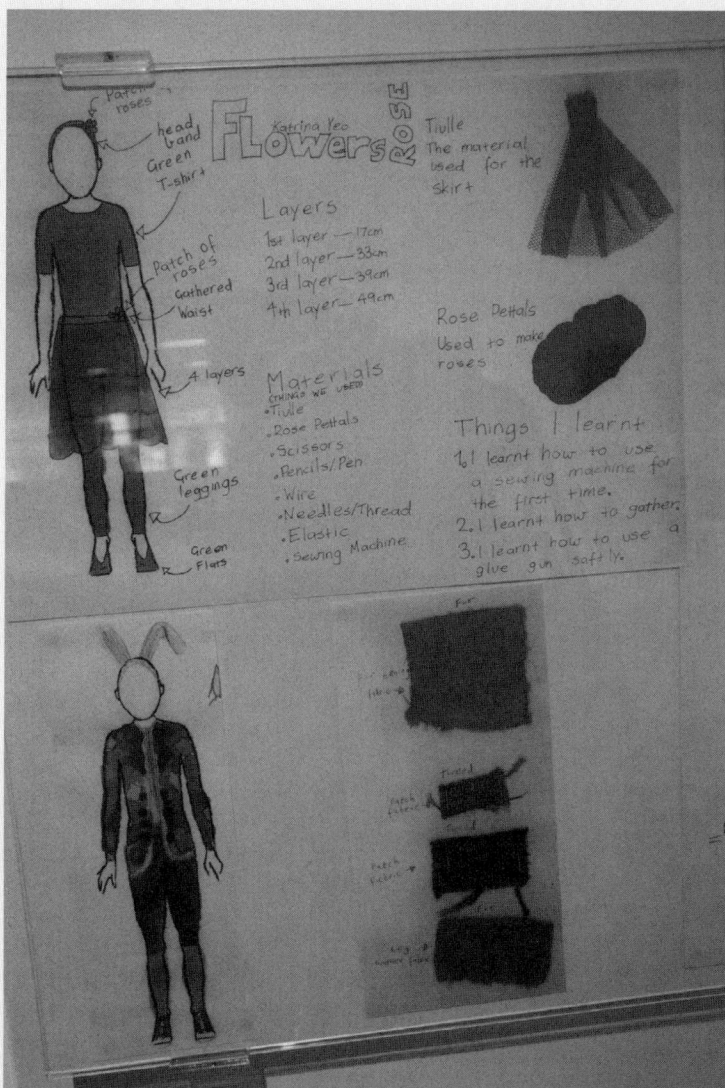

Figure 7.13 Developing the relations between the ideal and real form in the Collective Inquiry School – the costume design

It goes back to the discussions we had [Evening Research Group Meetings] . . . reflecting on the concept [of the relations between ideal and real development]. I wasn't conscious about how we do it, giving it a name, and labelling it. (Tim, lunchtime forum) (Fleer, 2015: 241)

Tim was able to make better sense of the teaching approach that he had successfully created and could now consciously use by drawing upon the concept of the relations between real and ideal forms of development. The ideal form of development that was hoped for was being created through the production of *Alice in Wonderland*. By

Figure 7.14 Developing the relations between the ideal and real form in the Collective Inquiry School – the final costumes on display

visiting a production company and a theatre from their local community, the children were able to use what they observed to set up their own departments – such as the costume department. These were also ideal forms of organising and working. In this process, the role of being the director of the production meant that Margie learned about the role of a director, but also that this was a career that she could consider. On leaving primary school and going into secondary school, Margie could already see a pathway for herself. Tim's role was to create the conditions that allowed for the ideal form of the theatre production, with the real form of development that the children were exhibiting through their motive orientation. In the case of Margie, a productive relation between the ideal and real form of development was created through a stimulating motive of visiting the theatre company. The project of *Alice in Wonderland* generated possibilities for the children (as Table 7.2 suggests) to develop their competencies through the support provided by Tim and the community in establishing and working within the different departments (as observed on their excursion) to successfully stage the production. The pedagogy and theorisation of child development evident in this case study help to explain the powerful reflections made by Margie about her own learning at this school. As Hedegaard (2002: 37) reminds us:

> Depending on how a person encounters knowledge in different societal institutions, he [sic.] will appropriate knowledge and thinking methods with subject domains which are characterized by one or more of these epistemologies and convert them into personal concepts and thinking modes.

Twenty-first century learning: A community of inquirers

Conclusion

In this chapter, you looked closely at how we as educators create the contexts and conditions for children's development. However, it was also shown that children have their own perspectives on what they like to do, and the motives they wish to develop. Our role as teachers is to introduce children to institutional practices of schooling, preschool and child care. As members of the Australian community, we also introduce children to societal values and beliefs simply by honouring the curriculum frameworks where we follow the rules for, and outcomes of, education. But we are not alone in our work. For instance, what we do now and how we work with children have a history, to which we and the children we teach are introduced:

> A child is born into a society where knowledge already exists. Knowledge exists as practice and procedures for tool use, tool production and interaction between

persons-both in the form of material tools and in different symbolic forms such as language, text diagrams, pictures, movies, computer programmes etc. Societal knowledge can be characterised as reflected knowledge, when it can be communicated, and thereby different forms of knowledge can be distinguished which can be connected to different trends in the scientific development. (Hedegaard, 2002: 20)

The drawings in this chapter show what some Australian children value. You were invited to examine these drawings and to consider the dominant or leading motives for these Australian children. Although some similarities between these motives and those discussed in Chapter 6 were evident, such as being a successful school child, others were quite different. This chapter signals that we must also be critical of the main theories of child development discussed in previous chapters because they were not researched in Australia. Although the main theories could nicely represent the communities from which the research was undertaken, the timeframe in which the foundational research was done might also suggest that other motive orientations should be considered. For example, different motive orientations might emerge because of digital technologies, new pedagogies, different life experiences of children, and families who are mobile and international. Table 7.2 (along with the way it was developed) illustrates one way by which you could find out children's motive orientations for the community in which you are or will be teaching. Table 7.2 and the concept of motives discussed in this chapter provide a way forward for better understanding children's development and the context of development you create for the children you teach.

In the next section of the book, you will be invited to think even more critically about the theories of child development discussed thus far.

References

Bozhovich, LI 2009, 'The social situation of development', *Journal of Russian and East European Psychology*, 47, 59–86.

Correa-Chavez, M, Mejia-Arauz, R & Rogoff, B (eds) 2015, *Advances in child development and behaviour: Children learning by observing and contributing to family and community endeavors: A cultural paradigm*, Amsterdam: Elsevier.

El'konin, DB 1971, 'Toward the problem of stages in the mental development of the child', *Voprosy psikhologi*, 4, 538–63.

Fleer, M 2014, 'The demands and motives afforded through digital play in early childhood activity settings', *Learning, Culture and Social Interaction*, 3(3), 202–9.

——2015, 'Developing an assessment pedagogy: The tensions and struggles in re-theorising assessment from a cultural–historical perspective', *Assessment in Education: Principles, Policy & Practice*, 22(2), 224–46.

Fleer, M & Hedegaard, M 2010, 'Children's development as participation in everyday practices across different institutions: A child's changing relations to reality', *Mind, Culture and Activity*, 17(2), 149–68.

Hedegaard, M 2002, *Learning and child development*, Aarhus: Aarhus University Press.

——2012, 'The dynamic aspects in children's learning and development', in M Hedegaard, A Edwards & M Fleer (eds), *Motives in children's development: Cultural-historical approaches*, New York: Cambridge University Press, pp. 9–27.

Hedegaard, M & Chaiklin, S 2005, *Radical-local teaching and learning: A cultural-historical approach*, Aarhus: Aarhus University Press.

Rogoff, B 2003, *The cultural nature of human development*, New York: Oxford University Press.

Sutton-Smith, B 1997, *The ambiguity of play*, Cambridge, MA: Harvard University Press.

Wong, PL & Fleer, M 2012, 'A cultural-historical study of how children from Hong Kong immigrant families develop a learning motive within everyday family practices in Australia', *Mind Culture and Activity*, 19, 107–26.

Vygotsky, LS 1966, 'Play and its role in the mental development of the child', *Voprosy psikhologi*, 12(6), 62–78.

CHAPTER 8

Ways of Knowing, Ways of Being and Ways of Doing

Introduction

In this chapter, we build upon the content of Chapter 7, where we introduced the idea of looking at the development of Australian children. This chapter examines how each of the main theories of child development positions children, families and communities – that is, how each theory describes children, how it discusses (or not) the place of family and communities in conceptualising child development, and how it considers the original contexts in which these well-known theories were developed. In this chapter, you are also introduced to the key thinking of leading Australian scholars, such as Associate Professor Peter Anderson (education specialist) and Professor Karen Martin (early childhood education specialist). Both are pioneers in child development theories for Australian children.

Through engaging with the content of this chapter, it is anticipated that you will:

- think about child development in the context of all families and communities, and the conditions that we as educators create in child-care centres, pre-schools and primary schools
- become aware of the importance of engaging with, making visible and listening to the voices of Aboriginal and Torres Strait Islander people in the context within which you will be teaching
- critique the theories of child development that continue to inform education in Australia and consider a rights-based approach to, and ways of knowing, ways of being and ways of doing, for driving the theorisation of child development.

To achieve the goals of this chapter, you will critique the theories of development discussed thus far, and the theories put forward in the Early Years Learning Framework (EYLF). In this chapter and Chapter 9, it is argued that some theories discussed in the EYLF are not child development theories, but rather are valuable tools for critiquing child development.

Learning theories are imposed from the North

In this section of the chapter, you will meet Associate Professor Peter Anderson, as he discusses his views on theories of development in the context of all Australian children. Before you learn about his thinking, let's meet him through his official biography.

Associate Professor Peter Anderson

Associate Professor Peter Anderson grew up in Sydney. His family is from the Northern Territory. His father is a Warlpiri man, originally from Central Australia. His mother is from Daly River (Nauiyu) in the Port Keats area (Wadeye). They grew up as part of the Stolen Generation on Melville Island, but found their way back to country.

Peter has worked in Aboriginal higher education in different positions over the past 15 years, with distinguished positions, such as a member of the Australian Council of Deans of Education, holding editorial responsibility for the *Journal of World Indigenous Nations Higher Education* consortium, and Chair of the Australian Indigenous Lecturers in Teacher Education. Peter was a Senior Lecturer and Coordinator of Indigenous Education and Leadership in the Faculty of Education at Monash University, where he taught in the areas of organisational leadership, Indigenous and traditionally-oriented peoples' education, and teacher and academic pro-

Figure 8.1 'Teachers are part of the "helping professions" and they can make a difference.'

fessional development. He has recently moved universities and is now at the Queensland University of Technology. Peter's original research has theorised the understandings of the organisational value of academic freedom in Australian universities and considered leadership and learning theories in the broader context of the polar south.

Peter's views on education

Peter was interviewed about his theory of child development in the context of his views on education generally for primary teachers and early childhood educators. In this context, Peter raises key points about learning and child development theories:

- Learning and child development theories are imposed on Aboriginal people.
- There is a need for visibility and presence.
- A rights-based approach is needed.
- Racist teaching practices still exist.
- An international best practice model is required.
- The colonial narrative still remains.
- Feeling safe is vital.
- Racist assumptions about learners still exist.
- Interpersonal relationships are important.

The territory that Peter covers is expansive, but the narrative he presents is about getting the Australian ship in order before we can sail ahead into the unchartered waters of new theories of child development. His insights set the stage for conceptualising a theory of child development for Australian children.

Learning and child development theories imposed on Aboriginal people

Peter makes the point that learning and child development theories are imposed on Aboriginal people:

> If we were to look at an Australian context for educational theory, and if we were to use the work of Raewyn Connell [2007] then existing theories don't make sense – in the way in which the theory was written – as it was developed in the Northern Hemisphere. When we look at the theorist, their world views and their experiences, such as Piaget – he was a European male – his theory is transported to the Southern Hemisphere. It doesn't make sense because the environments don't match. As a sociologist I am always questioning things that are developed in the Northern Hemisphere, where the academy has had centuries long traditions, and then you see they are actually transported through the university system into Australia – 220 years. It does not make sense theoretically in terms of context. Context and theory go together. Epistemology, ontological perspectives, just like dark grey Piaget. It is brighter in Australia, so he might have been a bit happier, if he had studied children in Australia.

Need for visibility and presence

As an educator, you will potentially be teaching in many different communities. Each community will have its own context. But this is a Southern Hemisphere context and, as Peter suggests, it may not 'match up' or align easily with those theories of child development that were developed in the Northern Hemisphere.

Peter suggests that it is important to question the need for visibility and presence:

> Having the space. I cannot divorce myself from the reality that Aboriginal people are still invisible in the academy. In this system, we are invisible. A way of learning – talking about that construct – is visibility and presence. Aboriginal children, if they are present, can see themselves in text, can see themselves positively, reflected in a classroom. That is so much more powerful than being bombarded – even at home, where they are seeing in mainstream media the sort of ills of Aboriginal culture, as such. Most Aboriginal people don't drink. We are actually getting this false understanding of identity of children. They are afraid and they think it is bad to identify as an Aboriginal person. So until we can create a space that is safe for them to identify as who they are, and they are respected for who they are. I can't have a conversation about learning and development as such, because we need these spaces first. And the presence first.

Peter is inviting us to consider our own experiences of Aboriginal Australians. Is our perspective informed by the media? He is asking us to reflect upon what perspectives we might bring to a conversation with Australia's first peoples. He is also asking us to consider what perspectives we bring as beginning teachers in early childhood education, and what spaces we create that are safe for identifying as Aboriginal. It is in these safe contexts that a genuine dialogue about teaching and learning becomes possible.

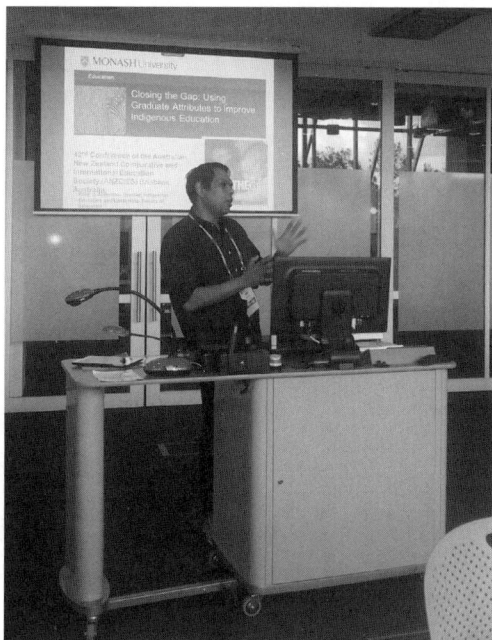

Figure 8.2 'In the teacher education space and in the classroom, we don't yet have Indigenous voices.'

A rights-based approach

On a rights-based approach, Peter says:

> Fundamentally, Australia is violating the human rights of Aboriginal and Torres Strait Islander peoples. We give our students an understanding of the rights of the child, the UN Declaration of Human Rights. These are foundational documents for our profession. Added to this is the UN Declaration on the Rights of Indigenous Peoples. There are two or three Articles (13 and 14), that speak around the role of education in terms of the benefits that it gives first nations peoples. This document is used internationally in the higher education space of all nations with Indigenous peoples. We have taken it up late: we were a signatory to it in 1999.

The Australian Human Rights Commission has posted 46 Articles. Articles 13 and 14 state:

Article 13

1   Indigenous peoples have the right to revitalize, use, develop and transmit to future generations their histories, languages, oral traditions, philosophies, writing systems and literatures, and to designate and retain their own names for communities, places and persons.
2   States shall take effective measures to ensure this right is protected and also to ensure that indigenous peoples can understand and be understood in political, legal and administrative proceedings, where necessary through the provision of interpretation or by other appropriate means.

Article 14

1   Indigenous peoples have the right to establish and control their educational systems and institutions providing education in their own languages, in a manner appropriate to their cultural methods of teaching and learning.
2   Indigenous individuals, particularly children, have the right to all levels and forms of education of the State without discrimination.
3   States shall, in conjunction with indigenous peoples, take effective measures, in order for indigenous individuals, particularly children, including those living outside their communities, to have access, when possible, to an education in their own culture and provided in their own language. (United Nations, 2007)

Peter reflects on this:

> Considering the violations, is a shift for pre-service teachers – it is an emotional shift, it is a psychological shift. This is the basis of the learning journey. The students are not at a point of being decolonised yet. Australia is not decolonised. Australia is still post-imperial. We are not a republic. So we cannot be post-colonial if we are not a republic. So we have to talk about post-imperial.

In the process of another cultural group taking over the land and culture of an established group (colonisation), a psychological violation is imprinted on that generation, but also is impacted intergenerationally. The British imperial system was the first political coloniser to invade the Australian continent, not just in its initial physical invasion, but also with regard to the rules and regulations that were put into place to reinforce that system. Decolonisation is to remove the affect of this colonisation – regardless of when the colonising act took place. This is thought about in two possible ways: (1) to physically remove the invaders; or (2) to psychologically remove the bondage. Peter is suggesting that in Australia we still have a long way to go in the decolonisation process where the original bondage is still in place.

To support the process of decolonisation, the Australian Human Rights Commission has also said that in its commitment to the UN Charter it is:

> *Affirming* that indigenous peoples are equal to all other peoples, while recognizing the right of all peoples to be different, to consider themselves different, and to be respected as such,
>
> *Affirming* also that all peoples contribute to the diversity and richness of civilizations and cultures, which constitute the common heritage of humankind,
>
> *Affirming further* that all doctrines, policies and practices based on or advocating superiority of peoples or individuals on the basis of national origin, racial, religious, ethnic or cultural differences are racist, scientifically false, legally invalid, morally condemnable and socially unjust,
>
> *Reaffirming* also that indigenous peoples, in the exercise of their rights, should be free from discrimination of any kind,
>
> *Concerned* that indigenous peoples have suffered from historic injustices as a result of, inter alia, their colonization and dispossession of their lands, territories and resources, thus preventing them from exercising, in particular, their right to development in accordance with their own needs and interests,
>
> *Recognizing* the urgent need to respect and promote the inherent rights of indigenous peoples which derive from their political, economic and social structures and from their cultures, spiritual traditions, histories and philosophies, especially their rights to their lands, territories and resources ... (United Nations 2007)

In considering Peter's comments and your own thoughts, you are now asked to record your understandings about Australia's first peoples and how you reached these in Child Development Reflection 8.1.

CHILD DEVELOPMENT REFLECTION 8.1: WERE YOU SUBJECTED TO RACIST TEACHING PRACTICES?

As part of Peter's approach to working with non-Indigenous pre-service teachers, he invites the students to reflect upon how they were taught about Aboriginal and Torres Strait Islander people in Australia. Write down three points that you recall from:

(continued)

- early childhood
- primary school
- secondary school.

What do you notice? Reflect upon what you have written in relation to what Peter says about this.

Peter considers the racist teaching practices of the past (which are still part of uninformed practice), the international best practice models we should be drawing upon and the colonising narrative still prevalent in society. He reflects further on how to feel culturally safe.

With regard to racist teaching practices, he says:

> The students unpack their learning at school. How do you know what you know around the Indigenous space? We map this. The usual suspects are there: 'We done dance'; 'We coloured in kangaroos and cut up boomerangs'; 'We learned at Aboriginal song'.
>
> Then we map the learning areas – it is always in visual art, dance, always history, but it is only a lesson. We unpack that, and discuss what they were taught.

On an international best practice model:

> What is key is to work at an international human rights level, because then we have best practice in the classroom. If your curriculum and pedagogy are linked to the international best practice models – such as Aboriginal and Torres Strait Islander people are consulted around the educational outcomes of their children, are consulted in terms of curriculum and development, are consulted and their voices are coming through – then you are teaching to an international best practice model.
>
> If you are teaching for depth of knowledge in classrooms, it shouldn't actually matter if you have an Aboriginal or Torres Strait Islander child in the class. If you are teaching all of your students, all of the children in the class using an international best practice model, a rights-based model, it doesn't matter if there is an Indigenous body there.

The colonial narrative

Peter discusses the colonial narrative:

> We have a colonial narrative of what an Aboriginal person is – that we all live in the Northern Territory, and that English is our second language. That narrative fits only 1 or 1.5 per cent of the population. Most Aboriginal people live in Sydney and Melbourne.

Feeling safe

Feelings of cultural safety are critical for a rights-based approach, as Peter notes:

> The way identity plays out is something deeply personal. It is racked with historical connotations. You do not know who is an Aboriginal or Torres Strait Islander person in your classroom until they self-identify. A child won't self-identify in a classroom

until the child feels that teacher is creating a safe environment, and talking about them in a positive way, and not in a stereotypical way. If a teacher is teaching well, then it does not matter if there is an Indigenous child in the class or not. Great if there is. If you are honouring their cultural perspectives, them as a person, and them as a learner, then they will feel safe to self-identify.

Peter's comments have also been reflected by others. For example, award-winning journalist and ABC Indigenous Affairs Editor Stan Grant writes:

I am afraid too. And that comes from the same place. I have known this fear all my life. When I was a young it used to make me feel sick, physically ill in the pit of my stomach. It was a fear of what could touch us – the sense of powerlessness, of being at the mercy of the intrusion of the police or the welfare officers who enforce laws that enshrined our exclusion and condemned us to poverty. It was a heavy hand that made people tremble. I see it still in my father. I see it as he tenses up just at the sight of a police car. He has done something wrong. But when he is pulled over for something as routine as a random breath test his heart beats faster and he fumbles his keys. We fear the state and we have every reason to. The state was designed to scare us. (Grant, 2016: 1–2)

CHILD DEVELOPMENT REFLECTION 8.2: A RIGHTS-BASED APPROACH

Peter introduces a rights-based approach and international best-practice model of teaching that are relevant for all children. He speaks to feeling safe, recognising and contesting the colonial narrative, being informed about the Aboriginal and Torres Strait Islander history of Australia, and recognising that child development theories have been imposed upon us through the academy of the university.

How might you be informed about each of these? Document the sources you would access:

1 feeling safe
2 recognising and contesting the colonial narrative
3 being informed about the Aboriginal and Torres Strait Islander history of Australia.

Knowing our history

Working with credible sources

As an early childhood educator or primary teacher, you may be wondering how to judge what might be a credible source for determining ways to contest the colonial narrative, to be informed about Australia's Aboriginal and Torres Strait Islander history and the best ways to feel safe. One way to do this is to follow the guidance offered by the Secretariat of the National Aboriginal and Islander Child Care (SNAICC) for planning for ways of knowing, being and doing that are supported by Aboriginal and Torres Strait Islander communities.

SNAICC is a national non-government peak body that advocates on behalf of Aboriginal and Torres Strait Islander children and families. SNAICC (2012a) advises that protecting the rights of Aboriginal and Torres Strait Islander children should centre on the right to:

- identify without fear of judgement and without being questioned
- uphold their connection to country, to maintain the kinship ties and sense of social obligation
- have access to and receive education from the Elders in their community
- access and receive information that is presented in a culturally sensitive manner (SNAICC, 2012a).

SNAICC (2012a) reports that for the right to feel safe to be upheld in early childhood settings, the following practices should guide best international practice:

- All services should be consulted in relation to cultural identity through language, traditional images, posters and celebrations.
- Using Indigenous languages in services supports the development of positive relationships with families.
- Families and children feel safe when cultural events are respected and celebrated.

SNAICC (2012a: 3) also advises that creating a culturally safe space involves educators

> engaging in high-level critical self-reflection to analyse how their behaviours and methods of interaction in the service reflect their own cultural assumptions and values, and how this communicates to peoples from different cultures.

Racist assumptions about learners

Like SNAICC, Peter Anderson also examines the cultural assumptions held by teachers. He argues that in the education space there are still many old views about Indigenous learners, which he says promotes a racist view of the Aboriginal child:

> No Indigenous person learns differently; every child learns in a way that is uniquely tailored. That means know the child and how they learn. This is basic Teaching 101. You must have professional relationships with the children as people in your classes, their parents, and Koorie educators. As part of the rights-based agenda, as a non-Indigenous teacher, it is about actually learning that you are not an expert in this space. You are an expert in education – absolutely.
>
> Sometimes people forget – they know they have an enormous HECS debt, that they have a four-year degree in education, but then when it comes to Indigenous children, they forget how to teach.

They think there is some mystical dot painting or a poster that will show you how to teach an Aboriginal child. Aboriginal children do not learn differently. All children learn differently. It is fundamentally racist – I can't say this enough – if you are thinking that an Aboriginal child learns differently, then that is a racist assumption: you may as well go back to eugenics and phrenology – that is where that conversation is at in terms of education. It has no place in modern classrooms.

SNAICC (2012a) draws attention to the term 'cultural proficiency' as a way forward. Cultural proficiency is defined by SNAICC as follows:

Cultural proficiency requires more than becoming culturally aware or practising tolerance. It is the ability to identify and challenge one's own cultural assumptions, values and beliefs, and to make a commitment to communicating at the cultural interface. (SNAICCa, 2012a: 1)

Further, 'cultural proficiency is a state of deep knowing and understanding of a culture where one continuously aspires to cultural proficiency and culturally proficient practice' (SNAICC, 2012a: 1).

Interpersonal relationships

In order to achieve cultural proficiency and to practise a rights-based approach to education as advocated by Peter Anderson, it is important to build interpersonal relationships. Peter speaks of the importance of interpersonal relationships:

It is about interpersonal relationships between the teacher and the learner; the teacher and the parent. It really does take a village to educate a child. We are starting to see schools take on the approach of education as being beyond the school gate, and think about how to create an understanding of the child as a whole. We see the expanding and contracting of the school as a whole, where many different groups and peoples are engaging – spaces where Indigenous people can engage.

There are resources to support you in working out how to build interpersonal relationships, how to rethink some of the basic assumptions about Aboriginal and Torres Strait Islander people and the children you will be teaching, and how to push against the colonial narrative mentioned by Peter. For example, some key points about different sources for building cultural competence are introduced by SNAICC (2012a):

1 Cultural competence means that an educator and the whole service are culturally aware and practising tolerance in ways that identify and challenge self and staff beliefs, assumptions, and values.
2 A commitment needs to be made to being at the cultural interface to promote tolerance and high cultural esteem.
3 It is important to analyse centre practices for barriers that prevent families from full participation, such as transport, perceived inappropriate cultural practices, fear of cultural discrimination, a sense of shame, a lack of Indigenous and Torres Strait Island educators in the centre and the consequences of stolen generation where there is a possible fear of children being removed from families.

....

Cultural competence – what does this mean for Aboriginal and Torres Strait Islander Australians?

....

SNAICC (2012a) states that respect is based on relationships. The early child-hood settings know the history of the children and families, intergenerationally and as a community, so that the impact of dispossession, family separation and the various forms of institutionalisation of families are understood and acknow-ledged. Relationship-building, based on real understandings of Australia's history, is important – but how can we systematically and credibly build these relationships?

You can build this through engaging in the process of developing a Reconcili-ation Action Plan (RAP). A RAP is key resource for documenting how you might work with Aboriginal and Torres Strait Islander families. This resource can support you with moving beyond the colonising theories from the Northern Hemisphere, as discussed by Peter, and begins to position you, the children you teach, and the communities in which you are teaching in new ways. Through the RAP, it is possible to learn other ways of conceptualising children's development, providing localised evidence for critiquing child development theories in relation to Australian children, families and communities. For example, the Narragunnawali RAPs (Reconciliation Action Plans) provide an education-based model for action using Reconciliation Australia's (2017) existing reconciliation framework (Relationships, Respect and Opportunities).

CHILD DEVELOPMENT REFLECTION 8.3: DEVELOP YOUR OWN RECONCILIATION ACTION PLAN

....

Reconciliation Action Plan

....

Download the RAP guidelines and the framework from Reconciliation Australia's RAP Hub (Reconciliation Australia's, 2017) and consider what your response might be to the following:

1 relationships in the classroom/early childhood setting, with community and around the school
2 respect in the classroom/early childhood setting, with community and around the school/centre
3 opportunities in the classroom/early childhood setting, with community and around the school/centre.

A RAP positions you as an educator to:

- establish a working group
- complete the reflection survey

- add actions to the RAP
- continue to revisit the plan and ensure actions are being implemented.

The RAP is one way to build relationships and to support the healing process in a genuine way, 'but it is up to you to do the hard work in implementing positive change' (Department of Education and Training, 2017). This means learning about how Aboriginal and Torres Strait Islander peoples have been positioned in the past, but also how this affects their present engagement with people in their community and sense of well-being.

Doing the right thing?

SNAICC (2012b: 1) has found that

> it has been observed that there may be some fear among those who work with Aboriginal and Torres Strait Islander children of 'doing the wrong thing' or uncertainty about 'where to start' when attempting cultural work with Aboriginal and Torres Strait Islander children.

As also suggested by Peter, non-Indigenous teachers can learn from their community by engaging and consulting with those groups who know the children best – the families. All children benefit when teachers consult and engage with all families.

SNAICC (2012b) gives a way forward for non-Indigenous teachers, suggesting that cultural knowledge is developed when teachers become aware of, and support children to engage with, their family history; where they come from (Aboriginal and Torres Strait Islander history); their personal identity – who they are, and their family, extended family and community as central to their sense of belonging; the places to which they belong – land and water; their participation and cultural expression; and their cultural values, beliefs and practices. Together, these elements form a child's cultural connectedness.

CHILD DEVELOPMENT REFLECTION 8.4: YOUR RESOURCE LIST

SNAICC (2012b) suggests that non-Indigenous teachers set up a resource guide, gathering contact details for their local community. It recommends the following:

- land councils
- national events
- state reconciliation council
- state community events
- Elders
- Aboriginal and Torres Strait Islander community-controlled organisations

(continued)

- local community events
- library
- art galleries.

What other groups do you feel you could consult and engage with, as you come to know the children and families in the community in which you are teaching?

In this section of the chapter, you have considered child development in relation to what it means for Australian children, families and teachers where a rights-based approach to education was considered. What you learnt was that the dominant theories that inform children's development in Australia have been developed in countries other than Australia.

A rights-based approach is relevant for all Australian children. We now look at a practice example of a rights-based approach in action to illustrate this key point raised by Peter Anderson.

A rights-based approach in action

Anderson has argued that a rights-based education is an expansive way of thinking and acting that must acknowledge the many different dimensions of Indigenous Australians. According to the Australian Museum (2017) the content should include:

- history
- social justice
- flags
- spirituality
- cultural heritage
- family
- the land.

A brief overview of these dimensions is provided in Table 8.1. Please consult additional sources to add to your understandings. The concepts are complex and require a great deal of researching and critical reflection. Identifying and learning about foundational knowledges that matter for Indigenous families in Australia is just the beginning of a rights-based approach. We must orient our focus directly to the community in which we are teaching.

CHILD DEVELOPMENT REFLECTION 8.5: EXPANDING OUR UNDERSTANDINGS

Select one of the case studies and consider what a rights-based approach might look like in practice. An example is shown in Table 8.1 below. Draw upon what you have learned from Peter Anderson's approach and apply this to:

- history
- social justice
- flags
- spirituality
- cultural heritage
- family
- the land.

Aboriginal and Torres Strait Islander peoples

Aboriginal and Torres Strait Islander people are culturally diverse. The content above will provide a foundation for undertaking this reflective task. But you could identify your own sources that are specific and relevant to your community. This is because you cannot consider Aboriginal and Torres Strait Islander people as one group. Aboriginal and Torres Strait Islander people live in different communities – urban, rural and remote. They use different languages (sometimes three or more) and sometimes have lost their heritage language and may be working to relearn it. It is important to focus on the cultural heritage of the local community in which you are teaching. Table 8.1 invites you to draw upon the generic research you undertook in Child Development Reflection 8.1 and to specifically consider the case studies to see how and where a rights-based approach could be considered. An example from the Resourceful Community case study is provided to get you started.

In drawing upon the UN Charter on the Rights of Indigenous Peoples (Table 8.2), take each of these ideas and investigate how you could affirm, reaffirm and recognise the history and cultural heritage of Australia's first peoples, engage with social justice and family, understand the significance of the Aboriginal flag and the concept of country, and examine spirituality.

Part of your journey through this chapter was learning about how important it is to take an international rights-based approach to education. But what research is being undertaken on child development in Australia to enable the current situation to change? We now turn our attention to this problem.

How do we research child development in Australia?

Historically, very little research has been done on child development in Australia. Baseline data for developing a theory of child development have not been gathered. Correspondingly, no child development theorist has written about Australian children's development. Australia does not have its own Vygotsky or a Hedgaard or a

Table 8.1 The content for a rights-based approach

	Resourceful Community	Culturally Diverse Preschool	Collective Inquiry School	Building Bridges Community
History	Learning about the past practices that violated Indigenous people's rights in the community. The local library has a historical society, but little is documented.			
Cultural heritage	Working with Elders to find out what matters for the Indigenous families living in the community – what is valued, significant and important and needing to be protected. The Elder in the community has entrusted an Indigenous early childhood expert with valued cultural knowledge that she shares with schools and preschools, supporting non-Indigenous teachers to learn and respect aspects of local cultural heritage.			
Flags	Noticing that the Aboriginal flag was not represented in the local community. Working with community to learn about the significance of the colours and symbols. Fundraising to erect a flag pole and flag in the school grounds.			
The land	Mapping the land and learning from Elders about country. Identifying local Aboriginal words for landmarks and using Aboriginal place names when referencing European place names. Hearing the stories. Listening. Waiting. Respecting.			
Family	Talking about family – what are the family interconnections in the community? Mapping family interconnections of all children. Noticing the complexity and expansiveness of family.			

(continued)

Table 8.1 The content for a rights-based approach *(continued)*

	Resourceful Community	Culturally Diverse Preschool	Collective Inquiry School	Building Bridges Community
Spirituality	Finding the deep spiritual connections – welcome to country; learning about the stories of the ancestors from that community; walking on country with an Elder or their representative.			
Social justice	Changing the colonial narrative in the school and preschool community and beyond. Creating spaces that are safe for Aboriginal and Torres Strait Islander families and their children. Learning and using local Aboriginal or Torres Strait Islander words. Making visible valued cultural heritage. Programs in school and preschool are connected and build upon knowledges and practices learned.

Knowing the history of the local community – teachers and children and their families – by interviewing the Elders and documenting as part of an oral history project, and displaying the documents in the school and preschool – and local library/hall and sporting clubs. | | | |

Rogoff. Although a range of important small-scale Australian studies can be found in the literature, it has only been since 2004 that the Australian Government has invested funds to support the study of a large sample of Australian children over time.

The Australian Institute of Family Studies (2017) website lists a range of studies that are related directly to the study of Australian children. For instance, there is a longitudinal study of Australian children that is following 10 000 children and their families. Children from a range of communities have been followed since 2004.

Further, a longitudinal study of Aboriginal and Torres Strait Islander children and their families has been undertaken since 2008. This study seeks to follow Aboriginal and Torres Strait Islander children in one group aged 6 to 18 months and in another group aged 3.5 to 5 years. It is known as Footprints in Time – the Longitudinal Study of Indigenous Children (LSIC) (Department of Social Services, 2017).

Table 8.2 UN Charter on the Rights of Indigenous Peoples: Enabling change

UN Charter (United Nations, 2007)	Example of practice you noticed in one of the case studies
Affirming that indigenous peoples are equal to all other peoples, while recognising the right of all peoples to be different, to consider themselves different, and to be respected as such.	
Affirming also that all peoples contribute to the diversity and richness of civilisations and cultures, which constitute the common heritage of humankind.	
Affirming further that all doctrines, policies and practices based on or advocating superiority of peoples or individuals on the basis of national origin, racial, religious, ethnic or cultural differences are racist, scientifically false, legally invalid, morally condemnable and socially unjust.	
Reaffirming also that Indigenous peoples, in the exercise of their rights, should be free from discrimination of any kind.	
Concerned that indigenous peoples have suffered from historic injustices as a result of, inter alia, their colonisation and dispossession of their lands, territories and resources, thus preventing them from exercising, in particular, their right to development in accordance with their own needs and interests.	
Recognising the urgent need to respect and promote the inherent rights of Indigenous peoples which derive from their political, economic and social structures and from their cultures, spiritual traditions, histories and philosophies, especially their rights to their lands, territories and resources . . .	

These important longitudinal studies provide insight into how young children are growing up in Australia. We learn whether families are reading books to children, and if they are, for how long. We gain understandings about how much screen time Australian children have. We also find out about the growth, and the health and well-being, of the children. There are a range of questions and corresponding data that are collected about the conditions for supporting the development of Australian children. Researchers go into family homes and interview parents and children, collect measurements of children's growth and, as the children grow up, find out from their teachers how they are going at school.

What knowledge of Australian children's development is being gathered and why do you think this is important? How can this research inform us about a theory of child development for Australian children? We now turn to the concept of relatedness as a first step in advancing an Australian theory of child development.

The concept of relatedness: Advancing an Australian theory of child development

In this section of the chapter, you will meet Professor Karen Martin through her writing and her biography.

Professor Karen Martin

Professor Karen Martin (also known as Martin-Mirraboopa) is a Noonuccal woman from North Stradbroke Island (South-East Queensland) with Bidjara ancestry (Central Queensland). Karen completed a Diploma of Teaching (Early Childhood) in 1988 and a Bachelor of Education in 1992 from Queensland University of Technology. Karen was awarded a PhD from James Cook University (JCU) for a dissertation titled 'Please Knock before You Enter: An Investigation of how Rainforest Aboriginal People Regulate Outsiders and the Implications for Western Research and Researchers'. These experiences contributed to Karen Martin's foundational research into the development of Aboriginal and Torres Strait Islander children.

Figure 8.3 A theory of relatedness as a foundation for children's development

She was awarded the JCU University Medal for this outstanding work in early childhood education and development. In 2007, she was also jointly awarded the Australian Association for Research in Education Doctoral Research in Education Award. Karen's teaching experience spans in excess of 15 years within Aboriginal community-controlled early childhood, primary and secondary schooling services, where she has taught in many areas, including child development. She also lectured in Indigenous studies at James Cook University, Townsville in the late 1990s and in teacher education at Queensland University of Technology. She was appointed an Associate Professor in Early Childhood at Southern Cross University, Lismore. Currently she is employed as a Professor in the School of Education and Professional Studies, Griffith University, where she designs and teaches child development courses.

Karen has been recognised for her national contributions to researching understandings of Aboriginal and Torres Strait Islander child development, as noted through being awarded the Barbara Creaser Memorial Award from Early Childhood Australia in 2005 and invitations to be a member of the Steering Committee of the Longitudinal Study of Indigenous Children through the Commonwealth Department of Families and Community Services and Indigenous Affairs and as a member of the Australian Institution of Aboriginal and Torres Strait Islander Studies (AIATSIS).

Ways of Knowing, Ways of Being and Ways of Doing

In the opening to the children's cultural needs document, SNAIC (2012b: 1) states that, 'Cultural knowledge needs to be in the control of Aboriginal and Torres Strait Islander people so that our children's cultural needs are met.' Martin (2008) has found that there are many contradictions in the knowledges, and in how knowledges are pitted against each other, that are unhelpful for conceptualising theories of learning and development. For instance, Martin says that Aboriginal knowledges are often considered dichotomous to 'Western scientific' knowledge. This perspective is presented as a dichotomy of universal validity versus validity embedded in context – Aboriginal knowledge being about generalisations and the short-term needs of people versus Western knowledge being abstracted from real life. However, these contradictions or binaries are viewed by Martin as unhelpful because they fail to recognise the similarities between knowledge forms. Consequently, Martin says that dichotomies have positioned 'Aboriginal knowledge as "non-science"' (Martin, 2008: 55).

Martin (2008) argues that Aboriginal knowledges need 'to be recognized as a valid body of knowledge [that] cannot be treated as an "add on" to Western scientific knowledge' (Martin, 2008: 56). Through extensive research and critique, Martin (2014) has developed both a theory of development and a methodology of research that is inclusive of Indigenous knowledges. She argues (2014: 294) that:

> Aboriginal knowledge is a way of life derived from an ontology that has sustained Aboriginal peoples for eons. Our Ways of Knowing (Martin, 2008) are more than information or facts and are taught and leaning in certain context, in certain ways. They are purposeful only to the extend to which they can be used.

Martin (2014: 294) says that knowledges are embedded in worldviews and are not artefacts, such as 'dance, technology and particularly visual art'. Knowledges and Ways of Knowing (Martin, 2008) are collectively understood, even though one individual may not have all the access of all the systems of knowledge. According to Martin (2014: 294):

> Our Ways of Knowing are consolidated through people exercising their connections to country. Every time we fish, gather, camp, talk about or walk on country we engage Our Ways of Knowing which shape for us our identities and particularly relationships to country, people and other Entities … Without 'knowing' we are unable to 'be' …

Martin (2008; 2014) conceptualises Ways of Knowing as part of her theory of child development and learning. She argues that 'the philosophical principles underpinning an Indigenous pedagogy propose that learning is a process of experiencing and a sharing of knowing from everything one does, from daily life events, and from those around oneself" (Martin & Rodriquez de France, 2007: 23). Hedegaard and Fleer (2013) also show how children's development takes place through everyday life. They show how everyday practices in the home, community and school create the conditions for children's development (see Chapter 6). But these everyday practices are invisible in research and in theories of child development. Martin and Rodriquez de France (2007) argue that in the context of the communities in which they research, and from the standpoint of Indigenous pedagogies and practices, everyday life events as the source of children's development challenge the dominant discourse and proposed models of the development of children, including those institutions charged with the responsibility for educating and developing Australian children. But this conceptualisation of children's development demands a new way of thinking about the knowledge of child development, particularly for Aboriginal and Torres Strait Islander communities. Martin (2008) argues that it is assumed that there is a 'lack of an overall conceptual framework within Aboriginal knowledges' and this leads to 'debates about substantive, methodological and epistemological, and contextual differences … subject content and characteristics between Aboriginal knowledge and western science knowledge' that have been unhelpful in the past (Martin, 2008: 55). Martin puts this ignorance to rest, because her theorising of Ways of Knowing as discussed here is a key dimension of a theory of child development that captures Aboriginal and Torres Strait Islander knowledges and practices, yet is expansive enough to capture the everyday practices of children, families and communities more broadly.

With regard to the play practices of children, Martin (2016a: 206) discusses how sociocultural perspectives and theories of child development 'instil the need to give as much attention to the *contexts* of the child and their family as is given to the play of an individual child or group of children'. She also notes (Martin, 2016a: 207) that:

> In developmental theories and perspectives, the individual child is the main and often sole focus. Play is often regarded as an outcome of their growth and learning and not as core to development. There is a lack of focus given to the role of the child's family and realities of their life.

Importantly, Martin (2016a: 207) argues that:

> In socio-cultural theories and perspectives, play is contextualized. Attention is given to the social *and* cultural aspects of the child *and* their family *and* the contexts in which they live. Therefore, socio-cultural theories and perspectives enable us to gain knowledge of play through the knowledge we have of the *contexts* and the conditions where they occur.

Generating knowledge: Foundational methods for Indigenous and Indigenist knowledge generation

> The essence of political integrity is power, Aboriginal agency and Aboriginal culturally safe and culturally respectful research that is achievable in privileging Aboriginal voices. (Martin, 2008: 59)

Martin (2008) has described Our Ways of Knowing, Ways of Being, and Ways of Doing as the three *knowledge bands* that collectively speak to a theory of child development for Australian children. But how are these knowledges, ways of being and ways of doing captured and theorised? Martin (Martin-Mirraboopa, 2003) has theorised an Indigenous research framework for studying the people of Far North Queensland, which adds to our understandings of researching child development discussed in Chapter 3.

Martin (Martin-Mirraboopa, 2003) identifies four key principles for undertaking research for knowledge generation that draw upon the strength of the researcher's Aboriginal heritage in ways that push against being positioned to resist or oppose Western research paradigms. Martin describes being a member of the Quanda-mooka Land Council, where Western research practices compromised her authority. Evidence was being sought for a native land claim:

> I watched with interest and listened to the ways in which our knowledges, cultures and beliefs were collected, analyzed, interpreted and presented for this claim. Placing some faith in the concept of Native Title, I wanted to contribute to the collection of evidence. Although I was interviewed, I felt that my knowledge and experiences were measured against pre-determined categories of culture to which it was deemed I could provide no new or convincing examples. Since I did not speak the language, I had not grown up on the island, nor had I at that time lived on the island, I was not considered a potential witness. (Martin-Mirraboopa, 2003: 204–5)

Martin's example is illustrative of how research can privilege some and discount others, but also how evidence is gathered and what constitutes valid evidence – valid for whom? Moreton-Robinson (2000: xxi) says that, 'The British invasion and subsequent colonisation of Australia began the process whereby whiteness became institutionalized'. Martin's example also shows how the research process itself becomes institutionalised in particular ways, even though the researchers themselves may well be unaware of how they are contributing to the institutionalised whiteness, through how they discount or allow particular forms of 'evidence' to come together under the banner of knowledge creation through research. Consequently, new frameworks are needed in research.

The principles of knowledge creation suggested by Martin include:

- recognition of our worldviews, our knowledges and our realities as distinctive and vital to our existence and survival
- honouring our social mores as essential processes through which we live, learn and situate ourselves as Aboriginal people in our own lands and when in the lands of other Aboriginal people
- an emphasis on social, historical and political context, which shape our experiences, lives, positions and futures
- privileging the voices, experiences and lives of Aboriginal people and Aboriginal lands (Martin-Mirraboopa, 2003: 205).

As with all research methodologies and method, there are protocols that must be followed for observing cultural validity and cultural reliability of data generated through the study. The research protocol prepared by Martin (Martin-Mirraboopa, 2003) includes:

- a relational knowledge system that is supported by a rational ontology, which focuses the research lens on interrelatedness and interdependence with the Entities (the land itself, the animals, the plants, the waterways, the skies, the climate and the spiritual system of the Aboriginal peoples living on that country)
- establishing through Law what is known about the Entities (Ways of Knowing)
- understanding the relations among Entities (Ways of Being)
- maintenance of the relations amongst Entities (Ways of Doing).

When you follow this protocol, it means you are studying *relatedness*. For instance, in research we begin by considering interrelatedness and interdependence with the Entities – that is, we do not focus on the person, but rather on the person in relation to the land itself, the animals, the plants, the waterways, the skies, the climate and the spiritual system of the Aboriginal or Torres Strait Islander people living on that country, therefore generating understandings of country and Aboriginal and Torres Strait Islander peoples as interrelated and interdependent. This approach and worldview are important for how we might connect with the communities in which we teach. The concept of relatedness as theorised by Martin (2008) is considered a powerful concept for explaining the forms of connectedness that exist within Aboriginal and Torres Strait Islander communities.

Martin (Martin-Mirraboopa, 2003) has also included in knowledge generation the dimensions of the *Ancestral Core*, the *Spirits* and the *Filter*.

The *Ancestral Core* gives identity to the people through the stories that are told, through the law formed and expressed by the Creators and the Ancestors. For example, Aboriginal and Torres Strait Islander families and communities pass on their stories about country to each other and their children (the land itself, the animals, the plants, the waterways, the skies, the climate and the spiritual system of the peoples living on that country).

It is important to respect (and know about) the spiritual system when teaching on country. The Spirit is a key dimension of the worldview of the people. The Spirit 'filters the power of the Creators and the Ancestor to ensure their messages are received' (Martin-Mirraboopa (2003: 66). The spiritual system is passed on through storying.

The *Filter* sustains the Entities (the land itself, the animals, the plants, the waterways, the skies, the climate and the spiritual system of the Aboriginal peoples living on that country), but also acts as a protector of the relations between all the Entities. Together, these dimensions of *Ancestral Core*, the *Spirits* and the *Filter* form the relatedness that is valued by many Indigenous peoples.

The generation of knowledge about researching is described by Martin (Martin-Mirraboopa, 2003: 206) as 'drawing upon the knowledges, beliefs, behaviours, experiences and realities from my own Quandamooka worldview'. This became 'the framework for Indigenist research', which generated the three bands of knowledges that underpin a powerful new theory of child development for which Martin has become known: Ways of Knowing, Ways of Being and Ways of Doing.

Ways of Knowing

Ways of Knowing are embedded in country through knowing who your people are, knowing where your country is located and, importantly, knowing your relationship to the Entities. As introduced above, the Entities include the land itself, the animals, the plants, the waterways, the skies, the climate and the spiritual system of the Aboriginal peoples living on that country. Martin (Martin-Mirraboopa, 2003) states that the ways of knowing are learned through the processes of:

- listening
- sensing
- viewing
- reviewing
- reading
- watching
- waiting
- observing
- exchanging
- sharing
- conceptualising
- assessing
- modelling
- engaging
- applying.

These processes contract and expand in relation to the political, social, historical and spaces in which they are enacted. However, as Martin argues (Martin-Mirraboopa, 2003: 209):

> It is more than just information or facts, and is taught and learned in certain contexts, in certain ways at certain times. It is therefore purposeful, only to the extent to which it is used. If it is not used, then it is not necessary.

Consequently, learning is purposeful and embedded in a system of relationships. The stories of relatedness are both collective and individual stories for a child. However, when taken together they map the person's identity. This means that our Ways of Knowing are foundational, and without this knowing, 'we are unable to "be", hence our Ways of Knowing inform our Ways of Being' (Martin-Mirraboopa, 2003: 209).

Ways of Being

Ways of Being signal that a person or a child is part of the world, but also that the world is part of the person or child. This means that a child born on country exists within a network of relations between the Entities of the land itself, the animals, the plants, the waterways, the skies, the climate and the spiritual system of the Aboriginal peoples living on that country. The contexts of these Entities matter because a child's relationship with the Entities is reciprocal. Rights are earned and bestowed during the processes of everyday life, where the rites to country, self and others are continually enacted. This collectively constitutes Our Ways of Being.

Our Ways of Being are always in motion, because there are transitions in life, such as movement from one life state to another. New situations create new conditions and new relations, and provide access to the need for new understandings of the Entities, where new roles are assigned to a child or adult. In each life-course change or new dynamic situation, Ways of Knowing are drawn upon to support knowing about how to be in these new situation – being respectful, being responsible and being accountable (Martin, 2008). This means not being above the Entities, but being a part of the Entities of the world. Martin (Martin-Mirraboopa, 2003: 210) suggests that children and adults draw upon what they know and have been taught 'from their Elders and family members as proper forms of conduct. Through this, our Ways of Being shape our Ways of Doing'.

Ways of Doing

Ways of Doing capture both Ways of Being and Ways of Knowing. Evidence of Ways of Doing can be seen through 'languages, art, imagery, technology, traditions and ceremonies, land management practices, social organization and social control' (Martin-Mirraboopa, 2003: 210). Ways of Doing are seen through individual and group identities, and the respective roles assigned where ways of conducting one self are observed. Ways of Doing are achieved through maintaining self-identity and being autonomous, but at the same time experiencing and living the relatedness and obligations to the Entities. Martin (2008: 79) explains this dialectic of autonomy and obligation through an example of being among the story of the willi-wagtail:

> The willi-wagtail [is] a small black and white bird that communicates by chittering and using its small body to tell its Stories. For us, the willi-wagtail is a messenger. When the willi-wagtail is excited and chitters fast, spreads its tail feathers and swings its tail from side to side, the message is more urgent. To 'interpret' its messages, the process is to come alongside, to immerse oneself in relatedness to the willi-wagtail and separate from one's embodied thoughts, words and language. Because the willi-wagtail assumes you can speak its language, it will repeat the message but will also grow impatient with each repetition until some acknowledgement or reply is given. Yet, it is just a message, it is never a full Story with all the details of who, what, where and when. Thus, by pausing and immersing oneself in relatedness, other messages come forth to confirm, or clarify the message from the willi-wagtail … In coming among, you learn more about this process of Ways of Doing by applying it in the range of contexts in which you live. It is highly contextual and involves engaging consciously and subconsciously in relatedness through processes of observing, discerning, filtering, applying reflecting, sharing and confirming.

Central to Martin's theory of Ways of Knowing, Ways of Being and Ways of Doing is the concept of relatedness. To draw upon Martin's theory as a theory of child development in early childhood and primary education means not just understanding the history of Indigenous peoples, not just colonisation (Martin, 2012, 2014, 2016b), but to also create the safe conditions for children through genuine consultation with families and communities. Martin's theory of child development in the context of Peter Anderson's rights-based approach to education offers insights into a new way of thinking about teaching and learning in Australia.

CHILD DEVELOPMENT REFLECTION 8.6: BUILDING RELATEDNESS AND TALKING UP STRENGTHS

What might be the activities you could organise so that you position Indigenous children in ways that highlight their strengths? Undertake the following activity with a group of children:

1 Invite children to draw a picture of their family, doing everyday things together that they enjoy.
2 What are the strengths shown in the children's drawings?
3 When you look at all of the children's drawings, what images of family and community are shown?
4 Use the concept of relatedness for your analysis. How is relatedness shown in the children's drawings?
5 Consider what message each drawing gives.
6 What might be the captions you could put with some of the children's drawings?

Building relatedness and talking up strengths

In this section of the chapter, you considered child development in relation to what it means for Australian children, families and teachers using the concept of relatedness. You learned how Ways of Knowing, Ways of Being and Ways of Doing can inform an Australian approach to conceptualising child development.

In the next section, we look closer at Martin's theory by drawing on her model of child development to better understand the case studies presented in this book.

The practices of Ways of Knowing, Ways of Being and Ways of Doing

The central child development idea discussed by Martin is the concept of relatedness. A practice-based example of this concept in action is presented through the four case studies in this book. In addition, a number of reflection questions are posed to help you to better understand the complexity of Martin's theory of child development.

Relatedness

Martin's (2016b) concept of relatedness helps us to think about how non-Indigenous educators might enter into a community. In the Building Bridges Community, people don't immediately ask the name of the newcomer, but rather ask about the newcomer's relationships, such as who their family are and where country is. Entering into someone's community and being a part of a community is about relatedness, which is a key concept in Martin's theory of child development.

CHILD DEVELOPMENT REFLECTION 8.7: ENTERING INTO A COMMUNITY/COUNTRY

If you are not a local to the community where you will be teaching, then telling stories of who you are, your country and the relationships you have in your community will open the space for a dialogue with the families and others you meet. They can then try to find connections with you, as they talk about country and their relationships in the community.

What is your story? Write down something about your family and your country/community that could be the basis of the story you share when you go into another community.

Stories of relatedness are both collective and individual stories for a child. Denise, an early childhood educator, discusses with Martin (2016b) the significance of a person being connected to country and what that means, even for educators:

> We are interested in you as a person – where you are from, your community, your family and your connection to this country … build up a relationship by getting to know you [teacher] first, so that we can establish trust and begin to relate. (Denise) (Martin, 2016b: 95)

It is through building trusting relationships that children and families together engage with you as their teacher. You may not be from that community or country, but you have your own story about your family and context. It is this story that others want to know about, so that they can create a space for you in their web of relationships. There are many different communities within Australia that we enter into as teachers, and the communities have their own Ways of Knowing, Being and Doing. We can only learn about these Ways of Knowing, Being and Doing when we are trusted enough to be gifted with these, as one part of establishing a sense of relatedness with community.

Entering into a community/country is always a two-way process. It is not linear, and it is not one way – that is, it is not just the community sharing with you, the teacher, their Ways of Knowing, Being and Doing. You begin with your story about your relationships, family and community/country (Martin-Mirraboopa, 2003).

Figure 8.4 What is your story?

Once you have told your story, then you watch, listen and wait. While you are watching, listening and waiting, the community will also be watching, listening and waiting – but in relation to you.

CHILD DEVELOPMENT REFLECTION 8.8: NEW WAYS OF THINKING ABOUT CHILD DEVELOPMENT WHEN USING THE CONCEPT OF RELATEDNESS

As you watch, listen and wait, you will be learning about many aspects of the families and community, and country. What are some ways in which you might document what you are learning? What might you document? Go back to Chapter 3 and consider the tools available there. Which of these might help you?

In drawing upon Martin's child development model (see Martin, 2007, 2008, 2014, 2016b), you would not just prepare observations of the children in your centre or classroom. You would prepare observations that were more akin to a sociogram (see Chapter 3) – that is, you would be documenting the relationships between the children and the families in the community. This is a different perspective on documenting children's development (Martin & Rodriquez de France, 2007).

The children in your centre will be part of a system of relationships, where members have obligations to each other. Learning about this system of relationships is key to finding your space in the community you have entered to be able to understand the children's development and your role in that development.

Relatedness is not a person-centric model, as we might be used to considering. Place is an important dimension of Martin's conception of child development. A child is not born as an individual, but rather is born into country, where a system of relations between the Entities exists. This point was also introduced at the beginning of this book, when you met the Building Bridges Community.

> Our children are part of nature, and therefore we are the symbols of nature too. We read ourselves, we read our families – in order to work out where we belong, who we belong to, and what our roles and obligations are to each other (Fleer & Williams-Kennedy, 2002: 23).

This worldview can also be found in the recently released curriculum in New Zealand, Te Whāriki (Ministry of Education New Zealand, 2017: 2), which states:

> In Māori tradition the child was a valued member of the Māori worlds before conception before birth, and before time. They began their journey in Rangiatea, homeland of the gods. Born into this world, they were nurtured like a precious seed to ensure their survival and inculcated with an understanding of their own importance.

CHILD DEVELOPMENT REFLECTION 8.9: INCLUDING THE CHILD'S RELATIONS WITH THE ENTITIES IN CHILD OBSERVATIONS

1   When you consider the following Entities, how do you document children's development so it includes these key dimensions of the child's relatedness?
2   Developing a sense of connectedness to country is about being a part of the Entities of:
    - the land itself
    - animals
    - plants
    - waterways
    - skies
    - the climate
    - the spiritual system of the peoples living on that country.

How does documenting the child's relatedness with these Entities help you to understand children's development in your centre or school? Record one key idea.

Martin (2016b: 98) says:

> For Aboriginal peoples, Places are valued because they are more than 'home'. They are Places of origin of Creators and also Ancestors. These Places are about one's DNA, they are essential to Identity and Connectedness.

In presenting the stories of Indigenous educators – their experiences and insights into what is meant by 'Places' – Martin (2016b) gives us insights into this dimension of relatedness. For instance, the spirit of country is felt, lived and embodied on country. The story of Vicki illustrates this:

> Until recently I felt that some of the qualities of the on-country experience could be replicated in early educational settings. After all, children can imitate the skills and action involved in hunting or preparing a fire ... and be thoroughly involved in that play. However, the feeling or the wellbeing that is felt and experience in nature or on-country cannot be transported into an artificial setting. (Martin, 2016b: 90)

These are important stories, and it is highly recommended that you read the stories found in Martin (2016b) because they provide insights into how relatedness is told through story.

CHILD DEVELOPMENT REFLECTION 8.10: CREATING YOUR OWN TOOL TO REFLECT MARTIN'S MODEL OF CHILD DEVELOPMENT

Return to the content above and create a mind map of the key dimensions of Martin's child development model. Use this mind map to create a child development pro forma that reflects your interpretations of Martin's model of child development.

As you create your tool, reflect on the central concepts in Martin's model, and consider how the tool you create can also be used for observing and planning in your community/centre/school.

Mapping Australia – Aboriginal and Torres Strait Islander perspectives

When we examine the AIATSIS map of Indigenous Australia (AIATSIS, 2017), it is possible to see a breadth of routes travelled across country, and a diversity of cultural communities that are far greater in number than the simple seven states and territories that are currently shown on maps of Australia. But we can also learn why so many Aboriginal and Torres Strait Islander Australians originally spoke a range of languages – so that they could interact with neighbouring communities. In Central Australia – Alice Springs – it is not uncommon for families today to speak a number of Aboriginal languages. The map shows the complex interplay of cultural diversity and invites us to reflect upon this important dimension of Australian history and geography that is not always known or acknowledged. However, it is not just geography and traditional history, but also recent history since colonisation, as discussed previously in relation to a rights-based approach.

A model of Ways of Knowing, Ways of Being and Ways of Doing

The concept of relatedness is captured in Table 8.3. It is a synthesis of Martin's child development model, which foregrounds Ways of Knowing, Ways of Being and Ways of Doing. It is presented here as a tool for you to use with the case studies discussed in this book, so that you can come to better understand the complexity of Martin's model of child development.

Table 8.3 Martin's model of child development: Capturing the development of relatedness

Summary of theory	Concepts	
Child development is about a relationships-centred worldview	The child development concept of relatedness captures: 1 connectedness to people 2 connectedness to country	
Theory	**Concepts**	**Educator pedagogy:** As an educator, how can you support the children's development that is aligned with the concept of relatedness?
Ways of Knowing The child is always becoming embedded in a system of relationships.	The development of connectedness to people	Learning the ways of knowing through: • purposeful listening • purposeful sensing • purposeful viewing • purposeful reviewing • purposeful reading

(continued)

Table 8.3 Martin's model of child development Capturing the development of relatedness (*continued*)

Theory	Concepts	Educator pedagogy: As an educator, how can you support the children's development that is aligned with the concept of relatedness?
		<ul><li>purposeful watching</li><li>purposeful waiting</li><li>purposeful observing</li><li>purposeful exchanging</li><li>purposeful sharing</li><li>purposeful conceptualising</li><li>purposeful assessing</li><li>purposeful modelling</li><li>purposeful engaging</li><li>purposeful applying.</li></ul>
Ways of Being A child is born on country, and becomes part of a network of relations. The child is developing as part of a reciprocal relationship between the self and the Entities.	Developing a sense of connectedness to country is about being a part of the Entities of: <ul><li>the land itself</li><li>animals</li><li>plants</li><li>waterways</li><li>skies</li><li>the climate</li><li>the spiritual system of the peoples living on that country.</li></ul>	Ways of Knowing are drawn upon by the child to support him or her to know how to be in new situations.
Ways of Doing Ways of Doing is captured through both Ways of Being and Ways of Knowing. The child develops an individual identity through developing a group identity.	Dialectics is about a dramatic tension between two apposing forces. The dialectic between autonomy and obligation is what creates the conditions for a child's development.	There is a tension between being autonomous and meeting community obligations. This tension is an active force in the development of self-regulation because children must observe the assigned role given, and conduct themselves in the way that is expected.

This is just a first step. You will have to find ways of engaging with Martin's model as is relevant for the communities in which you will be teaching or are currently teaching. It is an interpretation only, and extends upon the work you did in Child Development Reflection 8.10.

Figure 8.5 Understanding family – families live differently and have different values

BUILDING BRIDGES COMMUNITY CASE STUDY

PART 3: USING MARTIN'S MODEL OF CHILD DEVELOPMENT TO UNDERSTAND THE BUILDING BRIDGES COMMUNITY

> Education doesn't start when they get to school; they learn those signs; they use hand signals as they're talking; they read your body; and they read the land. (Laura) (Fleer & Williams-Kennedy, 2002: 40)

In considering Laura's comments, think about what learning the children in your centre might already have been exposed to, what is already well established, and what is yet to be understood but has been experienced as part of everyday life in that community.

Use the pro forma in Table 8.4 to analyse the Building Bridges Community. First, consider the main concepts and determine what examples of those concepts might be seen in practice in the Building Bridges Community. Then consider what role an

Table 8.4 Using Martin's model of child development for understanding the Building Bridges Community

	Concepts (List examples of these concepts in practice in the community)	**Educator pedagogy** (Give an example)
Ways of Knowing	The development of connectedness to people	
Ways of Being	Developing a sense of connectedness to country through the Entities	
Ways of Doing	What are the dramatic tensions that act as a force for development?	

educator might or does take in this example in supporting children's development. What are the conditions created by the community? What are the conditions created by the educators?

From the case study, we know that the educators and the project itself sought to identify worldviews, knowledges and Ways of Being. The key questions used by the educators to facilitate this were:

- What can everyone see?
- What can only the family see?
- What can we no longer see because it is so much a part of our lives?

When families video-record cultural practices that they value, then educators need to find the time to ask about these practices in ways that allow families to reflect upon these three key questions. A key learning from the Building Bridges Community was that the third question was the hardest to make explicit to people who had not grown up in the community. When practices are embedded in the everyday, it can be hard to see them, name them and talk about them.

Figure 8.6 Everyday practices – what can only the family see?

One of the tensions that presents itself in the Building Bridges Community case study relates to:

- view 1: children observing, listening and waiting
- view 2: asking questions, and knowing the questions to ask.

For instance, Vicky (mum) says that Gregory (child) asks a million questions. She video-recorded Gregory with his uncle, fixing up a car. Gregory asked questions about all the different parts of the car, which the uncle patiently named. He also asked questions about the relationship between the different parts of the engine, and how these parts work together. Vicky says that at school, when she was growing up, she didn't ask questions. Importantly, she said, she didn't know what questions to ask. So, for her, the tension between watching and listening, and asking questions, creates a developmental force for her son Gregory. He is learning both ways.

What were the stories told that showed a recognition of the different worldviews in the Building Bridges Community? We also learn that in the Building Bridges Community, many of the social mores that are essential for living and learning about country were evident. Can we find these in the Resourceful Community? We now turn our attention to this case study.

RESOURCEFUL COMMUNITY CASE STUDY

PART 6: USING MARTIN'S MODEL OF CHILD DEVELOPMENT TO UNDERSTAND THE RESOURCEFUL COMMUNITY

Returning to the families in the Resourceful Community, it is possible to see what is valued in the community – saving and creatively using the limited resources available – is also evident in the family home. This value of being resourceful shapes the lives of the families. We see that it is a way of knowing how to save resources, but it is also a way of being in the family home and community. Turning off lights, growing vegetables, walking everywhere, and looking after and recycling everything possible all help the families that live in their community.

How might this relate to a connectedness to the land? How does this worldview of living in a resourceful community relate to the Entities of the land itself, the animals, the plants, the waterways, the skies, the climate and the spiritual system of the peoples living on that country? Could this be something that could be foregrounded by the educator?

Consider these questions as you return to what has been written about the families, and document in Table 8.5 what you learn through your own analysis.

Table 8.5 Using Martin's model of child development for understanding the Resourceful Community

	Concepts (List examples of these concepts in practice in the community)	**Educator pedagogy** (Give an example)
Ways of Knowing	The development of connectedness to people	
Ways of Being	Developing a sense of connectedness to country through the Entities	
Ways of Doing	What are the dramatic tension that act as a force for development?	

COLLECTIVE INQUIRY SCHOOL CASE STUDY

PART 4: USING MARTIN'S MODEL OF CHILD DEVELOPMENT TO UNDERSTAND THE COLLECTIVE INQUIRY SCHOOL

The Collective Inquiry School sought to create the developmental conditions for children's own investigations, where their own autonomy and relatedness to each other were drawn upon to solve problems and to create group projects for deep learning. The school prides itself in using research protocols.

As you return to the different chapters where the Collective Inquiry School is discussed, analyse the research protocols used. What were the key systems of knowledge drawn upon? Were they individualistic or socially related? How did the children deepen their inquiries? What were the Ways of Knowing, Ways of Being and Ways of Doing that you noticed?

Table 8.6 Using Martin's model of child development for understanding the Collective Inquiry Community

	Concepts (List examples of these concepts in practice in the community)	**Educator pedagogy** (Give an example)
Ways of Knowing	The development of connectedness to people	
Ways of Being	Developing a sense of connectedness to country through the Entities	
Ways of Doing	What are the dramatic tension that act as a force for development?	

You may have noticed an emphasis on the social, historical and political context that shaped the children and teachers' experiences and classroom lives, and the positioning of children as strong and interdependent learners. Children learned about their past, but also projected into the future. What was important to the children, families and teachers was privileging the voices of people in the community, while simultaneously privileging the voice of the child as a legitimate researcher. Do you feel that the experiences and lives of Aboriginal people and Aboriginal lands could also be foregrounded in this school? What might be the possibilities for listening, observing and waiting so that relatedness to country can also be understood, valued and respected?

CULTURALLY DIVERSE PRESCHOOL CASE STUDY

PART 4: USING MARTIN'S MODEL OF CHILD DEVELOPMENT TO UNDERSTAND THE CULTURALLY DIVERSE PRESCHOOL

Many communities in Australia are culturally diverse. Generations of children and families have colonised Indigenous lands, and together we now experience cultural difference as the norm. In contexts of cultural diversity, how could the child development model created by Martin be used to better understand this diversity? How might her model help educators to build upon children's development? Using Table 8.7, go back to the text in the relevant chapters and determine how diversity is discussed in the pre-school, and how the educators create the conditions for the development of all the children.

Table 8.7 Using Martin's model of child development for understanding the Culturally Diverse Community

	Concepts (List examples of these concepts in practice in the community)	**Educator pedagogy** (Give an example)
Ways of Knowing	The development of connectedness to people	
Ways of Being	Developing a sense of connectedness to country through the Entities	
Ways of Doing	What are the dramatic tension that act as a force for development?	

By using Martin's theory of child development to inform our work, we can engage in active resistance to the colonising influence of theories from the Northern Hemisphere, as discussed by Peter Anderson.

Australian research

Conclusion

This chapter sought to engage you in the process of better understanding Karen Martin's theory of child development and Peter Anderson's conception of a rights-based approach. By synthesising the key ideas, you considered what might be the key concepts inherent in Martin's theory of child development and Anderson's rights-based approach. You were also invited to create your own synthesised model. Through this, you worked with a theory of child development relevant to Indigenous children, and their families and communities.

You also explicitly examined the concept of relatedness as the essence of Martin's theory and Anderson's rights-based model as the key to transforming change and critiquing mainstream child development theories, then you applied a pro forma of child development to all the case studies in this book.

In the next chapter, you will examine those child development theories and ways of critiquing that have not yet been discussed in this book, but that are included in the EYLF. Together, these theories have been included in the EYLF to inform educators in Australia. Some remaining questions about child development for Australian children are also explored.

References

Australian Institute of Aboriginal and Torres Strait Islander Studies (AIATSIS) 2017, *Map of Indigenous Australia*. Available at: https://aiatsis.gov.au/explore/articles/aiatsis-map-indigenous-australia [Accessed 20 August 2017].

Australian Institute of Family Studies 2017, *Child and adolescent development*. Available at: https://aifs.gov.au/our-work/research-expertise/child-development [Accessed 20 July 2017].

Australian Museum 2017, 'Education'. Available at: https://australianmuseum.net.au/education-services [Accessed 21 August 2017].

Connell, R 2007, *Southern theory: The global dynamics of knowledge in social science*, Sydney: Allen & Unwin.

Department of Education and Training 2017, *Narragunnawali: Reconciliation in schools and early learning*. Available at: https://www.education.gov.au/narragunnawali-reconciliation-schools-and-early-learning [Accessed 20 July 2017].

Department of Social Services 2017, *Footprints in Time – the Longitudinal Study of Indigenous Children (LSIC)*, Canberra: Australian Government. Available at: https://www.dss.gov.au/about-the-department/publications-articles/research-publications/longitudinal-data-initiatives/footprints-in-time-the-longitudinal-study-of-indigenous-children-lsic [Accessed 20 July 2017].

Fleer, M & Williams-Kennedy, D 2002, *Building bridges: Researching literacy development for young Indigenous children*, Canberra: Australian Early Childhood Association.

Grant, S 2016, *Talking to my country*, Sydney: HarperCollins.

Hedegaard, M & Fleer, M 2013, *Play, learning and children's development: Everyday life in families and transition to school*, New York: Cambridge University Press.

Martin, K 2007, 'Ma(r)king tracks and reconceptualising Aboriginal early childhood education: An Aboriginal Australian perspective', *Childrenz Issues*. 11(1), 15–20.

——2008, *Please knock before you enter: Aboriginal regulation of outsiders and the implications for research and researchers*, Brisbane: PostPressed.

——2012, 'Aboriginal early childhood: Past, present, and future', in J Phillips & J Lampert (eds), *Introductory Indigenous studies in education: The importance of knowing*, Sydney: Pearson Education, pp. 27–40.

——2014, 'The more things change, the more they stay the same: creativity as the next colonial turn', in A Reid, EP Hart & M Peters (eds), *A companion to research in education*, Dordrecht: Springer.

——2016a, 'Play, playing along and playing it up: Understanding the play of Aboriginal children', in M Ebbeck & M Waniganayake (eds), *Play and learning in early childhood education: Learning in diverse contexts*, 2nd ed., Melbourne: Oxford University Press, pp. 201–16.

—— 2016b, *Voices and visions: Aboriginal early childhood education in Australia*, Jamberoo: Pademelon Press.

Martin, K & Rodriquez de France, C 2007, 'Australian early childhood education and care: The fourth discourse', *Canadian Journal of Native Education*, 31(1), 19–27.

Martin-Mirraboopa, K [incorrectly published as Martin, K & Mirraboopa, B] 2003, 'Ways of Knowing, Being and Doing: A theoretical framework and methods for Indigenous and Indigenist research', *Journal of Australian Studies*, 27(76), 203–14.

Ministry of Education New Zealand 2017, *Te Whāriki: He whāriki mātauranga mōngā mokopuna o Aotearoa: Early childhood curriculum*, Wellington: New Zealand Government.

Moreton-Robinson, A 2000, *Talkin' up to the white woman: Aboriginal women and feminism*, Brisbane: University of Queensland Press.

Reconciliation Australia 2017, *RAP Hub*. Available at: http://www.reconciliation.org.au/raphub [Accessed 20 August 2017].

Secretariat of the National Aboriginal and Islander Child Care (SNAICC) 2012a, *SNAICC consultation overview report: Cultural competence in early childhood education and care services*, Melbourne: SNAICC. Available at: http://www.snaicc.org.au/wp-content/uploads/2015/12/02865.pdf [Accessed 20 July 2017].

—— 2012b, *Aboriginal and Torres Strait Islander Children's Cultural Needs*, Melbourne: SNAICC. Available at: https://www.snaicc.org.au/wp-content/uploads/2015/12/02932.pdf [Accessed 20 July 2017].

United Nations 2007, *United Nations Declaration on the Rights of Indigenous Peoples*. Available at: https://www.humanrights.gov.au/publications/un-declaration-rights-indigenous-peoples-1 [Accessed 20 August 2017].

PART III

Critiquing theory: Thinking critically about child development

CHAPTER 9

How do theories position children, families and communities?

Introduction

In this chapter, we examine those theories not yet discussed in this book, but that have been identified by the curriculum writers in the Early Years Learning Framework (EYLF) as important for the Australian context. However, rather than accept these theories uncritically, you will enter into an analysis of child development theories in relation to what these theories allow and how they inform your work as an early childhood educator or primary teacher.

In Chapter 1, the main theories of child development that underpin EYLF were discussed. The theories were:

- developmental theories
- sociocultural theories
- socio-behaviourist theories
- critical theories
- post-structuralist theories.

In various chapters throughout this book, we also acknowledged that the Australian curriculum appeared to follow a developmental trajectory.

In this chapter, we will explicitly look at each of these theories through the eyes of Amanda, Thin, Lauren, Tahlie and Shuang. This means that you will be introduced to three new theories in this chapter: socio-behaviourist theories, critical theories and post-structuralist theories. However, because the latter two theories are not child development theories, they will be examined only briefly. Further, socio-behaviourist theories do not constitute a single traditional child development theory, so will also only be introduced briefly. However, because each of these theories is included in the EYLF, it is important that they are discussed. Through reading this chapter and by undertaking the tasks identified in each Child Development Reflection, you will:

- become familiar with all the theories that are detailed in the EYLF
- critique each of these theories
- learn how theories determine what you see and how you act
- note how theories position children, families and communities.

Critiquing child development theories

In this section, you will be invited to think about how theories position children, families and communities in relation to Australian children.

CHILD DEVELOPMENT REFLECTION 9.1: EXAMINING CHILD DEVELOPMENT THEORIES IN THE CURRICULUM

An overview of developmental and socio-cultural theories (also named as cultural-historical theory) related to the EYLF is shown in Table 9.1.

Developmental theories and sociocultural theories have already been discussed in Chapters 3 and 6. Some general critique was offered in each chapter.

Drawing on the content of those chapters, record the names of those theorists associated with the particular theory presented and determine how you think children, families and communities are positioned. In order to determine this positioning, consider the following questions:

1   How does the theory name progression in terms of child development?
2   What are the central concepts that explain the theory?
3   What is the role of the adult in supporting children's development?
4   Does the community have a role to play in the child's development?

Figure 9.1 Amanda, Thin, Lauren, Tahlie and Shuang wonder how they are positioned as teachers in the EYLF.

Complete Table 9.1. It will provide you with a useful summary to which you can return when you need a quick reference.

Table 9.1 Two theories of child development as presented in the EYLF

Theory	Key characteristics	Who are the theorists?	How are children, families and communities positioned – your critique
Developmental theories	'focus on describing and understanding the processes of change in children's learning and development over time' (DEEWR, 2009: 11).		
Sociocultural theories	'emphasise the central role that families and cultural groups play in children's learning and the importance of respectful relationships and provide insight into social and cultural contexts of learning and development' (DEEWR, 2009: 11).		

In the next section, you are invited to critique the child development theories that are the basis of a socio-behaviourist theory: social learning theory and behaviourist theories. These two theories will be discussed briefly in relation to a series of Child Development Reflections that you will complete. You will document your critique in Table 9.2.

Divergent theories: Socio-behaviourist theory

The EYLF mentions the term socio-behaviourist theories. This term appears to capture two very different theories. The first is Bandura's social learning theory and the second is Skinner's theory of behaviourism. We will examine both and then discuss how they fit together (or not), to form socio-behaviourist theory as presented in the EYLF. The Australian curriculum does not refer to these theories. Rather, it draws only on developmental theories.

Social learning theory

We begin with social learning theory and examine this theory of learning and development. An introduction to social learning theory suggests Bandura's social learning theory proposes that people learn from one another by the means of observation, imitation and modeling (Bandura, 1977, 1986).

The key question asked by Albert Bandura was, 'How does watching people influence our behaviour?' Bandura chose to study aggression. In 1960, the general view held by the American public was that watching aggression calmed people (Bandura, 1977).

As you can see, Bandura's social learning theory has been around for a long time. His theory is still discussed in many child development courses. For example, when we invited student teachers to consider Bandura's theory, Amanda, Thin, Lauren, Tahlie and Shuang noted the following:

- Bandura is a social cognitive psychologist who is well known through his social learning theory, observational learning and self-efficacy concept.
- Bandura proposed that the extent to which children learn through observation of others does not depend only on what there is to observe around them. The end result will also be affected by what the children are focusing on (attention); what children remember (retention); what children can physically do when in the process of copying what others are doing (reproduction); and what they are interested or motivated to copy (motivation).
- Bandura (1977) believed that humans were active information processors and that they thought about the relationship between their behaviour and its consequences.
- Bandura is well known for his study of Bobo dolls, wanting to test whether aggressive behaviour would be observed and imitated. The inflated Bobo doll was assaulted by an adult. This was filmed and shown to children (see the companion website for details of the study).
- Social learning theory explains human behaviour in terms of continuous reciprocal interaction between cognitive, behavioural and environmental influences.

Bandura's original observational studies

Amanda, Thin, Lauren, Tahlie and Shuang draw attention to two key concepts in their child development research: *observational learning* and *mediational processes*.

Observational learning
The educators note that:

- 'Bandura's social learning theory focuses on the imitation of behaviours by children, imitating caregivers and peers, thus learning much about society and how it operates' (McLeod, 2016).
- Behaviour can be learned from the environment provided through the process of observation (McLeod, 2016). Indirectly, children are imitating the actions of adults who are known as models. Children have their own rules with regard to selecting people to be observed.

Mediational processes
Observational learning cannot occur unless cognitive processes are at work. These mental factors mediate (i.e. intervene) in the learning process to determine whether a new response is acquired. Therefore, individuals do not automatically observe the behaviour of a model and imitate it. There is some thought prior to imitation and

this consideration is called mediational processes. This occurs between observing the behaviour (stimulus) and imitating it or not (response). Bandura proposed four mediational processes:

- attention
- retention
- reproduction
- motivation.

You can see evidence of these mediational processes in original observations and analyses made by Bandura. Bandura looked closely at what children paid attention to, and then used his theory of social learning to explain why children retain understandings and ways of behaving (retention), how they used what they had learned and applied it elsewhere (reproduction), and how children became motivated (he suggested they became more violent after viewing certain aggressive acts).

CHILD DEVELOPMENT REFLECTION 9.2: WHAT MIGHT BE MEANT BY SOCIAL LEARNING THEORY? – PART 1

What was learnt about children's development through the original studies undertaken by Bandura?

When the children saw the Bobo doll being beaten by the adult or the child, they too hit the Bobo doll when it was introduced to them. Did you come to the conclusion that children modelled their behaviours on what they saw others do? What does this mean for children when viewing:

- TV programs
- advertisements
- video games
- smoking in the community
- drinking in the community
- eating junk food (or healthy food)
- media reports of global conflict?

Amanda, Thin, Lauren, Tahlie and Shuang have found that there are some criticisms of social learning theory because of the focus on the environment as the chief influence on behaviour. It is limiting to describe behaviour solely in terms of either nature or nurture, and attempts to do this under-estimate the complexity of human behaviour. They suggest it is more likely that behaviour is due to an interaction between nature (biology) and nurture (environment). Do you agree with Amanda, Thin, Lauren, Tahlie and Shuang? Use the resources on the companion website to help you.

Toddlers acting out a scene from the movie *Frozen*

CHILD DEVELOPMENT REFLECTION 9.3: WHAT MIGHT BE MEANT BY SOCIAL LEARNING THEORY? – PART 2

1 What are the different observational learning contexts in preschools and schools?
2 Consider the different contexts of the theories developed. Which country? When they were developed? What kind of research was undertaken?
3 How does what you have learned relate (or not) to Australian children, families and communities?

CHILD DEVELOPMENT REFLECTION 9.4: UNDERSTANDING SOCIAL LEARNING THEORY

Interview a teacher on your next professional placement about their understanding of the term 'social learning theory'.

1 How does the educator define this term?
2 How does the educator draw upon this theory to inform their teaching?

Social learning theory can be thought of as a bridge between behaviourism and cognitive learning theories because it encompasses attention, memory and motivation, and makes some links with stimulus–response processes. As you examine behaviourism in the section below, try to identify some practical examples of the characteristics of that bridge.

Behaviourism/behaviourist theories

We now turn to the term 'behaviourism'. This is a well-known theory in which scholars such as Piaget and Vygotsky were well versed (see previous chapters). Much of the justifications of sociocultural theory and developmental theory have been written in relation to behaviourism – that is, Piaget and Vygotsky both explained their theory in contrast to behaviourism. In essence, they argued against this theory informing child development and learning because they said it only focused on evidence of visible external behaviours.

Who were the theorists who developed behaviourism?

Although there were a number of researchers who would be classified as behaviourists, the main theorist who is primarily drawn upon by educationalists is BF Skinner. In this part of the chapter, we focus on his research and his theory. A brief overview is provided.

What are the main concepts of behaviourism?

The main concepts developed by Skinner (1954, 1968, 1986) that are relevant to education relate to behaviour modification. He introduced the concepts of positive and negative reinforcement, positive punishment, scheduled reinforcement and operant conditioning.

Positive and negative reinforcement

To *positively reinforce* means to reward an action that is desired. For instance, the child who tries to ride a bicycle for the first time might not do it well, but makes an effort and has some success. The extrinsic reward could be for someone who matters to the child, like a parent or sibling, to cheer and celebrate the desired behaviour. We also see this when teachers give children stamps or stickers for good work. The idea is to reinforce the desired behaviours.

To *negatively reinforce* means to modify behaviour through introducing something that is unpleasant and needs to be stopped. For example, by introducing a loud and unpleasant noise (stimulus), the sound stops when a lever is pressed (response).

To *positively punish* means to introduce something unpleasant when the undesired behaviour occurs – for instance, if a child is disruptive in a classroom, and each time this occurs the child experiences something they find unpleasant. To *negatively punish* means to remove something, such as when a child who is disruptive in class losing the opportunity to play with something they like, such as a particular toy.

A contemporary and fun example can be found in an episode of *The Big Bang Theory*. Sheldon positively reinforces the behaviours of Penny to shape how he wishes her to behave in his apartment (discussed also as operant conditioning – see further below).

Negative reinforcement versus positive punishment

There are two systems of behaviour modification that involve using positive and negative reinforcement: *operant conditioning* and *classical conditioning*. Operant conditioning is related to a learned response or learned modification of behaviour based on an immediate reward or punishment. This means that operant conditioning can be used to systematically shape a person's behaviour over time.

We can also compare negative reinforcement with positive punishment. As discussed earlier, negative reinforcement is the removal of a positive stimulus. To take a toy away or to give time out can help to stop some kinds of (negative) behaviour.

Operant conditioning is often discussed in the context of discussing classical conditioning. However, classical conditioning was known before Skinner's time. Still, it is worthy of mention here as a background to behaviourism. Ivan Pavlov found that when he presented dogs with some kind of stimulus that was not directly related to their behaviour, such as using a light or producing a sound when giving the dogs a treat, this acted as a simple conditioning of behaviour over time – that is, the dogs would see the light or hear the sound and begin to salivate in anticipation of a treat. The links between the stimuli (light/treat) and the response (salivating) is seen as a form of classical conditioning. These types of stimulus–response studies can also be seen in the foundational research of Skinner.

The foundational studies of Skinner

Skinner undertook many experiments to develop his theory of reinforcement or behaviour modification. Through classical experiments in laboratories using animals, he developed his theory of behaviourism.

Scheduled reinforcement

One of the studies by Skinner focused on observing pigeons and positively rewarding them with food for responding correctly to particular text. By positively rewarding the pigeons, he was able to speculate that positive reinforcement was important for changing the pigeons' behaviour.

Examine the YouTube video on the companion website, in which Skinner shows how he developed the concept of scheduled reinforcement. Pigeons are positively rewarded with food for responding correctly to particular text. A schedule of reinforcements (food) is planned. This idea has been used in education, where a schedule of reinforcement is planned in relation to the modification of a child's behaviour.

....

Skinner's original experiments

....

From looking at the material on the companion website, we have noted that Skinner's reinforced behaviour of pigeons was applied in other fields. We learned how addictions or simply an interest in gambling (variable ratio schedule) can arise. This is a contemporary example of how Skinner's original theory has been helpful for informing interventions.

CHILD DEVELOPMENT REFLECTION 9.5: WHAT MIGHT BE MEANT BY BEHAVIOURIST THEORIES?

If possible, interview the same teacher on your next professional placement about their understanding of the term 'behaviourism'.

1 How does the educator define behaviourism?
2 How does the educator distinguish between the contrasting 'socio' and 'behaviourist' parts of the term socio-behaviourist theory?
3 How does what you have learned relate (or not) to Australian children, families and communities?

Putting the two together

In this section of the chapter, we bring together the theories introduced – social learning theory and behaviourism – and discuss these in the context of socio-behaviourist theory. You probably would have noticed in your reading of the EYLF that when introducing the theories of child development, no detailed explanation of socio-behaviourism was given.

CHILD DEVELOPMENT REFLECTION 9.6: SOCIO-BEHAVIOURIST THEORY

Return to Chapters 2 and 6, where the 'socio' dimension is detailed. Consider how 'socio' is theorised and how it may relate to 'socio-behaviourists'. What are the key points you extracted from reading those chapters?

One of the key points that 'socio' brings to mind is the social dimensions of a context or behaviour. By bringing together 'socio' with behaviourism to make up the theory of socio-behaviourism, we meet an interesting contradiction – something that is about 'everyday social relations and life' and something that is about 'modifying behaviours' through scheduled or operant conditioning. Nolan and Raban (2015: 10) also observe this contradiction and reflect on this strange grouping of theories:

> It may seem odd to group social and behavioural theories together as they are two highly divergent approaches. However, the significant differences on which they are based – their view of the child, their view of knowledge and their view of the role of adults – make them arguably more interesting when placed in juxtaposition than when separated.

Socio-behaviourist theory as a term is new in the EYLF. It would appear that the term 'socio-behaviourist' is generally unknown outside of the EYLF. However, the term does appear in resources designed to support the EYLF.

CHILD DEVELOPMENT REFLECTION 9.7: UNDERSTANDING SOCIO-BEHAVIOURIST THEORIES

Understanding socio-behaviourist theories

1   Undertake a search for socio-behaviourist theory. Document what you find – if anything.
2   Interview a teacher on your next professional placement about how they use the theory of socio-behaviourism to inform their work.

- How does the educator define this term?
- How does the educator draw upon this theory to inform their teaching?

3   Did you find that the teachers you interviewed also found the term 'socio-behaviourism' confusing or divergent in its intent, or not relevant to Australian children?
4   Extract some key quotes from your interviews and place them into Table 9.2.

It is interesting that students and academic staff also seek to make sense of the incongruence of the 'socio' with the 'behaviourism'. You will find some mention of this problem when you examine a range of child development sources in Australia – but usually not elsewhere.

When the term 'socio'/'social learning' and 'behaviourism' are brought together, it can be argued that the focus is on:

- the child's experience
- receiving feedback for promoting learning
- reinforcement and punishment of some kind as part of explaining how behaviours are changed or continued.

However, there might also be differences, such as:

- The theories have a different conception of learning.
- Environmental, personal and social factors are considered to be fundamentally different.
- The ways in which reinforcement and punishment is considered in the theory are very different.

CHILD DEVELOPMENT REFLECTION 9.8: YOUR CONCLUSIONS

Through examining each of these terms – 'socio' and 'behaviourist' – and the associated theories – social learning theory and behaviourism – what conclusion can you draw about socio-behaviourist theories for Australian children?

The important thing to learn from this activity is that the term 'socio-behaviourist' brings together a cluster of child development theories.

Tools for critique: Critical theories and post-structuralist theories

The EYLF also introduces two other related theories that will be examined briefly in this section. They are critical theories and post-structuralist theories. You will critique both, aided by what you have learnt through the Child Development Reflections in this section of the chapter. Your critiques should be added to Table 9.2. Through this process, you will be able to compare all the theories that feature in the EYLF.

One key idea to consider as you read this section of the chapter is that critical theories and post-structuralist theories are not theories of child development.

Critical theory

Any overview of critical theory stresses the term 'critique'. This means a critique of society, of culture, of communications, of social class, of race, of the institution and so on. Only a brief overview is provided here.

CHILD DEVELOPMENT REFLECTION 9.9: WHAT MIGHT BE MEANT BY CRITICAL THEORIES AND POST-STRUCTURALIST THEORIES IN THE EYLF?

1　Examine the EYLF. Search this document electronically for the terms 'critical theory' and 'post-structuralist theories' and copy the text for analysis.
2　Who were the theorists who developed critical theories and post-structuralist theories?
3　Add what you learn to Table 9.2.

Critical theory began in Germany, in what is now famously known as the Frankfurt School. A group of scholars led by Max Horkheimer wanted to put into practice the philosophy of Marxism through critiquing Western science, as well as the research that informed this way of generating knowledge.

Understanding critical theory

Critical theory began with a critique of Marx's economy. Carl Marx noticed, among many things, that in many Western industrial societies the way the economy worked was through labour exchange, and this was important to study. He noted that for some industrial societies, it essentially enslaved the working class – sending children into mines and making them work long hours in cotton mills. His original works were foundational for many who were interested in social justice.

Critical theory seeks to critique the society and culture of a given economy, and where labour exchange is closely examined for inequality and equity. Although there are different views on the history and definition of critical theory, it has become an umbrella term for any theory that seeks to critique.

In education, critical theory asks key questions of:

- *domination:* who is in a position of power and control?
- *everyday practice:* understanding the relations between an individual situation and problems as embedded in everyday social contexts
- *gender:* who is being privileged
- *ruptures:* disrupting what is taken for granted
- *equity:* who wins and who loses
- *social class:* how societal structures are maintained.

CHILD DEVELOPMENT REFLECTION 9.10: SPECIAL NEEDS OR GIFTED AND TALENTED?

Dorinda Carter Andrews and the consciousness gap in education

In order to come to understand the central concepts in critical theory, you are invited to engage in a series of reflections where teachers and scholars have used critical theory to better understand their own experiences of being a teacher or a student. For example, Dorinda Carter Andrews gives a personal example of being labelled as in need of special education. Her Grade 1 teacher wanted to test her for special education performance, and Dorinda's mother insisted she be tested for gifted and talented performance.

> That teacher did not know what to do with my energy or my intellect. She had labelled me as a child in need of academic remediation, when in fact I needed academic challenge. I don't blame her solely for her behaviours, I think her teacher education program and her professional development as an in-service educator had not prepared her for these new experiences in the seventies, of teaching black youth. Her low level of critical awareness about issues of race, culture and power in teaching and learning, impeded her from providing me the resources I actually need. (Dr Dorinda Carter Andrews, 2014)

What are your thoughts on testing children who appear to be gifted and talented, or who just seem different?

CHILD DEVELOPMENT REFLECTION 9.11: UNDERSTANDING CRITICAL THEORY

If possible, interview a teacher on your next professional placement about their understanding of the term 'critical theory'.

1   How did the educator define this term?
2   How does the educator use critical theory for their work?
3   Did the educator mention:
    - domination
    - everyday practice
    - gender
    - ruptures
    - equity
    - social class?

Post-structuralist theories

In this section of the chapter, we examine post-structuralist theory. It is a very complex theory, and even a long look would not do justice to this theory. However, this theory is popular in early childhood education in Australia. As such, a little more text is devoted to this theory – even though it is not a child development theory.

It is argued in most books and articles that post-structuralism was named by a group of American academics to capture the theories that were popular in the 1960s and 1970s, and that were developed by French and continental philosophers and critical theorists. As a 'post' theory, post-structuralism can only be understood in the context of structuralism (in which the 'structure' of language and of 'texts' was examined and found to be inherently unstable and often contradictory). There are many theories of post-structuralism. All the theorists who come under the banner of post-structuralism have critiqued structuralism in some way.

Post-structuralists rejected the value-laden oppositional binaries that were foundational to structuralist thinking. For instance, 'high technology' is better than 'low technology', or jobs that involve the 'mind' (e.g. lawyer) are superior to those that primarily use the 'body' (e.g. labourer). There are many binaries in our everyday language, such as, 'evil' versus 'good' or 'girl' versus 'boy', which become problematic when one binary node is thought to be more valuable than the other. Post-structuralists examine and expose these value-laden relations. Deconstruction of the assumptions that underpin one node of the binary – such as 'soft' versus 'hard', where girls are soft and boys are tough – are considered by post-structuralists.

Michel Foucault (1977a, 1977b, 1980) is one of the best known post-structuralists. His philosophy has informed many educators in early childhood education and primary schooling.

Michel Foucault

Foucault examined the subtle social conditions in which we live, work and learn. For example, he studied and questioned the prison system. He introduced the concept of institutionalised surveillance to name a particular prison system that he studied. However, the prison is just an example of the institutionalised surveillance that occurs locally and globally.

MacNaughton (2005) wrote explicitly on how Foucault's work could inform education through critically examining and unsettling 'truths' that have come to be associated with early childhood education:

- minority world truth of the child – child development that 'builds universally applicable, factual and correct statements about how children develop' (2005: 23).
- developmental truths of the child and early childhood pedagogies – 'In much of the Minority World (e.g. Europe, North America, Australia and New Zealand), developmental psychology's authority is established so well that it is a foundational discipline of study of early childhood educators and other professionals who work with young children, and it is a pervasive influence on early childhood pedagogies' (2005: 25).

More recently, we have seen assessment approaches (e.g. the Australian Early Development Census (Department of Education and Training, 2016)), that seek to establish the truth about children's development, but in ways that reflect a universal trajectory through assessment technologies that mirror particular minority world truths about the child.

Analysing post-structuralist theories

The post-structuralist position of the politics of truth has informed early childhood educators. A post-structuralist view enables educators to take an active stance. Post-structuralism provides educators with tools for critique, which seek to:

- 'survey how and why critical and poststructuralist theories see truth as political'
- identify 'how scientific truths about children are used in early childhood studies to establish facts about children and to build pedagogies'
- show how truths about children are linked to culturally biased norms about how children should be
- explore how truths compete with each other for positions of privilege in fields of study, such as early childhood
- discuss how the 'winning' truths in this competition form, in Foucault's (1977a, 1997b, 1980) terms, a 'regime of truth' (MacNaughton, 2005: 19–20).

Further, post-structuralism:

- 'uses the case of developmental "regime of truth" of the child to highlight why disrupting regimes of truth is important to work for social justice and equity in early childhood studies'

- argues that the 'politics of truth in early childhood studies brings with it unavoidable political choices for activist educators' (MacNaughton, 2005: 19–20).

The following principles emerged through the process of critique in the original work of Foucault. These are concepts employed by MacNaughton in early childhood contexts in Australia.

Surveillance

In the example of the prison system mentioned above, it was possible to identify that institutions and other systems set up structures to closely observe and supervise people in reference to the expected 'truth'. For example, in early childhood settings and schools, there are codes of behaviour that must be followed, ways of identifying and assessing learning and approaches to teaching that are privileged. The premise of a quality education in Australia is based on assumptions about children's development. In schools, this primarily means following a curriculum that is based on age periods (National Curriculum) and organising learning spaces based on the age of the children – for example, all 6-year-olds are in the same classroom. Even though this view of organising learning through stages or milestones of development that has been put forward as a 'truth' about children's development has been critiqued, it continues to exist.

Figure 9.2 Surveillance or observing children?

Normalisation

This concept positions children and their teachers to always be comparing, conforming, and standardising against a particular 'truth'. For example, in early childhood education, this has meant checking infant records against the expected growth charts for weight and height (the truth), regardless of the cultural backgrounds of the children, who may be biologically heavier or lighter based on their family genetics and cultural histories.

Exclusion

This term captures the process of excluding or including an established truth about what is normal or desirable. In early childhood education, this could mean pathologising any form of development or behaviour that does not fit mainstream expectations. A possible result is the referral of a child to another service, or for the child to go out of the preschool into another space or venue for specialist support so they can better fit into the mainstream service. The truth is expected 'behaviour'.

Classification

Many organisations cluster people and activities through classification, such as job classification, travel class or type of school attended (private or public). In schools and early childhood settings, the clustering of children is based on their age. The truth is 'age'. There are schools that resist this developmental truth, such as the Collective Inquiry School.

Distribution

Ranking and arranging of people can occur through jobs held, their cultural groups, the class from which they are thought to come, years of education and so on. In early childhood settings, ranking and arranging of children can also occur in contexts of where the children live (e.g. their postcode) or based on an assessment score for their community, known as the Australian Early Development (AED) Index, or how they are classified in terms of special needs. These distributions can have the effect of determining the resources made available in the future for that family or community, or they could have the effect of stigmatising a particular community, resulting in a lower level of expectations being placed upon children growing up in that community and attending their local preschool and school. The child is assigned to particular groups that will or will not receive additional resourcing. Some teachers in the Resourceful Community case study had low expectations of the children, and this would have contributed to the AED assessment result.

Individualisation

This concept draws upon particular truths to separate individuals. A developmental truth about expected progression at preschool will be used to decide whether a child should stay an additional year in preschool and therefore not transition to school with the children in their social group or cohort. The mother in the Peninsula family in the Resourceful Community case study was worried about her child having to repeat a year at school.

Totalisation

Truth is used to build conformity. School and preschool practices build conformity through the implementation of a curriculum. Teachers use the curriculum to create the conditions for all the children to develop in particular ways. In the Resourceful Community case study, Andrew in the Peninsula family had to learn how to conform to the expectations of particular school behaviours.

Regulation

This concept captures the specific truth about controlling thinking and acting of people. In school and in early childhood settings, beliefs about children's needs – such as for an afternoon nap or snack, or for time to play – are based on a belief about children's development, such as that an 18-month-old needs a rest in the afternoon and 6-year-old children need a play period in the middle of the morning (between literacy block and a numeracy block) so they can concentrate on school learning better. The Human Services visits to the Peninsula family home in the Resourceful Community case study were not only a form of surveillance, but a form of regulation linked to developmental theory.

These are challenging concepts. However, they provide a powerful base from which to critique everyday practices that we no longer notice – as we saw in Chapter 3 in the Building Bridges Community case study, where we noticed how the teacher sat and read a story – an everyday practice – having never considered before what her body language was signalling to the Aboriginal children in the class.

Figure 9.3 Children being positioned with agency

Applying the tools to critique child development theories

Critical theories and post-structuralist theories are not theories of child development; rather, they are powerful tools that ask questions about development (and more). Asking questions about agency and power provides insights into contexts that afford development, but these two theories do not explain how children develop. Rather, the focus is on questioning opportunities for children's development – what does a particular theory privilege and what does it silence? What is afforded for the child?

In line with Peter Anderson's concerns (Chapter 8) for context when discussing child development, we also learn that the main theories that have dominated the literature and education in Australia were not developed in Australia. As such, the door is open for you to consider a potential theory of child development that speaks to, and makes visible, Australian children, families and communities – as Karen Martin did (see Chapter 8).

CHILD DEVELOPMENT REFLECTION 9.12: UNDERSTANDING CRITICAL THEORY

1   What might critical theory allow you to see, think and do?
2   Consider the different contexts in which critical theory was developed – in which countries were they located?
3   Why was critical theory developed?
4   What kind of research was undertaken?
5   How does critical theory relate to the Australian context and to Australian children?
6   How does what you have learned relate (or not) to Australian children, families and communities?

CHILD DEVELOPMENT REFLECTION 9.13: UNDERSTANDING POST-STRUCTURALIST THEORIES

1   What might the theories allow you to do?
2   Consider the different contexts of the post-structuralist theories developed. When and where were these theories developed? What kind of research was undertaken?
3   How do the theories relate to the Australian context and to Australian children?
4   Consider what you have learned and add it to Table 9.2.
5   How does what you have learned relate (or not) to Australian children, families and communities?

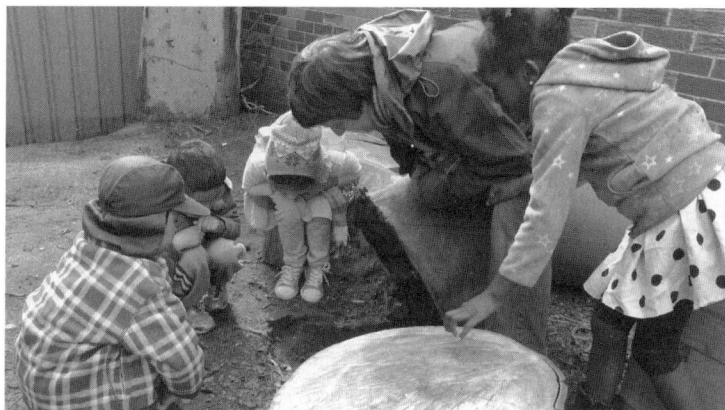

Figure 9.4 How does what you have learned relate (or not) to Australian children, families and communities?

What we learn when we look into the EYLF is that post-structuralist theories offer insights into issues of power, equity and social justice in early childhood settings (DEEWR, 2009).

CHILD DEVELOPMENT REFLECTION 9.14: THEORIES – WHAT HAVE YOU LEARNED?

Now that you have read about socio-behaviourist, critical and post-structural theories, consider Table 9.2. An overview of theories discussed in this chapter, as they relate to the EYLF, is provided. Consider what you have learnt about socio-behaviourist, critical and post-structural theories, and complete the table.

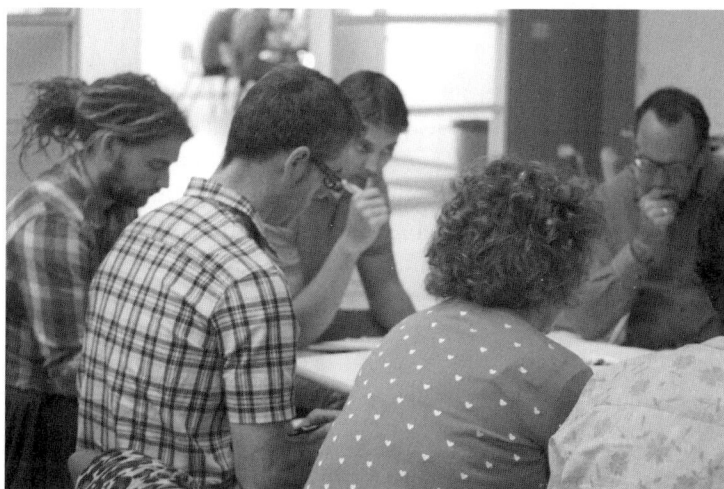

Figure 9.5 Studying concepts in curriculum documents

Table 9.2 Theories of child development presented in the EYLF

Theory	Key characteristics	Who are the theorists?	How are children, families and communities positioned – your critique
Developmental theories	'focus on describing and understanding the processes of change in children's learning and development over time' (DEEWR, 2009: 11).		
Sociocultural theories	'emphasise the central role that families and cultural groups play in children's learning and the importance of respectful relationships and provide insight into social and cultural contexts of learning and development' (DEEWR, 2009: 11).		
Socio-behaviourist theories	'focus on the role of experiences in shaping children's behaviour' (DEEWR, 2009: 11).		
Critical theories	'invite early childhood educators to challenge assumptions about curriculum, and consider how their decisions may affect children differently' (DEEWR, 2009: 11).		
Post-structuralist theories	'offer insights into issues of power, equity and social justice in early childhood settings' (DEEWR, 2009: 11).		

Conclusion

In this chapter, you were invited to examine three broad categories of child development: socio-behaviourist theories, critical theories and post-structuralist theories. We learnt that socio-behaviourist theories represent an unusual clustering of contradictory child development theories. We also learnt that the critical theories and poststructuralist theories are powerful tools for critique. In the next chapter, you will take a position on your beliefs about child development in relation to Australian children.

Acknowledgements

Special thanks to Dr Marie Hammer and her students, Amanda Wei Thin Hii, Lauren Intihar, Tahlie Arena and Shuang Zhao for sharing their research and comments.

References

Bandura, A 1977, *Social learning theory*, New York: General Learning Press.

—— 1986, *Social foundations of thought and action*, Englewood Cliffs, NJ: Prentice-Hall.

—— 1997, *Self-efficacy: The exercise of control*, New York: WH Freeman.

Department of Education, Employment and Workplace Relations (DEEWR) 2009, *Belonging, Being and Becoming: The Early Years Learning Framework for Australia*, Canberra: Commonwealth Government.

Department of Education and Training 2016, *Australian Early Development Census*. Available at: https://www.education.gov.au/australian-early-development-census [Accessed 21 August 2017].

Foucault, M 1977a, 'Truth and power', in C Gordon (ed.), *Power/knowledge: Selected interviews and other writings 1972–1977*, Sussex: The Harvester Press, pp. 109–33.

—— 1977b, 'Two lectures', in C Gordon (ed.), *Power/Knowledge: Selected interviews and other writings 1972–1977. Michel Foucault*. Brighton: The Harvester Press, pp. 78–108.

—— 1980, *Power/knowledge: Selected interviews and other writings 1972–1977*, New York: Pantheon.

MacNaughton, G 2005, *Doing Foucault in early childhood studies: Applying poststructuralist ideas*, London: Routledge.

McLeod, SA 2016, 'Bandura – social learning theory'. Available at: http://www.simplypsychology.org/bandura.html [Accessed 20 June 2017].

Nolan, A & Raban, B 2015, *Theories into practice: Understanding and rethinking our work with young children*, Sydney: Teaching Solutions. Available at: http://www.earlychildhoodaustralia.org.au/shop/wp-content/uploads/2015/06/SUND606_sample.pdf [Accessed 20 June 2017].

Skinner, BF 1954, 'The science of learning and the art of teaching', *Harvard Educational Review*, 24, 86–97.

—— 1968, *The technology of teaching*, New York: Appleton-Century-Crofts.

—— 1986, 'Programmed instruction revisited', *Phi Delta Kappan*, 68, 103–10.

CHAPTER 10

Future directions: How theories support ongoing change

Introduction

In this chapter, you will take a position on the theories of child development you believe are best for you. You may have more than one favourite. Having read through the content of this book, you now have the background required to make an informed decision about each of the child development theories discussed.

To support you with this penultimate goal, you will begin this chapter by critiquing the theories of child development, deciding on what they offer and what they silence. You are then invited to return to your reflections made in Chapter 1 and compare your original thinking with where you are now. The chapter, and hence the book, finishes with you preparing a philosophy statement about child development.

Through engaging with the content of this chapter, it is anticipated that you will:

- take a position on the value of the major theories of child development that have traditionally informed education in Australia
- make a commitment to listening to the voice of the Indigenous communities in which you will be teaching
- think about child development in the context of Australian families and communities and the conditions that we as educators create in child-care centres, preschools and primary schools.

Critiquing theories

You have now read through the content of this book and engaged in detail with the theories of child development that are widely used in early childhood and primary education. The theories were:

- maturational theory of child development (e.g. milestones; biology is the focus; age is the criterion for progression)
- sociocultural theory, as presented by Barbara Rogoff (learning by observing and pitching in; three lenses for analysing children's development – personal, interpersonal and contextual/institutional/cultural)
- Piaget's theory of child development (great developmental periods: the sensorimotor level; the concrete operations of thought and interpersonal relations; and the preadolescent and propositional operations)
- Bronfenbrenner's bioecological model of human development (propositions to capture the interrelatedness of individual and context; proximal processes; earlier versions including the chronosystem and time; and the first version of his model, a nested system of microsystem, mesosystem, exosystem and macrosystem)
- Vygotsky's (periodisation; drama as the force for development; a revolutionary view of child development), Hedegaard's (personal, institutional, societal – values, demands and motives) and Kravtsova's (stable and dramatic periods) cultural-historical theory of child development
- Anderson's rights-based approach to learning and development (decolonisation; feeling culturally safe; being agentic; recognition of history and country)
- Martin's theory of relatedness (Ways of Knowing, Ways of Being and Ways of Doing)
- Bandura's social learning theory (four mediational processes: attention; retention; reproduction; and motivation)
- Skinner's theory of behaviourism (positive and negative reinforcement; positive punishment; scheduled reinforcement; and operant conditioning)
- critical and post-structuralist theories for asking questions about child development (asking questions of child development and its affordances).

You have also briefly examined other theories that inform curriculum and that are referenced in the EYLF, or that underpin the scope and sequence approach in the Australian curriculum. Finally, you have read two chapters on theories of child development that speak directly to the Australian community. Together, these readings will allow you to make judgements about what a theory allows you to see and what a theory silences.

You are now invited to reflect upon the content of each chapter and to critique the theories as a whole (see Table 10.1). To do this, it is suggested you return to each chapter and your documented reflections in your journal, and consider what the theory appears to allow you to do. Then document your thoughts in Column 2 in Table 10.1.

To do this, draw upon the essence of the theory. For example, a maturational or developmental view of child development focuses on ages and stages of development. This means that this theory will encourage you to look for evidence of particular milestones of development. Try this approach with the other theories. Then consider what might be missing and what the theory does not easily allow you to consider. For example, in a maturational view of child development, the focus is

Table 10.1 Critiquing theories

Theory	What the theory makes visible	What the theory silences
Maturational theory of child development (Chapter 3)		
Rogoff's theory of child development (Chapter 3)		
Piaget's theory of child development (Chapter 4)		
Bronfenbrenner's theory of child development (Chapter 5)		
Vygotsky's theory of child development (Chapter 6)		
Kravtsova's theory of child development (Chapter 6)		
Hedegaard's theory of child development (Chapters 6 & 7)		
Anderson's rights-based approach to learning and development (Chapter 8)		
Martin's theory of relatedness (Chapter 8)		
Bandura's social learning theory (Chapter 9)		
Skinner's theory of behaviourism (Chapter 9)		
Critical and post-structuralist theories (Chapter 9)		

on the individual child, their age and what stage they might be in. But this does not provide insights into how the context, rather than their age, might shape the child's development. Now critique the other theories of child development. Document what is missing or silenced by the theory in the final column of Table 10.1.

By critiquing what a theory affords and silences, we can better understand the theory of child development and know when and how to use the theory to guide our approach to observing children. But we can also reflect on when a particular theory is helpful for curriculum planning and when it is not. Your view of child development determines how you plan for children's learning. It shapes how you conceptualise progression. It frames what content you select from the EYLF and the National Curriculum. If you believe that children's development follows a maturational approach, then you are likely to match the curriculum to where a child is at. If you believe in a cultural-historical approach, you will select content above where the children are at, and will create the conditions that are motivating for children to learn the content.

The EYLF provides some support for this, critically reflecting on the study of child development theory. For instance, in Chapter 1 you were asked to reflect on five key strategies from the EYLF. They are reproduced here for your convenience. Consider these questions again.

> Drawing on a range of perspectives and theories can challenge traditional ways of seeing children, teaching and learning, and encourage educators, as individuals and with colleagues, to:
>
> • investigate why they act in the ways that they do
> • discuss and debate theories to identify strengths and limitations

- recognise how the theories and beliefs that they use to make sense of their work enable but also limit their actions and thoughts
- consider the consequences of their actions for children's experiences
- find new ways of working fairly and justly (DEEWR, 2009: 11)

Compare the reflections you have just made in relation to the journal entry you completed when you read Chapter 1 and first engaged with these strategies. What do you notice about your own thinking? How has it changed?

Prepare a poster of the theoretical perspectives of child development that you believe will be most helpful for you with regard to understanding children in school and preschool. Draw out the key points, as shown in Figure 10.1.

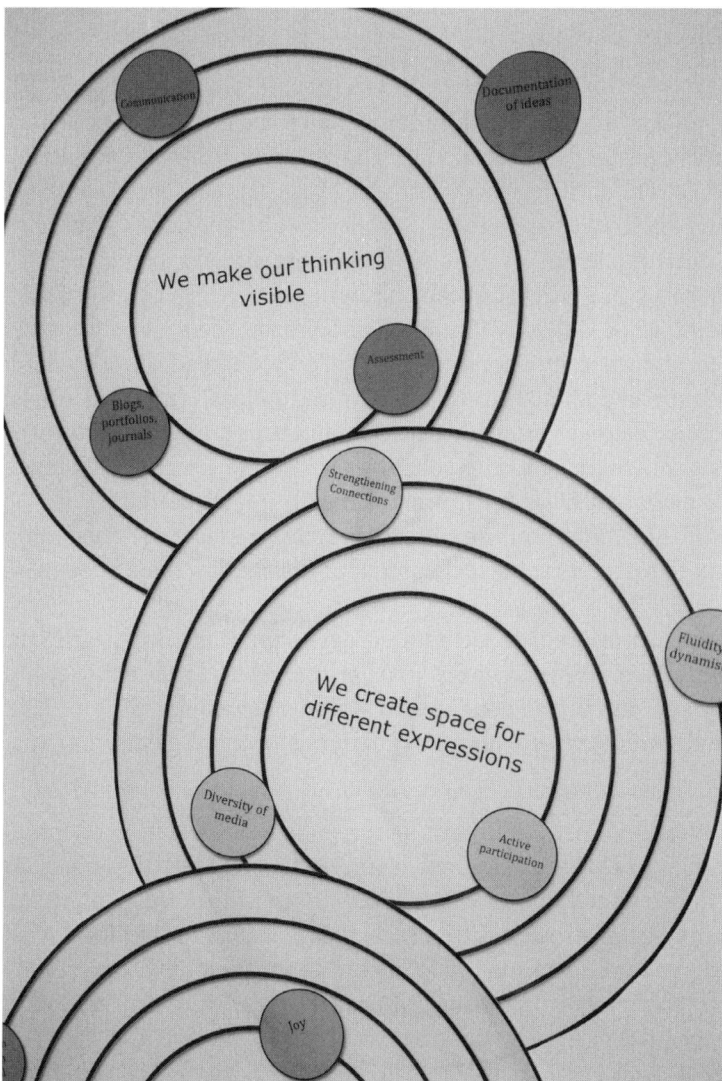

Figure 10.1 Poster critiquing the theories of child development that we use

Using theories

As a result of your study of the different theories of child development, and through using the different theories to analyse the case studies, you will now be in a more informed position about how theories support your thinking about children, families and communities.

Each of the four case studies in this book showed how theoretical lenses shaped what could be talked about. Different theories resulted in completely different readings of each of these four case studies:

- the Resourceful Community – the Peninsula family and the Westernport family
- the Collective Inquiry School
- the Culturally Diverse Preschool
- the Building Bridges Community.

Through using theory in conjunction with the case studies, we had the opportunity to gain some key understandings about Louise and Andrew from the Peninsula family that were invisible to staff from government agencies, who worried about Louise not walking and Andrew's teachers being concerned that Andrew could not focus at school. An unsuitable theory of child development was being used to interpret the observations being made of both children.

We could also see how the Collective Inquiry School used theory to change its pedagogical practices – it turned its approach upside down. Instead of following a step-by-step approach (behaviourist-framed learning sequences), the school used cultural-historical theory to create more authentic complex and meaningful learning experiences for all the children in the school – as we saw when the teachers redesigned one of the neighbourhood communities into a theatre company.

The observations of the children in the Culturally Diverse Preschool opened up discussions about how to read the ecological context of the children being observed (Chapter 3).

The Building Bridges Community reflected and made conscious important cultural knowledge about which non-Indigenous teachers need to be aware if they are to see and make informed decisions about their children's development.

In studying these different cases, some key learnings become evident, as discussed below.

- *Key learning* 1: Working with different theories broadens our conceptual toolkit. Over the course of the book, we examined a range of theories that closely mirror those listed in the EYLF, and that inform the Australian curriculum. The theories provide different insights, act as lenses for seeing children and help us make informed judgements about their development. By considering each theory in relation to the case studies, we can foreground what each theory privileges and what each silences. Through this, we can make judgements about which theories to use, and when, to frame our conception of children. But importantly, by engaging with the different theories, we can start to question their origins and their relevance.

- *Key learning 2: Core theories.* The core theories introduced in this book reflect what is currently being used in the field and currently being used by researchers in early childhood education. The selection is reflective of what matters now. It is important to keep an open mind to other theoretical conceptions of child development. The theories introduced by Karen Martin and Peter Anderson are based on their work in Australia. They offer new directions for the field. They speak to all children through the rights-based model, but are also specific to Australia's first peoples.

- *Key learning 3: Where were the theories developed and what evidence has informed the models?* The dominant theories were not developed on research based on an Australian context or in contemporary times. A rights-based approach and the concept of relatedness as introduced here represent the first steps towards building an Australian theory of child development. However, more needs to be done if we are to have sufficient evidence to create a model of child development appropriate to Australian children.

- *Key learning 4: Selecting the right observational approach to study children's development.* In Chapter 2, you were introduced to observational principles and practices for making high-quality observations of young children. We noted how child studies are labour intensive, but offer a rich basis for making interpretations of children's development. However, we also learned that laboratory-based studies create the same conditions for studying children's development. It was much faster and more reliable. Yet we found that these laboratory based settings possibly did not speak directly to the broad contexts in which we find children, such as the sandpit or the PE gymnasium. Both approaches offer possibilities and limitations.

Through these four key learnings, you should now be in a position to critically reflect upon what theory of child development you find to be the most helpful for your study of children.

CHILD DEVELOPMENT REFLECTION 10.1: WHAT THEORY OF CHILD DEVELOPMENT INFORMS YOUR WORK?

1 What theory of child development do you find most helpful for your study of children?
   a developmental or maturational theory of child development (Chapter 3)
   b Piaget's theory of child development (Chapter 4)
   c socio-cultural or cultural-historical theories: Vygotsky's theory of child development (Chapter 6); Rogoff's theory of child development

(continued)

(Chapter 3); Kravtsova's theory of child development (Chapter 6); Hedegaard's theory of child development (Chapters 6 and 7)

d   socio-behaviourist theories: Bandura's social learning theory (Chapter 9); Skinner's theory of behaviourism (Chapter 9)

e   critical theories (Chapter 9)

f   post-structuralist theories (Chapter 9)

g   Bronfenbrenner's theory of child development (Chapter 5)

h   Anderson's rights-based approach to learning and development (Chapter 8)

i   Martin's theory of relatedness (Chapter 8)

2   What is your reason for selecting this theory of child development?

3   How does the theory help you to analyse children's development?

4   What method of observation will you use and why?

Future directions

As you continue your studies and begin/return to working with children and families, you will take with you what you have learnt about child development. However, theories and understandings about how children develop continue to evolve as we learn more through research. One of the gaps that has existed until now is a theory of child development researched in our Australian community. In Chapter 8, you were invited to consider the theories of child development in the context of Australian children, families and communities. Peter Anderson presented a rights-based approach to education and the writings of Karen Martin conceptualised development and learning through the concept of relatedness, where Ways of Knowing, Ways of Being and Ways of Doing informed a theory of child development. Each researcher discussed context as critical for development and learning. Context was also discussed in Chapter 7, where the motives of some Australian children and families were presented through an analysis of the case studies introduced in Chapters 2 and 3.

The case studies and the content of Chapter 8 pave the way forward for teachers in Australia because they discuss the cultural contexts of Australian children, families and communities. As Peter Anderson points out in Chapter 8, before we can conceptualise a theory of child development for our particular context, we need to:

- notice how theories from the Global North were originally developed – for which children, which families and which communities
- examine the time period in which these theories were developed – some of the theories still discussed were developed in the 1950s
- consider the population of children who were the focus of the original studies, and who informed the theory – Swiss families (Piaget), with specific

child-rearing practices that are very different from the culturally diverse communities that make up the contemporary Australian population.

It is also important to notice our own personal histories as we discuss different theories. Some of you reading this book will come from a position of privilege, while others may not. Yet others will be considering your cultural heritage and what you bring to the Australian community. My own position is as a daughter of a poor immigrant family, with intergenerational discord due to my extended family living on the border between the Netherlands and Germany during a time of conflict, where many atrocities were committed. I bring to my critique something my mother once said to me as a child: 'Have an education. Once you have an education, it can never be taken away from you.'

Figure 10.2 A position of privilege

Moreton-Robinson (2000: xx) reminds us that when we critique child development theories, we must engage with our history. What is your history? What do you bring to the study of child development? What have you been sensitised to because of your own history? For some, this privileged history is in the form of 'whiteness': 'white race privilege makes a difference to women's life chances. Yet these authors fail to appreciate that their position as situated knowers within white race privilege is inextricably connected to the systemic racism they criticise but do not experience' (Moreton-Robinson, 2000: xx).

Further, we must think about theories of child development in terms of what they represent. 'One dimension is to perceive representation as "speaking for"; the other is to comprehend representation as involving interpretation" (Moreton-Robinson, 2000: xxii). In Chapter 8, various ideas were presented about how to connect with local Aboriginal and Torres Strait Islander communities in order to understand children's cultural communities, and to draw upon this understanding when studying children's development. This idea also applies to working with a broad range of cultural communities that make up the diversity of peoples found in Australia today. By working with and connecting with community, we are better able to understand the development of the children we observe and for whom we plan.

The theorists whose work is detailed in Chapter 8 take this step by critiquing the theories of child development that we have inherited in Australia, and begin to speak of a future theory of child development for Australian children, families and communities.

CHILD DEVELOPMENT REFLECTION 10.2: WHAT THEORIES DO YOU BELIEVE ARE RELEVANT TO THE STUDY OF AUSTRALIAN CHILDREN?

1 If you were one of the writers of the EYLF, how might you explain, edit, re-categorise and rename all the different theories presented in Table 10.1?
2 If you were to use a different theory of child development to provide a new foundation for the Australian curriculum, how might the scope and sequence of the content look? How might the Australian curriculum be framed?

Figure 10.3 What theories do you believe are relevant to the study of Australian children?

Conclusion

It is through using theory that it becomes possible to reimagine the learning journey of children. As educators, it is important to declare what theory of child development you believe will work best for you and your cultural community. The key is knowing what a particular theory will make visible in your study of children, and what it will silence. In Part II of this book, you had the opportunity to see how each theory that was presented in each of the chapters made particular forms of development visible. But these case examples also highlighted some omissions – development we could not see. Determining your preferred theory of child development risks sanctioning a particular truth (Chapter 9). However, in studying many different theories, you will now be better informed about what a particular theory privileges and silences. With this understanding of child development, you will be making the best possible choice for the children you teach. At the end of the day, you still need a theory of child development to guide you in planning for learning and evaluating progression. You cannot work without theory. But you must also use it critically, and not accept it as the 'single truth' about how children develop.

References

Department of Education, Employment and Workplace Relations (DEEWR) 2009, *Belonging, Being and Becoming: The Early Years Learning Framework for Australia*, Canberra: Commonwealth Government.

Moreton-Robinson, A 2000, *Talkin' up the white woman: Indigenous women and feminism*, Brisbane: University of Queensland Press.

Index